EAC occasional paper no 3

Listing Archaeological Sites, Protecting the Historical Landscape

Listing Archaeological Sites, Protecting the Historical Landscape

EAC occasional paper no 3

Edited by Peter A.C. Schut

EAC occasional paper no 3

Listing Archaeological Sites, Protecting the Historical Landscape

Edited by Peter A.C. Schut

Europae
Archaeologiae
Consilium

Cultural Heritage Agency
Ministry of Education, Culture and Science

www.e-a-c.org

ISBN 978-90-579-9144-8

EAC, Association Internationale sans But Lucratif (AISBL), Siège social

Koning Albert II-laan 19	Avenue Roi Albert II 19
P.O. Box 10	Boîte 10
1210 Brussels	1210 Bruxelles
Belgium	Belgique

Page design and composition by Studio Imago, Jaap Wolters, The Netherlands

Cover design by Studio Imago, Jaap Wolters, and Peter Schut

Production by Studio Imago

Cover illustration:
The Netherlands Winsum - Harssensbosch. Two former *borg* sites (houses of Groningen
nobleman) and a road from the 14th and 16th century still visible in the polder landscape
north of Groningen.
Photo: Paul Paris, Amstelveen

Contents

Fig. I Târgovişte, Romania: The EAC symposium (Ovidiu Cîrstina)

Foreword

Approaches to archaeological heritage management in Europe have evolved over time, with different approaches in the various countries reflecting diverse legislative traditions. Archaeologists have relied on the provisions of heritage legislation, where present, to protect archaeological remains. On a common European level, concerns about the protection of archaeological heritage and the development of legislative responses have arisen from the growth of archaeology as an academic branch of learning. Archaeology has evolved from a discipline studying individual artefacts to one that takes a more holistic approach to events and actions in the past. To understand the past we need to look not only at its monuments but also the whole environment.

Preserving monuments and archaeological sites is of manifold importance, the need to cater to today's academic demands being one. In a rapidly changing world we have to decide what to protect for the future. In what kind of context will the public be able to understand the past when presented with archaeological sites? Our generation has a responsibility to preserve the archaeological heritage for future generations. One of the important tools employed in the protection of archaeological heritage is the inventory of sites. But do we focus on relevant issues in compiling inventories and other systems for protecting the archaeological heritage? As part of its mission to support the management of archaeological heritage throughout Europe, the Europae Archaeologiae Consilium (EAC) took as the theme for its annual Heritage Management Symposium the issue of monument protection and the role of site inventories in this work. The meeting was held in Târgoviște, Romania on the 6th – 7th March 2008.

The symposium "Listing archaeological sites, protecting the historical landscape" aimed to identify the latest developments associated with the task of formulating an integrated, interdisciplinary approach to the various systems of listing monuments and sites and historical landscapes. The symposium offered 17 papers from 14 different countries. Geographically it ranged from Spain, via Central Europe to Russia and Northern and Western Europe and presented different views on the issue. The successful symposium was arranged by Peter Schut, the Cultural Heritage Agency, The Netherlands and Dr. Mircea Angelescu, head of the Directorate of Historical Monuments and Museums in the Ministry of Culture and Religious Affairs of Romania.

The EAC was invited by the Ministry of Culture and Religious Affairs of Romania to hold its General Assembly and Heritage Management Symposium in that country in 2008. The annual meeting was a great success due to the unequalled generosity and hospitality of the Romanian government and the regional government in Dambovita. On behalf of EAC, it is my great pleasure to express my deepest gratitude to Dr. Mircea Angelescu, to Dr. Virgil Nitulescu, general secretary of the Ministry of Culture and Religious Affairs, to the president of the district council of Dambovita, Ing. Georghe Ana, to Ing. Dr. Aurelian Popa from the prefect institution of Dambovita, to the mayor of Târgoviște, Ing. Iulian Furcoiu and to Dr. Ovidiu Cîrstina, Director of the regional museum of Dambovita. The conference and the field excursion were run with great efficiency and courtesy by Ioana Robu, Emilian Gamureac and Gheorghe Olteanu. We are all very grateful to them.

Europae Archaeologiae Consilium has as an aim the publication of the papers presented at its annual symposiums. It is an occasion of pride that this has been achieved so soon after the 2008 symposium. This publication presents an account of the proceedings of the symposium. In addition, it goes even further by publishing papers on the situation in countries that could not be represented at the conference. I trust the reader will appreciate this opportunity to gain an insight into the role of inventories from almost all parts of Europe. Peter Schut, the editor of this volume, has unselfishly carried out the laborious undertaking of collecting the papers and editing them. Without his crucial contribution the symposium volume would not have been realized. I am therefore deeply indebted to him for all his work. Last, but by no means least, my thanks goes to all the contributors, both those who attended the conference at Târgoviște as well as those who, though not at the conference, were so good as to contribute a paper to the volume.

Helsinki, 12th January 2009

Marianne Schauman-Lönnqvist

President of EAC

II Listing archaeological sites, protecting the historical landscape

There are two parts to the title of the 9th EAC Heritage Management Symposium held in Târgovişte, Romania (6th-7th March 2008). The first refers to listing in the sense of the administration of the assessed archaeological sites. This, of course, covers a great number of areas, ranging from legislation and registration, each with its own meaning and context for every participating country, to issues to do with data-structures and hardware infrastructure, with the internet serving as an indispensable medium for dissemination of information.

The second part, the historical landscape, also has quite different meanings for and attracts different levels of attention in the various countries. It is a topic which is gaining increasing attention, although the approaches to it in the different countries vary in line with regional historical developments. Similarly, there is a varied degree of co-operation and integration within countries between all those who are involved in the management of the historic landscape.

In the call for papers the symposium theme was introduced as follows:

Various approaches to the listing and protection of archaeological remains exist, and challenging new developments are still occurring. Up-scaling and integration dominate the debate.

Over the years, numerous systems have been developed for drawing up site invento-ries. Given that archaeological remains are important both to academics and to society as a whole, both sets of interests play a role in such exercises. One question arising in this context concerns the extent to which it is desirable and, indeed, possible to develop systems for assessment and selection that rise above 'trends', both among academics and in the public perception of the historical landscape. In both academic archaeology and archaeological heritage management, a shift from the site to the (historical) land-scape as a whole can be discerned. This requires both archaeologists and archaeologi-cal heritage managers to take a more integrated, interdisciplinary approach. The desire of academic archaeologists and, more especially, society for coherent parts of the his-torical landscape to be preserved for the future calls for the development of integrated, heritage-wide, landscape-oriented approaches to assessment and selection.

Selection methods from adjacent disciplines such as archaeology, historical geography and art or architectural history must be used in an integrated manner.

The aim of the symposium is to identify the latest developments associated with the above themes in the different countries of Europe and to discuss the matter. The aim is not to focus on legislation, but to examine how, in the context of existing structures; we can operationalise the process of protecting sites and landscapes.

The following questions were posed so as to focus the introduction:
- *For whom are site inventories produced and who is in charge of such operations?*
- *Who takes what role in terms of academic and social responsibility?*
- *What criteria (for sites and landscapes) exist for assessment and selection and what procedures can be used in practice?*
- *How does one obtain the data needed for assessment and selection?*
- *Does one consider only proven values or also predicted values (role of predictive modelling)? In other words: is it reasonable to impose restrictions in terms of owner-ship purely on the basis of archaeological predictions?*
- *In which manner is the process of listing related to the so-called 'Malta archaeology'? Can archaeological information which is elicited during planning procedures (at the cost of a developing party) be used for aims of protection?*
- *Is opportunism acceptable (selection of sites/landscapes that are 'promising' in terms of protection)?*
- *Expert judgment versus objective criteria and parameters*

- *To what extend should protection programs be strategically driven? And which strategic choices can be made: should we go for what is in danger or should we focus on the opportunities for long lasting preservation?*
- *Best practises for the organisation of a protection program.*
- *Managing protected sites: which developments can be permitted? Compensation of owners? Monitoring the quality of sites?"*

Given the wide scope of the central theme it is inevitable that the different contributions vary in their approach. Nevertheless, within this variety the central issue is addressed.

The listing of sites and the way individual sites are protected in different countries varies in line with the provisions and requirements of the national legislation. The procedures around site protection differ greatly. Sometimes every newly-discovered site is automatically protected, while in other countries a complex process is necessary to achieve the same effect.

The site directed tradition as practiced in many countries is now moving more and more towards a landscape approach where sites, singly or in groups, are regarded as part of a natural landscape in all its aspects. Sometimes the landscape as a whole may be scheduled, but often the scheduling of individual sites is combined with other mechanisms such as spatial planning to protect the landscape.

Two aspects can be distinguished in the landscape approach. Firstly, there is the situation where the protected landscape may contain no visible remains. Such landscapes, while a valuable information source for archaeologists and scientists in related disciplines, are not readily appreciated by the general public who are not easily convinced of the value of protecting 'invisible monuments and landscapes', especially in densely populated areas. Secondly, there are situations where relict traces of sometimes more than a thousand years of development are still recognizable in the modern field and property boundaries and road-ways, while megaliths, burial mounds, castles, churches etc. form visible landmarks in a changing landscape. Where both aspects described are present in combination we may justifiably claim it as a situation of utmost value, the biography of the landscape in its true sense.

The historical landscape can be a powerful source of knowledge and inspiration, not only for archaeologists, but also for those who are involved in spatial planning for the future and whose decisions must be informed by archaeology. There needs to be an integrated approach to such issues, involving co-ordination and co-operation between specialists of very different backgrounds. The result may be that archaeological remains can remain *in situ* as landscape features in new residential areas. In this way, those who dwell in these new communities can encounter the past on a daily basis (fig.II). This is protection by development in its true sense, not as the antithesis of traditional protection, but as a solution in a society under construction. Development of an integrated approach to archaeology, built heritage and the historic landscape will contribute to an enhanced awareness of the historic environment on the part of present and future generations.

In the papers in the volume, various national approaches to protection are described. During the symposium at Târgovişte, the different approaches gave rise to interesting discussions about the issues raised. It is only possible to mention some of the subjects raised here. Among them were:

The way classification and selection of archaeological sites take place;

The consequences of publication of the location of sites to the public via the Internet or other means, in particular the risk that sites might be looted by treasure hunters;

The consequences of decentralisation and its implications for scientific research (upload of knowledge).

These are subjects that merit further discussion.

The papers provide an overview of the legislation, listing and landscape approaches in many European countries. Since most of the contributions deal with all three of these topics it was not possible to group them strictly by subject. The papers describe the situation in the different countries at the date of the Symposium. This is a period of rapid change for many heritage management agencies and so this volume must be regarded as an instantaneous snapshot of the situation in 2008.

Many people were involved in the success of the Symposium and this volume. In the preface the President of the EAC mentioned those who organized the successful Symposium in Târgoviște. The excellent organization of the event and the warm reception accorded to all made it an event the participants will not easily forget. The individual authors who, in the face of heavy work-schedules and the persistent questions of the editor, delivered their texts in a timely manner, deserve special thanks for their time and patience. The papers are marginally edited so that the work of the authors is fully respected. Without the indispensable assistance of Eamon Cody (Dublin), David Cowley (Edinburgh), Claire Driver (London), Marie-Jeanne Ghenne (Brussels), Phil Mason (Ljubljana), Sue McDonnell (Utrecht) and Bernard Randoin (Paris), all of whom played an important role in English and French editing, it would not have been possible to produce this volume. It was a pleasure to work with these colleagues. Bea, Lonneke and Vincent for allowing me to work quiet a few evenings and weekends at this volume.

Peter Schut

Cultural Heritage Agency, Amersfoort

Fig. II The Netherlands, Utrecht - De Meern: The location of the Roman limes road along a quayside and a Roman vessel. The road was deliberately marked in the town planning by making a break in the buildings and situating a footpath above the Roman remains (Cultural Heritage Agency, Amersfoort).

1 | Value and values in archaeology and archaeological heritage management in the Netherlands

Jos Bazelmans

Archaeology and archaeological heritage management have experienced something of a boom in the Netherlands since the early 1990s. The introduction of new forms of funding and of a combination of market forces and societal control have led to a series of changes in the archaeological establishment, in terms of funding, organisation, implementation and intended results. Viewed against the history of Dutch archaeology over the past two hundred years, these changes can rightly be dubbed revolutionary. I believe that we are not fully aware of the implications of this revolution. This essay sets out to discuss these implications. I will call for an analysis which is based on the ethnographic study of the care for heritage and on the anthropology of value and values (Barraud, De Coppet, Iteanu and Jamous 1994). A brief discussion will provide insight into who determines archaeological value and values in Dutch archaeology, and why and how they do so, as well as the investments that lie behind these decisions. From this perspective, it seems obvious to me that archaeologists must provide a much more confident and critical contribution to the debate on the essence and values of our modern and future society. In more specific terms, this means for example that archaeologists must take on a much more prominent role in the creation of the Dutch historical canon: the dynamic open and multiform body of knowledge about our past that functions as our collective memory.

Growth and institutional reform

To give you an idea of the radical changes that have occurred in Dutch archaeology over the past decade, I should like to describe the developments in terms of the money circulating in archaeology. At the moment, some €70 million a year is spent on archaeology in the Netherlands. It is important, for my argument, to know where this money comes from. Prior to the 1990s, it was mainly public money made available by the central and local government. Nowadays it comes from also from a different source: the profits on land sales by local authorities and direct payments from private parties commissioning archaeological excavations and studies required by law. This change to the financing system has implications in terms of direction and control, and thus, I think, for the nature and purpose of archaeological research. To my way of thinking, these implications are by definition controversial because, in our society, one cannot simply assume that private money will be used for public ends. What do the fundamental changes to the funding of research and conservation mean for our idea and knowledge of the past, and the way we manage our cultural heritage?

Culture, economics and money

As I have said, the use of large amounts of money in archaeology from *new sources* should not be considered an unproblematic issue. In our society, the relationship between the market, on the one hand, and society, politics, art, culture and religion on the other is problematic, particularly when money, services and objects are transferred from one sphere to the other. To elucidate this matter, I should like to draw on the anthropological study of the 'keeping and giving' of alienable and inalienable goods in non-modern societies (Weiner 1992). This will clearly reveal how value and values are created in our sector of cultural preservation, as well as the controversial but essential role one particular form of value – that is money – plays in this process.

In our society we refer to the domain within which money, services, labour and goods exchange hands in accordance with the principles of supply and demand as the 'economy' – the 'market' in the figurative sense of the word. The modern economy is separate in institutional and conceptual terms from the domains where the interpersonal (family, neighbourhood, clubs etc.) or politics, art and culture and/or religion dominate. In these domains, too, money, services, labour and goods play a role, but the rules governing how they are handled differ significantly from those in the market. At the same time, in these not strictly economic spheres we find things that should not circulate in the form of gifts, merchandise or spoils – think, for instance of crown jewels or family heirlooms By analogy with this modern distinction between the economy in the strict and broader senses of the word, anthropologists draw a distinction for every society, in ideal terms, between a domain for the exchange of alienable goods or wares, and a domain in which more or less inalienable goods are kept and exchanged (Parry and Bloch 1989). In the first, our 'market' of supply and demand, the exchange of goods, services and labour – again, according to the ideal – will be relatively anonymous and rapid, and geared towards the ultimate acquisition of commodities and personal gain. In the second – in our society the interrelated domains of politics, art and culture, and religion – we find long-term social relationships of keeping and giving geared to the long-term survival of various social ties, ranging from the family and the neighbourhood to the state. While the first domain – also known as the short-term order – is non-ethical by nature, in a society the second – the long-term order – is a matter of ethics.

Although these two domains are inextricably linked, and each presupposes the existence of the other, in virtually every society, including our own, the conversion of objects from one to the other always gives rise to problems and debate. Actual conversion is therefore often regarded as impossible – or at least problematic – on moral and ethical grounds, or even as a loss. It requires special 'purifying' actions. In our society, money is the object of exchange that plays a role in and links both domains. This also seems to be the source of its ambiguous nature in the western world. In one domain money is seen as the perfect means of guaranteeing the prosperity of society, since money allows individuals to seek profit. In the second, however, its anonymous and impersonal nature makes it, in its extreme form, a diabolical thing that can destroy social relationships and the shared values that underpin them (Le Goff 1986). One good illustration of this, and of the conceptual boundary that exists in our society between the market and other domains, is the fact that the exchange of money turns intimate relations between two individuals into prostitution, and that if a citizen pays money to a public servant, it is regarded as corruption.

Although it features not very prominently in public debate a similar issue currently exists in archaeology. I should like you to consider what you think of the idea that not only should the principle of 'the developer pays' apply in archaeology, but also the principle of 'he who pays the piper calls the tune'. In other words: imagine if those who finance the surveying, excavation and conservation of archaeological sites were to have the power of determining whether sites are worthy of protection and could influence the research agenda. In more abstract terms: how would you feel about money from the economy in the strict sense of the word dominating the domain of art, science and culture? Although I assume that most people would instantly reject this idea, it is a pity that this issue has never been properly aired in the archaeological debate, partly because it could help define responsibilities within the archaeological system.

I believe the problem runs deeper than the question of public or private responsibility. Taxpayers' money earmarked for culture – a 'purifying' transformation of money by the state from the short-term to the long-term order – is a special type of funding that can be used without restrictions in the archaeological sector. However, money that comes directly from the economy is not. This idea requires careful consideration in the debate about culture and the economy in general, and particularly in the context of the major changes in the sources of funding in Dutch archaeology. Whereas archaeology used to be performed by several dozen archaeologists working for universities and the state – using government money and subsidies strictly earmarked for cultural purposes – it is now performed by over a thousand qualified archaeologists who are dependent on money from a range of civil-society, public-sector and private-sector parties both old and, above all, new. It will be clear, from a sociological or academic historical perspective, that these institutional and financial developments must have enormous impact on the discipline. What is not clear, however, is precisely what that impact will be.

How the discipline changes will depend to a large extent on the input of the various 'principals'. Hopefully, academic archaeologists on the one hand will not retreat into a new ivory tower. It is to be hoped that they will not focus exclusively on their own research agenda, and be accountable only to the academic community. Academic archaeologists must exploit the fact that, despite their small numbers, they have always been credible partners who speak with authority on the past and the best way to acquire knowledge of it. They must cherish and constantly review this position, as it cannot be taken for granted. On the other hand, however, commercial parties who work for clients/developers must not use their growing powers of negotiation to sideline public partners, with a view perhaps to keeping down costs. Given my analysis of the role of money in both domains and its conversion from one to the other, this would almost by definition lead to major problems.

Value and values

I have chosen, in this essay, to take a social anthropological perspective, in the hope of elucidating how, in our society, the appreciation and preservation of the heritage is rooted in broader systems of exchange, how management of the heritage relates to the economy in the strict sense – the market, in other words – and above all how the way we treat our heritage is an expression of key social values. At first glance, this last point jars with our own self-image and appears to hold little relevance for the way we treat the heritage today. After all, according to prevailing opinion among academics and policymakers, our appreciation of the heritage springs entirely from the actual – 'objective' – potential that archaeological remains offer for the academic narrative of our past. That is why, in our society, experts play an exclusive role in the process of assessment and selection. However, I doubt whether this covers all aspects of our modern perspective. I believe that crucial social values are at stake in our management of the heritage, and that our treatment of the past is closer to non-modern societies in that respect than we might at first be prepared to admit (Latour 1993). As we have already seen, producing an expert narrative of the past is not an aim in itself, it is an intrinsic part of a much bigger project, the aim of which is to pass on from one generation to the next the heritage that represents the state and society. To show what I mean, I should now like to examine two related themes. The first is the meaning of the concepts of 'value' and 'values' and developments in their meaning; the second is the continuing, and recently revived, dominance in the Netherlands of the national perspective on the cultural heritage and heritage management.

Value and values are among the most frequently used terms in Dutch archaeology: valuation ('waardering') being an all-important step in the Dutch cycle of archaeological heritage management (Groenewoudt 1994 and Willems 1997). The Collins English Dictionary gives a dozen definitions. We are concerned with two of them which, though interrelated, are also substantially different. The first is value as 'the desirability of a thing, often in respect of some property such as usefulness or exchangeability'. Here, 'value' is synonymous with 'price', 'an amount, especially a material or monetary one, considered to be a fair exchange in return for a thing'. In this sense, value is the key feature of dealings in the modern short-term order of exchange, the market. We also use the term 'value' in an entirely different sense, however, in its plural form. We often hear talk of our society's 'values', its ethical standards, the benchmark for choosing between different modes of action. Our 'values' include happiness, respect for others, sustainability (Bloemers 2003) etc. Here, 'values' is a fairly recent sociological abstraction that harks back to a much older meaning.

This second meaning of value is not reflected in the modern use of the term 'price', but it is reflected in the verb 'to prize'. In this second sense, 'value' or 'values' specifically refers not to quantities created in the interplay of supply and demand, but to 'significance by virtue of quality'. This meaning refers both to material quality, as in things like gold and silver, and inner quality, as in 'to value someone or something highly'. In other words, value refers to the qualities that distinguish one thing from another, or to the reputation a person enjoys, or the respect someone deserves, on the basis of the qualities that society holds dear. In other words, this meaning of value refers to the qualities that determine the *reputation* of a thing or person. I think that this still plays a role in shaping values away from the context of the market, and thus also in shaping the cultural heritage. These qualities are commonly regarded as an intrinsic, natural or preordained element of the thing or person in question (Bazelmans 1999). However, it is good to realise that revealing and shaping those qualities often takes a great deal of effort and investment.

The Dutch banknotes in circulation from the 1950s to the 1980s serve as a nice example of both meanings (fig. 1.1). They depicted a series of great men, i.e. men with reputation: Grotius, Boerhave, Huygens, Erasmus, Rembrandt (all designed by Eppo Doeve), Vondel, Hals, Sweelinck, De Ruyter and Spinoza (all designed by Robert (Ootje) Oxenaar). These images must not be regarded merely as decoration. Of course money derives its value from, among other things, the national reserves of currency and precious metals, and from national monetary and economic policies. However, its value also derives from political, historical and religious notions as symbolized

by the great figures depicted on the banknotes. In other words, the value of money has its origins in both orders of exchange and is therefore not merely synonymous with exchange value but is also inextricably linked to the core values that the state regards as crucial for the survival of society.

Historical awareness and the historical experience

The question is: what value and values are created in archaeology? I would suggest that, in this respect, there is not much difference between us and many non-modern societies, and what was depicted on the old Dutch banknotes. In archaeology, too, the acquisition and maintenance of standing or reputation is key, as part of the greater project of writing the historiography of groups. To my mind, this is evident in the treatment of the past in the developing nation states of Europe in the 19th and 20th century. In this context it is striking how actively and consciously many historians in the Netherlands become involved in the debate on the historical canon (www. entoen.nu), and over the question of what values are rooted in our national history (Van Es and de Rooij 2005, Van der Horst 2005, Lendering 2005, Palm 2005 and Pleij 2005, for a critical stance see Ribbens 2004). No historian will ever say it is possible to write a complete narrative of Dutch history, but I believe that their collaboration on the creation of a canon implies that consensus is possible, at least along broad lines, taking the boundaries, institutions and communities of the Dutch nation state as a starting point. Many historians do not even shy from describing the origin of the values regarded as so important in our current society: individual courage, tolerance, common sense, exemplary rebelliousness, consensus-mindedness etc. This surprises me, especially the particularism that some historians display. I have come to the conclusion that this debate cannot be left solely to historians. I should like to urge archaeologists to take a much more prominent role.

Fig. 1.1

Fig. 1.2

Before I can examine this role, I must first consider two factors that hamper the involvement of archaeologists, or at least appear to do so. Without wishing to do an injustice to theologists', artists' and philosophers' centuries of intensive reflection on the essence of nature (Schouten 2005), I detect in our society an increasing tendency to base our individual and collective identity and our core values in nature. Some cultural philosophers even refer to nature as the new religion. Symptomatic of this are the Dutch efforts to reshape our landscape into what it was before man had an impact (Van Schendelen 1999 230-232), by literally 'de-poldering' it in the name of nature development, with some a-historical wilderness as the point of reference (Vera 1997 and Keulartz 2002), and by reintroducing animals that are extinct in this country. Another example is the humanisation of animals (Cliteur 2001) in our food production system – by word, at any rate, if not by deed. Again, it is interesting to look at money, and specifically at a series of banknotes used in the Netherlands from the 1980s up to the introduction of the euro in 2002. The celebrated men of the past who once graced the money in our pockets were replaced by images of nature: the kingfisher, the robin, the sunflower (fig. 1.2), the snipe, the little owl and the lapwing (all designed by Jaap Drupsteen). I interpret this change of imagery as a change in the value orientation of our society, as authenticity, naturalness, diversity, beauty and purity came to dominate.

Secondly, I have observed that the collective memory, and therefore also the individual historical experience, has become more superficial over time in the Netherlands. It is an undeniable fact that important values are increasingly rooted in more and more recent periods of history. Historians have played a leading role in this. In the sixteenth and seventeenth centuries, in the developing Republic and later in the Dutch state and its cultural elite, Tacitus' Batavians of the Roman period were crucial to the way the Dutch nation defined itself and to important values such as independence and bourgeois virtues (Langereis 2004 and Van der Woud 1998). In the nineteenth century, the Dutch took as their example artistic and scientific ideas and the pragmatic and heroic behaviour of stadholders, merchants, discoverers, scientists and artists in the Golden Age (Bank 1990). Nowadays, core values seemed to be defined almost exclusively in relation to the behaviour of those who resisted or collaborated with the Nazis in the Second World War (Van der Heijden 2001). The public's enthusiasm for what I, as an archaeologist, call the history of yesterday – the history of families, professions, companies, streets, villages and regions in the 19th and 20th centuries – is also part of this trend. This is all about feeling at home in your immediate environment, in your own dialect, in your own family and circle of friends, in a globalising world in recession, where different value systems are diametrically opposed to each other. The values at stake here are probably not those of the state and its cultural elite.

This historical, popular scientific and public focus on the familiar is not a problem as far as I am concerned, it is more an inevitability inherent to human nature. No form of political correctness can change any aspect of the construction of an exclusive identity. However, I believe this particularist perspective does need to be accompanied by a focus on the complex contemporaneous and historical relationships with other social entities and thus automatically by an awareness of the historicity of our identity. When it comes to writing the history of the nation, for example, this entails putting the concepts of the Netherlands, the Dutch state and the Dutch community into perspective.

Placing things in perspective like this opens up a series of themes that lie further back in pre- and protohistory, and which are interesting not only from an academic point of view, but also bring us face to face with important issues in our own society. I am thinking, for example, of the origin of mankind, man's colonisation of the planet, the domestication of animals and crops, the creation of a family of Indo-European languages and cultures, the creation of the first states and empires etc. These processes confront us directly with our ideas and our appreciation of the contrast between humans and animals, between indigenous and foreign, between hearth and home and the outside world, between the individual on the one hand and society and the state on the other etc. *This is about combining humanity and cultural diversity, self-awareness and openness, and a sense of community and individual autonomy.* These are crucial pairs of social values, about which archaeologists also have plenty of interesting things to say. These frameworks seem to have been clearly defined at the international level. The Valletta Convention states that protecting the archaeological heritage will help in the creation of a European collective memory, and allow us to retrace the history of mankind. Again, this is reflected in the money we now use.

The paper denominations of the Euro, with their explicit and somewhat clichéd reference to successive European architectural styles from the Roman period onwards, clearly show that the creation of value and values is now part of a political and cultural project to shape a European community (Klamer and Van Dalen 1998). However, according to the European Central Bank, the 'windows, doors and bridges' on these banknotes not only symbolise an exclusive European identity, but also 'the spirit of openness and cooperation in the EU and in communications between peoples' (www.ecb.int/bc/banknotes/looks/). I believe that there could be no better invitation to historians – and also to archaeologists – to make an active contribution to the retracing of our history and the values it represents.

Note: this essay is an abridged version of Bazelmans 2006.

J.Bazelmans@cultureelerfgoed.nl

References

Bank, J. 1990: *Het roemrijk vaderland : cultureel nationalisme in Nederland in de negentiende eeuw,* Den Haag.

Bank, J., Es, G. van & Rooij, P. de 2005: *Kortweg Nederland. Wat iedereen wil weten over onze geschiedenis,* Wormer.

Barraud, C., Coppet, D. de, Iteanu, A. & Jamous, R. 1994: *Of relations and the dead. Four societies viewed from the angle of their exchanges,* Londen.

Bazelmans, J. 1999: *By weapons made worthy. Lords, retainers and their relationship in Beowulf,* Amsterdam.

Bazelmans, J. 2006: Value and Values in Archaeology and Archaeological Heritage Management. A Revolution in the Archaeological System, *Berichten van de Rijksdienst voor Oudheidkundig Bodemonderzoek* 46, 13-26.

Bloemers, J.H.F. 2003: *Op weg naar een duurzaam archeologisch-historisch landschap in 2015?,* Amsterdam.

Blom, H. 1983: *In de ban van goed en fout? Wetenschappelijke geschiedschrijving over de bezettingstijd in Nederland,* Bergen.

Cliteur, P. 2001: *Darwin, dier en recht,* Meppel.

Goff, J. le 1986: *La bourse et la vie. Économie et religion au Moyen Age,* Parijs.

Groenewoudt, B.J. 1994: *Prospectie, waardering en selectie van archeologische vindplaatsen een beleidsgerichte verkenning van middelen en mogelijkheden,* Amersfoort.

Heijden, C. van der 2001: *Grijs Verleden, Nederland en de Tweede Wereldoorlog* (Amsterdam, 2001)

Horst, H. van der 2005: *Het beste land van de wereld. Waar komen onze normen en waarden vandaan?,* Amsterdam.

Keulartz, J. 2000: Naar een 'beschaafde' strijd om de natuur, in Keulartz J. (ed.), *Rustig, ruig en rationeel.Filosofische debatten over de verhouding cultuur-natuur,* Baarn.

Klamer, A., & Dalen, H. van 1998: *Het verhaal van geld,* Amsterdam.

Langereis, S. 2004: Van botte boeren tot beschaafde burgers. Oudheidkundige beelden van de Bataven, 1500-1800, in Swinkels L. (ed.), *De Bataven. Verhalen van een verdwenen volk,* Amsterdam.

Latour, B 1993: *We have never been modern,* Harvard University Press, Cambridge Mass., USA.

Lendering, J. 2005: *Polderdenken. De wortels van de Nederlandse overlegcultuur,* Amsterdam.

Palm, J. 2005: *De vergeten geschiedenis van Nederland. Waarom Nederlanders hun verleden niet kennen,* Amsterdam.

Parry, J., & Bloch, M. 1989: Introduction: Money and the morality of exchange, in Bloch M. & Parry, J. *Money and the morality of exchange,* Cambridge, 1-32.

Pleij, H. 2005: *Erasmus en het poldermodel,* Amsterdam.

Ribbens, K. 2004: 'De vaderlandse canon voorbij? Een multiculturele historische cultuur in wording', *Tijdschrift voor Geschiedenis* 117 (2004) 500-521

Schendelen, M. van 1999: De strijd om Arcadië: natuur en landschap als domeinen van ruimtelijke ordening, in Kolen, J.& Lemaire, T. (eds.), *Landschap in meervoud. Perspectieven op het Nederlandse landschap in de 20ste/21ste eeuw,* Utrecht, 217-234.

Schouten, M.G.C. 2005: *Spiegel van de natuur. Het natuurbeeld in cultuurhistorisch perspectief,* Utrecht.

Vera, F. 1997: *Metaforen voor de Wildernis. Eik, hazelaar, rund en paard,* Den Haag.

Willems, W.J.H. 1997: Archaeological heritage management in the Netherlands: past, present and future, in Willems, W.J.H., Kars, H. & Hallewas, D.P. (eds.), *Archaeological heritage management in the Netherlands fifty years State Service for Archaeological Investigations,* Assen, 3-34.

Woud, A. van der 1998: *De Bataafse hut. Denken over het oudste Nederland (1750-1850),* Amsterdam.

2 | Perspectives sur les relations entre la gestion du patrimoine archéologique et la gestion du paysage en Région wallonne (Belgique)

Axelle Letor et Marie-Jeanne Ghenne

Résumé: La gestion du paysage historique peut être opérée à différents niveaux, via la régulation de l'impact de l'aménagement sur le patrimoine d'une part, et via la prise en charge générale du paysage d'autre part. Au premier niveau, la Région wallonne a développé des processus de contrôle et des outils d'identification communs à la plupart des pays européens, tels que les inventaires. Ceux-ci ont un rôle à jouer dans la promotion du patrimoine auprès du public, des aménageurs et des autorités. Toutefois, il est évident qu'en plus d'être le reflet de la recherche, ils offrent une vision morcelée du patrimoine qui n'appréhende pas le paysage résultant des activités humaines au cours du temps. Les avis émis par les archéologues lors du processus de planification se concentrent donc sur les sites et leur environnement immédiat; l'attention portée à l'ensemble du paysage historique est insuffisante. Au second niveau, les documents et les procédures ayant une incidence sur le paysage, ainsi que les travaux d'identification et de qualification paysagère destinés à mettre en œuvre la Convention européenne du paysage de Florence (2000), intègrent la dimension historique de façon variable. Dans les deux cas, il est crucial de proposer des moyens de mesurer le degré d'historicité du paysage actuel, d'en intégrer les résultats dans les instruments de gestion, d'en encourager l'utilisation. Une démarche consistant à partir du paysage présent et à s'insérer dans les outils préexistants, comme l'entend la caractérisation historique du paysage en Angleterre (HLC), nous paraît novatrice en Région wallonne.

Préambule

Le but de cette contribution est de mettre en évidence l'importance de l'intégration globale du patrimoine dit culturel (au sens ici restreint de patrimoine bâti, paysager et archéologique), vulnérable et non renouvelable, dans les procédures d'aménagement du territoire grâce à un inventaire archéologique élargi comme aide à la décision, dans une perspective de protection mais aussi de développement durable.

L'accent sera principalement mis sur la gestion du patrimoine archéologique par le biais de l'inventaire archéologique et des relations qu'il entretient avec le paysage. Nous évoquerons par ailleurs une des applications implicites de la Convention européenne du paysage de Florence (2000), à savoir la question de l'intégration de l'archéologie dans l'analyse et dans l'évaluation paysagère.

L'évolution de la notion d'inventaire dans le cadre de l'intégration de l'archéologie dans les procédures d'aménagement du territoire

Outils et procédures

Depuis 1989, la Belgique est devenue effectivement un état fédéral composé de trois régions : Bruxelles, Flandre et Wallonie et de trois communautés : la communauté française, la communauté flamande et la communauté germanophone. Quatre entités ont la charge de la matière archéologique : les trois régions, compétentes en matière de biens immobiliers (fouilles archéologiques) et la communauté germanophone, partie intégrante du territoire wallon mais possédant sa propre compétence archéologique depuis 2000. Les biens mobiliers (musées) relèvent de la tutelle communautaire. En Région wallonne, l'ensemble du patrimoine, dont l'archéologie, est géré sur une superficie d'environ 16.000 km^2 par la Direction générale de l'Aménagement du territoire, du Logement et du Patrimoine du Ministère de la Région wallonne désormais il faut par la DGATLP, la DGO4, Direction générale opérationnelle 4 (1er août 2008) et par Ministère de la Région wallonne, le Service public de Wallonie.

Dès le 19ème siècle, les sociétés savantes se sont penchées sur la distribution des sites archéologiques sur leur territoire de prédilection. Le Service des Fouilles des Musées royaux du Cinquantenaire de Bruxelles devenu le Service des Fouilles de l'Etat a développé les premières cartes archéologiques méthodiques. Le Service National des Fouilles qui lui a succédé reçut, en 1973, la mission de réaliser un répertoire cartographique des sites connus pour le Ministère des Travaux Publics. Des répertoires bibliographiques des trouvailles archéologiques par province furent en outre publiés par le Centre national de Recherches archéologiques en Belgique, satellite du SNF depuis 1963 (Matthys 1997).

Dans la deuxième moitié des années '80, deux projets cartographiques destinés à étayer la connaissance et la protection des sites archéologiques en milieu urbain et rural dans le cadre de l'octroi des permis de bâtir voient le jour. Ils sont réalisés par l'Université catholique de Louvain pour la Communauté française et de la Région wallonne. Il s'agissait d'une première passerelle vers une gestion du patrimoine archéologique en tant que composante de l'Aménagement du territoire. Progressivement, l'archéologie sortait du milieu exclusivement culturel et surtout académique. Cette initiative était devenue nécessaire dans la mesure où des cellules d'intervention rapide (Services SOS Fouilles) avaient été mises en place sous la direction scientifique des universités francophones depuis 1980.

Les Atlas du Sous-Sol archéologique des Centres urbains anciens, inspirés des travaux d'H. Galinié à Tours et cartographiés à l'échelle cadastrale se composent de trois parties graphiques, outre un fascicule de synthèse : la carte des archives du sol (interventions archéologiques, état du sous-sol, espaces jadis bâtis, aujourd'hui accessibles), la carte de destruction et de protection, et la carte des zones soumises à information d'un archéologue agréé du Ministère (Remy & Ghenne 2002).

La Planification wallonne des Sites d'Intérêt archéologique, contemporaine des Atlas, se concentre sur le milieu rural. Elle se compose d'un fichier informatisé, d'une cartographie des sites par province conçue au 1/25000e afin de se superposer à l'échelle du plan de secteur, document d'occupation du sol opposable au tiers. Elle comporte un fascicule explicatif qui décrit le potentiel archéologique (chercheurs, inventaires, potentiel, état de la recherche), l'érosion (destructions et menaces), la protection des sites, et évalue les politiques et décisions d'urbanisme relatives aux sites archéologiques.

A partir de la régionalisation en 1989 et surtout à partir de la publication du premier décret archéologique en 1991 (révisé en 1999), intégré au Code wallon de l'Aménagement du territoire, de l'Urbanisme et du Patrimoine (CWATUP), un inventaire systématisé des sites archéologiques se développe sur la base des travaux cités ci-dessus et du fonds d'archives du Service National des Fouilles. Presque simultanément, la signature de la Convention de La Valette en 1992 (ratifiée depuis 2004) par la Région wallonne vient appuyer cette démarche. C'est ainsi qu'afin de réguler l'impact des travaux d'aménagement sur le patrimoine archéologique, des procédures d'information, similaires à la plupart des régions et pays européens, se mettent progressivement en place en Région wallonne, par le biais de la consultation des permis d'urbanisme au regard des recensements des sites archéologiques. Ce processus est soutenu par un article du décret archéologique qui permet de « subordonner la délivrance d'un permis d'urbanisme ou de lotir à l'exécution de sondages archéologiques et de fouilles » (CWATUP, Livre III, Titre IV, Chapitre II, Article 235). Les permis sont consultés par la Direction de l'Archéologie du Ministère de la Région wallonne. Ils sont également visés par la section fouille de la Commission royale des monuments, sites et fouilles, à titre consultatif. Les archéologues ont donc été amenés à émettre un avis fondé sur l'inventaire conçu comme outil de gestion.

L'inventaire permet une protection indirecte, en tant que référence à des sites connus ou présumés mais n'est pas, sous sa forme actuelle, opposable au tiers. Les seules protections effectives des biens archéologiques se situent au niveau de l'inscription sur une liste de sauvegarde (valable un an et pouvant aboutir à un classement) et par classement (CWATUP, Livre III, Titre II, Chapitre 1er, Section 2-7), sous la forme d'un arrêté ministériel et d'une publication au Moniteur belge.

Toute trace de l'activité matérielle humaine est répertoriée dans l'inventaire et cartographiée en tant que « zone » de potentialité archéologique (Remy & Ghenne 2002), sans distinction particulière des espaces menacés. Des enquêtes documentaires ponctuelles approfondies sont toutefois menées dans le cadre des études d'incidence. Les archéologues tiennent bien entendu compte du fait que l'inventaire reflète avant tout l'état des connaissances; ils peuvent favoriser les zones vierges dans leurs prises de décision. La réalisation et l'accès à l'information sont organisés au niveau des Services de l'Archéologie provinciaux du Ministère. Une centralisation des données est prévue, à travers la banque de données informatisée commune et une méthode d'enregistrement uniformisée. Un thesaurus permet de contrôler les entrées, tout en s'adaptant localement.

Produit à l'origine sous forme de fiches et de cartes réalisées manuellement, l'inventaire a progressivement pris la forme d'une base de données informatisée, ponctuellement liée à un Système d'Information géographique (SIG). Il implique le dépouillement systématique des diverses sources bibliographiques, archivistiques, cartographiques et iconographiques disponibles, ainsi que des enquêtes de terrain. La collaboration avec les prospecteurs ou les chercheurs bénévoles locaux s'avère cruciale dans ce processus qui fait appel à une connaissance concrète des territoires étudiés. L'enregistrement des données tend vers la multidisciplinarité en incluant dans la base de données des informations géomorphologiques, le résultat des prospections géophysiques, les datations absolues, etc.

De 2000 à 2006, en participant aux deux volets du projet européen Planarch visant à promouvoir des solutions au niveau de la gestion du patrimoine archéologique dans le cadre des procédures qui l'unissent à l'aménagement du territoire, la Direction de l'Archéologie a développé, à la faveur des échanges et dans des conditions optimales, un inventaire élargi répondant à des normes transnationales (Letor 2007b).

La base de données informatisée a été perfectionnée, enrichie en étant directement liée au SIG, lui-même alimenté par de nouvelles sources cartographiques et par la prise en compte de la photographie aérienne. La méthode cartographique a fait l'objet d'une réflexion en profondeur (Letor 2007a). Elle s'est affinée en s'adaptant aux usages pratiqués par les services de l'Aménagement du territoire. Au plan des territoires rural ou périurbain, les sites archéologiques jadis indiqués par des points ou des périmètres approximatifs ont été transformés en polygones qui suivent les limites de toutes les parcelles cadastrales touchées par l'étendue d'un site avéré ou présumé. Les anciennes informations sont néanmoins conservées sous la forme d'une couche cartographique d'archivage. Cette approche permet une protection plus large et une vision plus claire, évitant ainsi toute forme de recours puisque les permis d'urbanisme sont octroyés en fonction du parcellaire par les services de l'Aménagement du territoire.

Une série de cartes et d'études propres à la gestion du patrimoine archéologique urbain ont également été produites. Elles constituent des documents plus complets que les Atlas publiés dans les années '80/'90 décrits ci-dessus car, par rapport à ceux-ci, elles ont été augmentées d'études thématiques ciblant l'évolution des quartiers, notamment ceux concernés par les plans communaux d'aménagement ou ayant subi de profondes modifications au cours des temps, de cartes géotechniques (épaisseur des remblais, profondeur de la nappe aquifère, stratigraphie. Fig. 2.1) et de cartes d'évolution des zones de culture et de friches.

Un premier pas dans le sens d'un élargissement de l'enregistrement archéologique *stricto sensu* a été mené en concevant, à titre expérimental, deux cartes du potentiel lié à l'environnement, superposables à la carte des zones archéologiques. Ces données doivent être utilisées avec précaution pour éviter le déterminisme écologique. Cependant, il a été tenté de mettre en évidence les zones estimées favorables à l'activité ou à l'installation humaine, d'un point de vue géologique (présence de matières premières telles que le silex), pédologique (sols fertiles) et paysager (rivières, sources, confluents, gués, ou hauteurs). La carte du potentiel de conservation (Fig. 2.2) établit quant à elle les zones favorables ou défavorables à la conservation des vestiges archéologiques, selon des critères essentiellement pédologiques (épaisseur des sols, qualité du drainage, perturbations, colluvionnement, …).

Tous ces documents servent d'assise au choix des interventions à mener en amont des aménagements, à la préparation des archéologues en cas d'intervention préventive, aux négociations avec les aménageurs et avec les pouvoirs décisionnels. Enfin, bien que conçus dans une optique d'aménagement du territoire, ils constituent une base utile à la recherche scientifique.

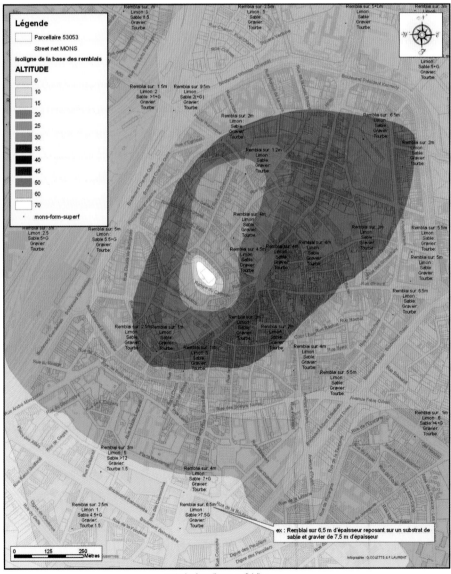

carte des formations superficielles

Fig. 2.1: Carte géotechnique des formations superficielles, Mons (Province de Hainaut). Auteur : Olivier Collette d'après une documentation de Serge Ghiste, infographie: Fabrice Laurent et Olivier Collette.

La prise en compte du paysage dans le cadre des inventaires
Aussi sophistiqués soient-ils, il est évident que les instruments qui inventorient le patrimoine archéologique, en plus d'être le reflet de la recherche, en offrent une vision morcelée qui ne rend pas compte de la stratification, de la complexité (changements, continuités, réutilisations), et de la globalité (paysages ordinaires, « endommagés », ...) du paysage. En conséquence, les avis rendus par les archéologues durant le processus de contrôle de l'aménagement se concentrent sur les sites et leur environnement immédiat ou sur des paysages thématiques, voire des « reliques » imaginaires. C'est le cas du classement des biens archéologiques qui ne considère le paysage historique qu'en tant qu'environnement d'un site ou en tant que témoin d'un événement historique (par exemple, le site de la bataille de Waterloo). Les études d'incidence présentent la même lacune. Cela a été mis en évidence dans le cadre du projet européen Planarch 2, lorsque 100 dossiers d'études d'incidence en Région wallonne, couvrant une période allant de 1997 à 2004, ont été examinés de manière à estimer le rôle de la composante patrimoniale dans ces études (Jones, Slinn *et al.* 2006). Il apparaît que pour le paysage, ces dernières « sont caractérisées par une approche traditionnelle comprenant la géologie, la géographie, l'agronomie ou l'écologie.

Souvent aussi ce sont l'approche visuelle et les critères de qualité qui prévalent sans tenir compte des liens entretenus par l'homme et la nature tels qu'évoqués dans la Convention européenne du paysage » (Ghenne 2008).

La place accordée au paysage dans sa globalité lors de la gestion du patrimoine, insuffisante dans la pratique, est toutefois bien définie au niveau législatif en Wallonie, et ce avant la publication du texte de la Convention européenne du paysage (2000).

Depuis le 27 novembre 1997, la notion de paysage est introduite dans le CWATUP (« Le territoire de la Région wallonne est un patrimoine commun de ses habitants. La Région et les autres autorités publiques chacune dans le cadre de ses compétences et en coordination avec la Région, sont gestionnaires et garantes de l'aménagement du territoire. Elles rencontrent de manière durable les besoins sociaux, économiques, patrimoniaux et environnementaux de la collectivité par la gestion qualitative du cadre de vie, par l'utilisation parcimonieuse du sol et de ses ressources et par la conservation et le développement du patrimoine culturel, naturel et paysager » : CWATUP, Livre Ier, Titre Ier, Chapitre 1er, Article Ier, paragraphe 1er (Devillers & Deconinck 2004, Melin *et al.* 2001)

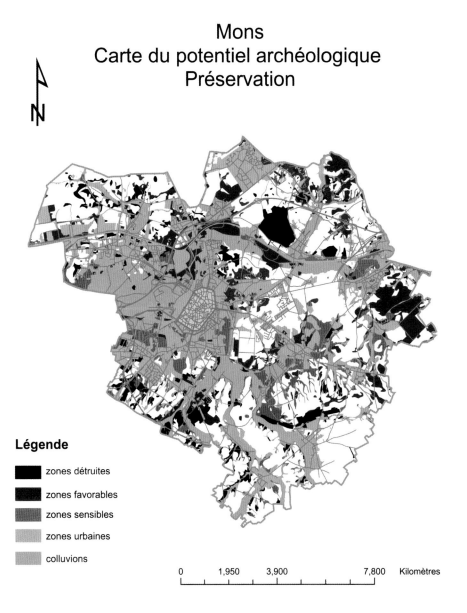

Mons
Carte du potentiel archéologique
Préservation

N

Légende
■ zones détruites
■ zones favorables
■ zones sensibles
□ zones urbaines
□ colluvions

0   1,950   3,900   7,800   Kilomètres

Fig. 2.2: Carte du potentiel de conservation archéologique lié à l'environnement dans la commune de Mons (Province de Hainaut). Auteurs : Olivier Collette et Axelle Letor, infographie : Olivier Collette et Luc-Emmanuel Venditti.

Table 2.1

Documents	Valeur	Niveau	Dimension hist. du paysage		
			Présente	Absente	Eventuelle
Diplôme européen des espaces protégés	Orient.	Suprarég.			X
Convention pour la protection du patrimoine mondial, culturel et naturel (UNESCO)	Orient.	Suprarég.			X
Convention Benelux en matière de conservation de la nature et de protection des paysages	Orient.	Suprarég.			X
Directive de la Communauté économique Européenne Faune-Flore-Habitat	Orient.	Suprarég.		X	
Stratégie paneuropéenne de la diversité biologique et paysagère	Orient.	Suprarég.			X
Schéma de Développement de l'Espace communautaire	Orient.	Suprarég.			X
Loi sur le remembrement de biens ruraux	Réglem.	Régional			X
Procédures de classement	Réglem.	Régional			X
Plan de secteur	Réglem.	Régional	X		
Règlements Régionaux d'Urbanisme	Réglem.	Régional	X		
Études d'incidence sur l'environnement	Orient.	Régional			X
Plan d'Environnement pour le Développement Durable	Orient.	Régional			X
Code wallon de l'Aménagement du territoire, de l'Urbanisme et du Patrimoine	Réglem.	Régional	X		
Schéma de Développement de l'Espace Régional	Orient.	Régional	X		
Contrat d'Avenir de la Wallonie	Orient.	Régional		X	
Décret du Gouvernement wallon relatif à la conservation et à la protection du patrimoine	Réglem.	Régional	X		
Plan wallon de Développement Rural	Orient.	Régional			X
Schéma de Structure communal	Orient.	Comm.		X	
Règlement communal d'Urbanisme	Réglem.	Comm.		X	
Plan communal d'Aménagement	Réglem.	Comm.			X
Procédure de délivrance des permis	Réglem.	Comm.			X
Plans de développement	Orient.	Comm.		X	

D'autre part, le décret du Gouvernement wallon relatif à la conservation et à la protection du patrimoine, adopté le 1er avril 1999, propose une définition du patrimoine intégrant l'intérêt paysager (« L'ensemble des biens immobiliers dont la protection se justifie en raison de leur intérêt historique, archéologique, scientifique, artistique, social, technique ou paysager ». CWATUP, Livre III, Titre 1er, Chapitre 1er, Article 185).

Le paysage et le patrimoine culturel ont été établis comme facteurs à envisager au cours des études d'impact sur l'environnement depuis les directives européennes de 1985 et 1997 (« Directive européenne sur l'évaluation des effets de certains projets privés et publics sur l'environnement » 85/337 du Conseil des Communautés européennes du 27 juin 1985, amendée par la Directive 97/11. (Feltz 2004; Jones Slinn *et al.* 2006; Melin *et al.* 2001; *Textes juridiques sur le paysage en Belgique, Région wallonne*, s. d.).

La place de la dimension archéologique/ historique dans la gestion du paysage en Région wallonne

Les documents et procédures

Si la prise en compte de l'archéologie du paysage par les acteurs de la gestion du patrimoine archéologique demeure déficiente, nous pouvons nous interroger sur la manière dont la dimension archéologique ou historique est considérée lors de la gestion du paysage.

Les documents et procédures administratifs et légaux ayant une incidence sur ou un lien direct avec la prise en charge du paysage en Région wallonne sont présentés ici sous la forme d'un tableau (Table 2.1) tentant de mettre en évidence leur degré d'intégration de la dimension historique ou culturelle (ces documents ont été inventoriés par la Conférence permanente pour le Développement territorial (CPDT) : (Billen *et al.* 2004; Devillers 2004; Devillers & Deconinck 2004; Feltz 2004; Melin *et al.* 2001; *Textes juridiques sur le paysage en Belgique, Région wallonne*, s. d.). Le classement est effectué selon trois catégories :

- « présente » : la dimension historique est mentionnée explicitement ou évoquée, la procédure ayant un réel effet d'intégration de cette dimension,
- « absente » : les dimensions historique ou culturelle ne sont pas citées, le paysage est considéré d'un point de vue écologique ou visuel,
- « éventuelle » : la dimension historique n'est pas directement mentionnée mais le document ou la procédure peuvent être utilisés à des fins d'assimilation de cette dimension, ou la dimension culturelle est citée, dans laquelle peut être incluse la dimension historique (encore faut-il s'accorder sur les définitions de paysages culturels ou historiques).

La valeur d'orientation ou réglementaire des outils est spécifiée, ainsi que le niveau de compétence : suprarégional, régional ou communal.

La dimension historique du paysage est bien représentée au niveau régional. Toujours « présente » (5 cas sur 11) ou « éventuelle » (5 cas sur 11), elle n'est « absente » que d'un document, non réglementaire.

Au niveau suprarégional, la dimension historique n'est jamais clairement indiquée, mais elle est le plus souvent « éventuelle » (5 cas sur 6), en accordant une place importante à la dimension culturelle. On constate par contre une faiblesse au niveau communal, où la dimension historique n'est jamais « présente ». Elle est « absente » d'un document réglementaire essentiel : le règlement communal d'urbanisme. Ceci est d'autant plus dommageable que

dans le cadre de l'optimalisation du CWATUP, une autonomie croissante est accordée aux communes wallonnes.

La Convention européenne du paysage et les travaux d'identification et de qualification du paysage

La ratification de la Convention européenne du paysage par la Région wallonne depuis le 20 décembre 2001 (et par la Belgique depuis 2004) incite à l'exécution de travaux d'identification et de qualification, répondant à la mesure particulière n°3 (Con*vention européenne du paysage, Florence, 2000.* Article 6 – Mesures particulières). Si le document européen ouvre des portes à la prise en compte de la dimension historique, ne fût-ce que par sa définition du paysage, celle-ci n'est pas clairement exprimée. Il revient aux archéologues et historiens de se positionner eux-mêmes en tant qu'intervenants dans sa mise en œuvre (Ghenne 2006).

Les initiatives entreprises dans cette voie reconnaissent manifestement la dimension historique et prônent son assimilation aux études d'identification et de qualification. L'ouvrage déterminant « Des paysages : pour qui ? Pourquoi ? Comment ? » publié par G. Neuray en 1982, fait la part belle à l'évolution du paysage. En 1998, une Conférence permanente pour le Développement territorial (CPDT) a été établie par le Gouvernement wallon. Depuis 2001, le thème n°4 « Gestion territoriale de l'environnement » de la CPDT consacre ses actions au patrimoine paysager.

Fig. 2.3a et b: Évolution du paysage de la localité de Marcinelle de 1845-1855 à 2000 (Commune de Charleroi, Province de Hainaut). Auteure : Anne-Cécile Ghigny, infographie : Anne-Cécile Ghigny et Luc-Emmanuel Venditti.

La dimension historique y est envisagée de façon tangible (Billen *et al.* 2004): «L'apport de l'histoire notamment permet de comprendre l'évolution et ainsi de relativiser le caractère naturel ou immuable de certains paysages »), entre autres :

- dans le cadre des mesures de protection des paysages patrimoniaux;
- au cours d'études d'incidence préalables aux demandes de permis;
- dans le cadre de la création de chartes du paysage;
- pour la délimitation des périmètres paysagers du plan de secteur;
- pour la définition de projets par les acteurs communaux (Billen *et al.* 2004). Toutefois, dans ce cas : « La commune dispose généralement de diverses études qu'elle peut rassembler pour constituer un dossier de base : il peut s'agir d'analyses de paysages déjà réalisées dans le cadre d'opérations précises (rénovation urbaine, remembrement,...); il peut aussi s'agir d'inventaires existants (inventaire des sites, du patrimoine,...) » (Billen *et al.* 2004). Or, nous avons vu que ces inventaires ne suffisent pas à la compréhension historique du paysage présent, considéré dans sa globalité.

De la même façon, les principaux outils développés par la CPDT, tels que la carte des territoires paysagers de Wallonie, les atlas de paysage et l'étude des paysages patrimoniaux font bien appel à l'analyse historique, notamment lors de la reconnaissance des «aires paysagères» et des «paysages témoins patrimoniaux» (Feltz 2004; Kummert & Quériat 2004) mais n'appréhendent pas encore la totalité du paysage historique.

Cette faiblesse résulte d'ailleurs d'une représentation de l'archéologie véhiculée notamment par les archéologues eux-mêmes qui tendent à se focaliser sur les sites et leur environnement immédiat, sur les notions de paysages thématiques ou témoins, dont ils oblitèrent volontiers des pans d'évolution pour les transformer en gardiens figés d'un passé imaginaire.

Pour une prise en compte complète du paysage historique

Le rôle de l'archéologue et de l'historien est d'insister, selon les termes de la Convention européenne de Florence, sur la notion que le paysage présent est le fruit des interactions entre l'homme et son environnement, et que par conséquent, à l'exception de quelques rares espaces encore totalement naturels, la globalité du paysage actuellement visible est historique.

Il leur revient surtout de mettre en place des moyens concrets qui permettent de comprendre, en le mesurant systématiquement, le degré de profondeur historique de l'ensemble du paysage actuel. Les résultats devraient d'une part être intégrés à l'inventaire archéologique afin d'atteindre les processus de contrôle (tels que les études d'incidence ou la délivrance des permis d'urbanisme) et d'autre part être mis à la disposition des analyses paysagères et des instruments réglementaires ou de guidance ayant une incidence sur la prise en charge du paysage en général (tels que les divers plans et schémas locaux ou régionaux).

Au-delà de l'intégration de l'information, son utilisation régulière par les aménageurs, les bureaux d'étude d'incidence et les services d'aménagement du territoire locaux ou régionaux constitue un enjeu important. Le dialogue devrait être intensifié pour encourager ceux-ci à consulter régulièrement les Services de l'Archéologie et pour définir le type de renseignements entrant en adéquation avec leurs besoins.

Les mêmes questions se posent d'ailleurs au niveau de la sensibilisation du public, les voies menant à une meilleure communication et à la participation citoyenne devant être explorées plus avant.

Enfin, il nous semble que les liens entre le autorités régionales et la recherche académique pourraient être plus profondément exploités en vue de la production d'informations utiles à la gestion et à la conservation quotidienne du patrimoine.

Les tables rondes sur le paysage tenues au cours des réunions de l'*European Archæologists Association* (*EAA*, Cork 2005, Cracovie 2006), la publication de l'*Europæ Archæologiæ Consilium* (*EAC*) «*Europe's Cultural Landscape*» parue en 2002 (Fairclough & Rippon 2002), de même que la réflexion menée lors du Symposium de l'*EAC* en 2006 à Strasbourg, ont fait évoluer notre approche.

La géographie historique déploie depuis longtemps des moyens d'analyse du paysage et la majorité des projets archéologiques incluent désormais un examen du contexte environnemental. Mais une démarche consistant à partir du paysage présent et à s'insérer dans des outils de gestion préexistants, comme l'entend la méthode de caractérisation historique du paysage (*Historic Landscape Characterisation/HLC*) pratiquée en Angleterre, nous a paru novatrice en Région wallonne. Durant le projet Planarch 2, une analyse du paysage en zone périurbaine a été tentée, s'inspirant des principes de la caractérisation historique du paysage. En superposant les cartes anciennes et plans cadastraux successifs (Fig. 2.3 a et b), elle a permis de mettre en évidence l'évolution du parcellaire et l'utilisation du territoire au cours du temps. Il s'agissait d'un exercice annexe qui, faute de temps, n'a pas été poussé jusqu'à la caractérisation proprement dite.

C'est pourquoi la caractérisation est à présent testée sur une portion limitée mais significative du territoire wallon, dans le cadre d'une thèse en archéologie à l'Université libre de Bruxelles. La pertinence des résultats sera évaluée selon un angle d'approche scientifique et stratégique. Le degré de faisabilité et d'utilité que présente une caractérisation du paysage historique pour la prise en charge du paysage et du patrimoine en Région wallonne sera envisagé; la démarche répond-elle aux besoins :

- des archéologues,
- des services ministériels,
- de la Conférence permanente pour le Développement territorial (CPDT),
- des autorités locales,
- des fondations de développement urbain ou rural,
- des aménageurs,
- des bureaux d'études d'incidence ?

Au sein de quels documents et procédures réglementaires ou d'orientation les résultats de la caractérisation peuvent-ils être introduits le plus efficacement ? Quels en sont les intérêts et les limites au niveau stratégique ?

L'objectif de cette recherche est d'améliorer les prises de décision en matière de gestion du patrimoine et, partant, ne fût-ce que très localement, de susciter une interaction avec les organes gouvernementaux ainsi qu'avec les travaux d'identification et de qualification répondant à la mesure particulière n° 3 de la Convention européenne du paysage.

Remerciements

Nos remerciements s'adressent à Mesdames Hélène Remy, Mireille Deconinck (Ministère de la Région wallonne, Direction Générale de l'Aménagement du territoire, du Logement et du Patrimoine, Jambes et Université Libre de Bruxelles), Gislaine Devillers (Ministère de la Région wallonne, Direction Générale de l'Aménagement du territoire, du Logement et du Patrimoine, Jambes), Marie-Françoise Godart (ULB, Institut de Gestion de l'Environnement et de l'Aménagement du Territoire) et Messieurs Olivier Collette (Géologue indépendant), Graham Fairclough (*English Heritage*), et Didier Viviers (ULB, Centre de Recherches archéologiques).

aletor@ulb.ac.be

Bibliographie

Antrop, M. 1989 : Het *landschap meervoudig bekeken*. Monografieën Stichting Leefmilieu, 30, Kapelle.

Antrop, M., De Maeyer, P., Vandermotten, C. & Beyaert, M. 2006 : *La Belgique en cartes. L'évolution du paysage à travers trois siècles de cartographie*, Bruxelles.

Aldred, A. & Fairclough, G. 2003 : *Historic Landscape Characterisation. Taking Stock of the Method*. http://www.english-heritage.org.uk/sevrer/show/nav.1293. Dernier accès en juin 2007.

Billen, C., Feltz, C., Godart, M.-F., Melin, E. (dir.), Neuray, C., van der Kaa, C. & Rousseaux, V. 2004 : *Pour une meilleure prise en compte des paysages.* CPDT, plaquette n° 4, Namur.

Clark, J., Darlington, J. & Fairclough, G. 2004 : *Using Historic Landscape Characterisation*, Londres.

Convention européenne du paysage, Florence, 2000. Conseil de l'Europe, Série des Traités européens, n° 176, Strasbourg.

CWATUP. Code wallon de l'Aménagement du territoire, du Logement et du Patrimoine, 2000, Namur. http://wallex.wallonie.be. Dernier accès août 2007.

Devillers, G. 2004 : Les paysages culturels au niveau de la Région wallonne et au niveau international, in : *Actes des 4es rencontres de la Conférence permanente du développement territorial. Territoires, urbanisation et paysages. Liège, Palais des Congrès, 19 novembre 2004*, Namur, 128-130.

Devillers, G. & Deconinck, M. 2004 : La mise en œuvre de la Convention européenne du paysage en Région wallonne. *Les Cahiers de l'Urbanisme* 50, 6-11.

Fairclough, G. & Rippon, S. (éd.) 2002 : *Europe's Cultural Landscape : archœologists and the management of change. EAC Occasional paper 2*, Exeter.

Feltz, C. 2004 : Paysages et aménagement du territoire en Wallonie en 2004 : état de la législation, avancement des recherches de la CPDT et réflexions sur les enjeux et outils de gestion en Wallonie, in : *Actes des 4es rencontres de la Conférence permanente du développement territorial. Territoires, urbanisation et paysages. Liège, Palais des Congrès, 19 novembre 2004*, Namur, 19-29.

Gilman, P. *et al.* 2006 : *Development of sites and Monuments Records (SMRs) in the Planarch Area of North West Europe*, Maidstone.

Ghenne, M.-J. 2006 : Le territoire comme palimpseste : les résultats du projet Planarch – planification, archéologie et paysage (II), in : *Les objectifs de qualité paysagère : de la théorie à la pratique. Cinquième réunion des ateliers pour la mise en oeuvre de la convention européenne du paysage. Actes. Girona, 28-29 septembre 2006*, Girona, 85-88.

Ghenne, M.-J. 2008 : Enquête sur la prise en compte du patrimoine culturel dans les études d'incidence en Wallonie (1999-2003). Les Cahiers de l'Urbanisme 67, 92-98.

Ghenne, M.-J. & Remy, H. 1997 : Planification et gestion du patrimoine archéologique. *Les Cahiers de l'Urbanisme* 19-20, 30-37.

Ghenne, M.-J., Remy, H., Soumoy, M., Collette, O.,
    Ghigny, A.C., Letor, A. & Tilmant, P.H. 2001 :
    Wallonia Final Report, in : Cuming, P., Evans, K. &
    Williams, J. (éd.): *The Planarch Project in Belgium
    (Flanders and Wallonia), England, France and the
    Netherlands. Final report on actions undertaken by
    the partners*, Maidstone.

Jones, C., Slinn, P. *et al* 2006 : *Cultural Heritage and
    Environmental Impact Assessment in the Planarch
    Area of North West Europe*, Maidstone.

Kummert, M. & Quériat, S. 2004 : L'identification de
    paysages patrimoniaux en Wallonie : les paysages
    liés à la représentation et les paysages témoins,
    in : *Actes des 4es rencontres de la Conférence
    permanente du développement territorial.
    Territoires, urbanisation et paysages. Liège, Palais
    des Congrès, 19 novembre 2004*, Namur, 131-134.

Laurent, R. (dir.) 1980 : *Sources de la géographie
    historique en Belgique : exposition, 26 avril – 31
    mai 1979, à l'occasion du colloque organisé par
    les Archives du Royaume et l'Association des
    Archivistes et des Bibliothécaires de Belgique, 25-27
    avril 1979*, Bruxelles.

Letor, A. 2007a : Le SIG du projet européen Planarch 2.
    Inventaire du patrimoine archéologique en province
    de Hainaut (Belgique). *Culture et Recherche* 111, 22.

Letor, A., 2007b : Mise en œuvre des quatre actions
    du projet Planarch 2 en Wallonie, in : *Le projet
    Planarch 2. Archéologie et Aménagement du
    territoire. Les Cahiers de l'Urbanisme, Hors-série*,
    87-98.

Matthys, A. 1997 : La Direction des fouilles : Histoire et
    devenir. *Les Cahiers de l'Urbanisme* 19-20, 8-17.

Melin, E., Feltz, C., Ertz, D., van der Kaa, Cl.,
    Demesmœcker, A. & Kummert, M. 2001 : *Rapport
    final de la subvention 2000. Septembre 2001.
    Thème 5.1. Le patrimoine naturel et les paysages*
    (MRW, CPDT), s. l. http://www.lepur.geo.ulg.ac.be/
    telechargement/recherches/finalisees/subv_00-01/
    rapport/th5/00-01-th5.1-annexes.pdf, téléchargé via
    le site : http://www.cpdt.wallonie.be. Dernier accès
    en juin 2007.

Neuray, G. 1982 : *Des paysages : pour qui? Pourquoi ?
    Comment ?*, Gembloux.

Remy, H. & Ghenne, M.-J. 2002 : Inventaire des sites
    archéologiques en Wallonie, in : *Le projet Planarch.
    Archéologie et aménagement du territoire, Les
    Cahiers de l'Urbanisme, Hors-série*, Hors-série,
    124-131.

*Textes juridiques sur le paysage en Belgique, Région
    wallonne. Prise en compte du paysage dans les
    documents réglementaires et stratégiques en
    Région Wallonne.* Conseil de l'Europe, Strasourg,
    s. d. http://www.coe.int/t/f/coopération_culturelle/
    environnement/paysage/politiques_nationales/
    Textes_Région_wallone.asp#TopOfPage. Dernier
    accès en juin 2007 (adresse supprimée).

3 | From the archaeological heritage inventories to the historical landscapes of Spain

Silvia Fernández Cacho and David Villalón Torres

Abstract: In Spain, although there have been various initiatives for the development of Cultural Heritage registers, it was not until the 1980s that a specific national inventory of Archaeological Heritage began to be developed. This inventory was completed in some provinces, based on the documentary information available (interventions, bibliography, references, etc.) without ever comparing the data with ground observations. In 1985, heritage policy was transferred to the 17 autonomous regions of Spain. Since then, each region has set its own pace in the development of inventories and the conceptual and technical criteria for their implementation. Thus, while some of them have developed an advanced information system for the processing of the archaeological information available, generating new models of management, others have not. Moreover, rapid and aggressive landscape change is affecting the Archaeological Heritage (intensive farming, urbanization, large infrastructures, etc.) and it is increasingly necessary to identify and preserve Historic Landscapes. Some Spanish regions have already begun to use the new modes of research and management tools. In this context, cooperation between research institutes and agencies that manage the Cultural Heritage is crucial.

Historical introduction

The need for new inventories of the assets that make up the Spanish Historical Heritage has become obvious ever since the new regulatory initiatives to protect and preserve them were passed. If we acknowledge that passing new legislative measures to satisfy the need for Artistic Heritage inventories arises from the authorities concern about such matters, we can then say that such concern was first endorsed in the Spanish royal document *Real Cedula* dated June 6, 1803 that includes rules on how to register and preserve old monuments (Pereda, 981: 25).

However, it was not until the beginning of the 20th century that the creation of a register of the Historical Heritage assets was at least theoretically promoted. Indeed the Royal Decree dated 1 June 1900 provided for the creation of a Monument and Artistic Catalogue and in 1933, through the Spanish act on the defence, preservation and growth of the National Historical-Artistic Heritage (*Ley sobre Defensa, conservación y acrecentamiento del Patrimonio Histórico-Artístico Nacional)*, the making of an asset inventory was once again suggested. This inventory, though, was not made due to the difficult post-war situation in Spain, despite the fact that between 1940 and 1953 a series of decrees on the making of a catalogue of Spanish monuments were published. In 1940, the task of editing and publishing that catalogue in those provinces where it had not been done before was assigned to the Diego Velazquez institute and in 1953, that same work was assigned to the Spanish Ministry of National Education (*Catálogos e Inventarios de Patrimonio Histórico)*; in both cases as an urgent task that had to be accomplished without delay (Hernández, 1998).

In all these works, the type of information that had to be registered was specified. In most cases what was required was the site location and a brief description of the sites, as well as the graphical information available (plans, photographs, drawings, etc.). However, the most direct precedent for the current management model of archaeological data in Andalusia is the archaeological site inventory of the Spanish Ministry of Culture from 1980. As in previous cases, this inventory was done on a provincial basis and consisted of two phases (Fernández-Posse – Alvaro, 1993; Sánchez-Palencia, 1981; Ruiz Zapatero-Jimeno, 1999: 37-38).

The first consisted of a search of the available documentation to find general information on all the known archaeological sites and, secondly, to review and update the inventory, with a focus on the declared or government-owned sites, to explore the less researched areas and to create a data bank. Only the first stage was concluded and it revealed different results in different provinces all over Spain. In order to carry out this first stage, an easy-to-complete form designed to gather very general data was used. Some of the basic sections of the entry form used standardised fields with later computerization in mind (Sánchez-Palencia, 1981).

The form essentially contained administrative information fields, related to the location of the site and its legal situation. There was only one information field where more specific details of the site could be provided. This field related to the site's cultural classification, which was also standardized. The entry form had a total of 27 classifications. There was no functional typology field nor was there a field for the location characteristics. More-over, completion guidelines were provided to ensure, as far as possible, that there was some homogeneity in the data (Sánchez-Palencia, 1981). This increasing interest in producing an archaeological site inventory for the whole country, however, did not influence the 1985 act on Historical Heritage (*Ley de Patrimonio Histórico Español de 1985*), which does not envisage the production of a general real estate inventory but one of goods and chattels (Fernández-Posse – Alvaro, 1993: 68), perhaps as a result of a concern with the illegal traffic of art objects. The acts passed by the different Spanish autonomous regions have now led to a slow but steady improvement in the situation by adding some legal protection measures for the inventoried archaeological sites.

As we have previously said, the decentralization of the cultural competences in Spain militates against the creation of standard criteria for a common archaeological site inventory for the whole of Spain. Each autonomous region can decide on the priority to be accorded to this work in its own area. Heritage protection strategies have been developed along similar lines in the different autonomous regions but each with its own slant and influenced by the size of each region, its archaeological potential, and in accordance with the different priority each of them gives to the Archaeological Heritage. Therefore, the first feature that characterises the management of the Archaeological Heritage in Spain is its heterogeneity, arising from the transfer of competences to the 17 autonomous regions in the 1980s (fig. 3.1).

The competences of the Spanish autonomous regions are in the hands of the regional governments, which assign them to the different Ministries. The management of the Archaeological Heritage is part of the cultural management scope. However, only three out of the seventeen autonomous regions have a ministry with an exclusive competence in Culture (Andalusia, Castile-La Mancha and the Basque Country). In the others, the cultural management is one element of a ministry which may also be responsible for other matters, such as tourism, sports

and education (Table 3.1).Each ministry is organised, in turn, into specific departments (Protection, Preservation, Planning, etc.) with provincial offices, giving a distributed management within the territory. Despite the fact that there have been several unsuccessful attempts, the central government has not taken on the coordination of all the autonomous regions. As a result of this, the differences among them are very marked.

Archaeological entities listed in inventories

A fundamental issue for the making of archaeological inventories, and one of the main aspects that must be dealt with right from the beginning, is the definition of the type of entities to be included in them. In the past, when an inventory was made using an information register on a paper format, specifying the type of entity was not so necessary. However, as soon as inventories became computerised and digital cartography became available, specifying the type of registered entity is of particular importance, especially if the data are to be used to carry out spatial analysis using GIS technology.

In Spain, there are very few cases that clearly mention the archaeological entities that are registered in the inventories. In the few publications that tackle this issue, the traditional connection of an information register (whether on a paper format or a database register) with an archaeological site is made, like in the cases of Catalonia and Madrid (Antona, 1993; Blasco-Baena, 1999). The problem is that archaeological site types are not normally defined and sometimes the same site may appear under different headings, such as isolated findings, town plots, etc. As mentioned, this limits the value of the data for use in GIS.

Research bodies can have a role to play here. The archaeological inventory project of Aragon was developed thanks to collaboration between the regional government of Aragon and the University of Saragossa. Their respective project heads specified that the registrations referred to *archaeological sites and findings* (Burillo y otros, 1993; Burillo-Ibáñez-Polo, 1994), and also that for certain analysis, such as those regarding site density, the findings

Fig. 3.1: Autonomous Communities of Spain.

Table 3.1: The responsibility for cultural management in the regions.

Autonomous region	Administration who manage archaeological heritage
Castilla y León	Culture & Tourism
Galicia	Culture & Sports
Andalucía	Culture
Murcia	Culture, Youth & Sports
Valencia	Culture & Sports
Cantabria	Culture, Tourism & Sports
Asturias	Culture & Tourism
Madrid	Culture & Tourism
Canarias	Education, University, Culture & Sports
Baleares	Education & Culture
Castilla-La Mancha	Culture
La Rioja	Education, Tourism & Culture
Aragón	Education, Culture & Sports
Extremadura	Culture & Tourism
Cataluña	Culture & Media
País Vasco	Culture
Navarra	Culture & Tourism

made within the urban areas of Saragossa, Huesca, Teruel, Daroca, Tarazona and Jaca were to be considered as a single archaeological site (Burillo y otros, 1993: 21). Other internet-accessible inventories make no express mention of this issue. So for instance, a find within a town context and the town could be registered independently or an archaeological site and some of its elements, such as a building, a necropolis, etc., all could also be registered independently.

Different university research groups have come up with archaeological classifications for general inventory systems, such as the University of Granada (Andalusia) or Santiago de Compostela (Galicia). The former has adopted the expression 'archaeological entity' to define the elements that make up their proposal for an archaeological information system (Molina y otros, 1996: 82). Some of these entities include archaeological movable materials, as well as the following categories:
- *Movable property*: a good that must undergo special treatment.
- *Site*: a place where evidence of human activity can be found.
- *Archaeological area*: a physical space where one or more sites have been found, and the territory –in the archaeological sense- used by the communities of these sites.

The main difficulty with these definitions is that the definition of a real property could be used for an archaeological area and the other way round. The definition of a site could also be used for an archaeological site, which is also a place where evidence of human activity can be found.

As for Galicia, a classification model has been defined for archaeological registration in the information systems applied to the management of cultural resources.

This model, that can be defined as 'a formalization of the structure of a part of the observed reality,' shows a hierarchical structure where 'the objects of a specialised class are also objects of the generic class' (González Pérez-Bóveda, 1999: 13). The main classes relating to Artistic Heritage elements are:
- *Material entities*: tangible objects, whether intentional ones or not, that include movable elements as well as real property.
- *Spatial entities*: areas that can be delimited in space. This class includes archaeological sites, aggregation areas and heritage assets.
- *Archaeological container*: an abstract class that includes all the previous ones plus stratigraphic entities.
- *Contextual analysis entities:* any element that provides information on an archaeological container. It includes environmental samples and conditions.

This classification has the inconvenience that, using the suggested definitions, a site could also be classified as a heritage site, that is, they are not univocal expressions. Moreover, value criteria (heritage site) are mixed with spatial criteria (a site included under aggregation sites).

In the pre-computerization phase of the Archaeological Heritage inventory making in Andalusia, archaeological entities classifications were not made. Each entry was generically considered as an archaeological site although, in practice, it could well refer to an archaeological area, a part of it or to an isolated finding. However, at the design and development stage of the Andalusian Information System on the Archaeological Heritage (Fernández Cacho, 2002a; 2002b), each registration was linked to an archaeological entity, defined as the territorial scope where material remains of human activities are found and for the analysis of which an archaeological methodology is essential.

Table 3.2: Density calculation of archaeological enitities per square kilometre.

Autonomous Region	Area (kms²)	Archaeological entities registered	Density
País Vasco	7.234	5.000	0,691
Madrid	7.995	4.500	0,562
Galicia	29.574	15.000	0,507
Canarias	7.447	2.913	0,391
Valencia	23.255	7.986	0,343
Cataluña	32.114	11.000	0,342
Murcia	11.317	1.995	0,176
Andalucía	87.597	14.000	0,159
Aragón	47.719	5.000	0,104

To transfer the data into a GIS, it was deemed convenient to classify the entities into the following classes according to spatial criteria:

- *Isolated finding:* a place where goods and chattels or scattered architectural elements unasssociated with archaeological sites and/or inventories have been found.
- *Archaeological unit:* a part of an archaeological site that meets at least one of the following criteria:
  ◆ Legal criterion (compulsory): those that are protected.
  ◆ Town-planning criterion (compulsory): those that are included in the historical scope of a current town/city.
  ◆ Functional (discretional): it is based on the macro functional characteristics of the body or its potential town-planning inclination.
- *Archaeological site:* territorial boundary with a physical continuity of the material remains of human activity, or with an impact in their correct interpretation; for its analysis it is essential to use an archaeological methodology.
- *Archaeological area:* a series of archaeological sites that integrate a territory made up by a landscape whose cultural value shows differentiated characteristics.

In this case, we have decided to use a hierarchical relationship among the archaeological entities except for the case of an isolated finding. An archaeological unit is part of a place which, in turn, can be part of one or several

areas. This way the criteria set by the European Council in their definition of basic data in archaeological registers are met (European Council, 1999). None of these classifications is problem-free because archaeological entities are not always easy to interpret in *situ and* therefore associating them with one of the previously defined types is not easy either. In any case, defining the criteria that have been taken into account is essential in order to be able to use the information properly.

The number of archaeological entities registered in the Spanish inventories is also variable. In order to compare the information available, Table 3.2 shows the density calculations of archaeological entities per square kilometre (EA/Km²). As you can see, only the Spanish autonomous regions of the Basque Country, Galicia and Madrid show 0.5 EA/Km². A second group is made up by those regions showing between 0.3 and 0.4 EA/Km². Thirdly, there are those that do not reach 0.2 EA/Km².

In the region of Murcia, the 'modernization' of the archaeological chart and the design of their information system resulted in an increase in the number of archaeological entities. In 1986 the archaeological entities registered were 800, and in 2003 they were 1971 (San Nicolás-Lacárcel, 2003).Outstanding increases in archaeological information were also obtained during the making of the Aragon inventory in the 1990s. In the Daroca area, for

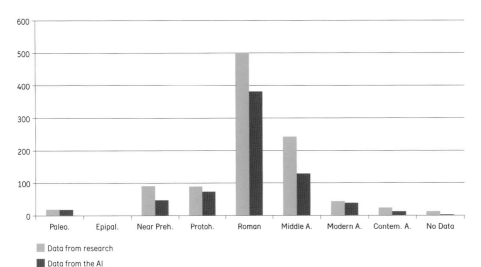

Fig. 3.2: Registered entities in Seville metropolitan (IAPH, 1999: 214).

example, there were 62 archaeological entities in 1987 included in the inventories; this figure increased to 214 in 1991 after archaeological explorations, the aim of which was to update the inventory, had been carried out. This represents an increase of 345%.

Some of the main reasons for this disparity in the number of registered archaeological entities are as follows: the surface area of the Spanish autonomous regions is very variable. Andalusia and Aragon are respectively almost twice and six times as big than the Basque Country or Madrid. In the latter, inventory compilation was by means of a series of archaeological survey campaigns of the whole territory. This is much more difficult in larger regions. Sometimes to the results of ongoing archaeological explorations and excavations are not fed into the archaeological inventory. This was the case for the Seville metropolitan area (Andalusia) where research in the cultural administration archives led to a 162.27% increase in the number of registered entities. (IAPH, 1999) (fig. 3.2). Apart from such large information dumps the number of registered entities increases at a gradual pace (fig. 3.3).

In no other cases can the densities registered in the inventories of Spain's autonomous regions be compared to those obtained after carrying out intensive archaeological explorations (Ruiz Zapartero 1996). For example, in the northern part of the Sierra de Baza mountain range (Andalusia) there is a registered density of 1.7 EA/Km² (Sánchez Quirante, 1991), in Bocelos and Valle de Furelos valley (Galicia) 2.5 EA/Km² (Criado et al., 1989), in some areas of Sierra Norte de Sevilla mountain range (Andalusia) there is 2.6 EA/Km² (García Sanjuán, 2004; García Sanjuán-Vargas-Wheatley, 2004), in Perales de Tajuña (Madrid) 2.8 EA/Km² (Almagro-Benito, 1993), in Valle de Abdalajís valley (Andalusia) 3.6 EA/Km² (Martín Ruiz-Martín Ruiz-Sánchez Bandera, 1999), etc. The implication of these densities is that the currently known number of registered archaeological entities for the whole of Spain should be multiplied by ten.

Information compiled for the registered archaeological entities

One of the most discussed issues when it comes to compiling the cards or entries for an archaeological inventory is that regarding the data to be compiled for the individual archaeological entities. In 1991, in the course of the first major meeting of representatives of the autonomous regions to coordinate policies in this matter, there was a debate on the different information requirements for archaeological research on the one hand and for heritage management on the other (Del Val et al., 1993).

The inventories have been promoted by the administrations that manage cultural policy and therefore preference is usually given to data arising from such management, rather than to a detailed characterisation of the listed archaeological entities themselves. In Aragón, where the inventory was made by university experts, data relating to the features of the physical environment of each site predominate, and no reference is made to land ownership or planning decisions that could affect it. These last aspects are taken into account in the registration entries of the inventories of Madrid, Valencia, Andalusia and Murcia. Sometimes, as in the case of Murcia, there are multiple entries in the inventory for the same entity, particularly in the case of towns. In Andalusia, however, the municipal archaeological charts - which are mainly focused on town areas - are made on an independent basis and are not well integrated with the regional inventory.

In general, basic information on a territory is usually provided rather than any detailed knowledge of specific areas. The increasing use of computing systems - with their capacity to add new information fields and modules - is enabling better integration of data. In this respect the Andalusian inventory, integrated in the Andalusian Historical Heritage information System, is one where the research objectives and the archaeological heritage management objectives are in reasonably close correspondence (Ruiz Zapatero-Jimeno, 1999: 44; Fontes, 2001: 162; Giannotti, 2005: 33; Vegas, 2005: 122; Barreiro, 2006).

However, it is difficult to put in place a system that will ensure that all the information deemed necessary will be included in an inventory. For example, in Andalusia a catalogue of caves with rock paintings made by specialised researchers focused on the paintings while teams co-ordinated by the regional authorities to make the inventory devoted more attention to issues relating to the preservation of the caves and their protection (Fernández Cacho-Mondéjar-Díaz Iglesias, 2002a). In fact, it is perhaps a utopian ideal to hope to produce a single inventory that meets the needs of all professionals. What does seem to be unquestionable is that the technical and scientific criteria underlying inventory production must keep pace with developments in the field. It is necessary and surely possible, as a basic minimum, to agree on the types of listed entities, time-function classifications and spatial delimitations to be employed in inventory production. The lack of precision in the locational data for archaeological bodies has been pointed out in the case of Andalusia (Amores et al., 1999; Fernández Cacho-Navascués-Blasco, 2000). The definition of such criteria is essential so to provide comparable basic data for the inventories of all the Spanish autonomous regions that, as of today, are incompatible due to a lack of standardization in the information fields and documentary languages.

The dissemination of archaeological inventories

Only six out of the seventeen Spanish autonomous regions make inventory data available on the Internet (Table 3.3).

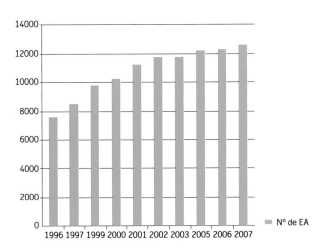

Fig. 3.3: **Number of Archaeological Entities in SIPHA.**

Table 3.3: (Information on the Internet).

Autonomous community	Declared real states	Inventoried real states
Andalucía	YES	YES
Aragón	NO	NO
Asturias	YES	NO
Baleares	NO	NO
Canarias	YES	YES (Restricted)
Cantabria	YES	NO
Castilla-León	YES	NO
Castilla-La Mancha	NO	NO
Cataluña	YES	YES
Extremadura	NO	NO
Galicia	NO	NO
La Rioja	NO	NO
Madrid	NO	NO
Murcia	YES	YES
País Vasco	YES	YES
Navarra	NO	NO
Valencia	YES	YES

Some of them, under legislation, restrict access to the data so as to prevent the pillaging of archaeological sites in their territory. This is so in the Canary Islands, where archaeological maps can only be accessed 'if it is due to a legitimate interest, and therefore can be done on a regulation basis' (Spanish act Ley 4/1999 of March 15, on the Historical Heritage of the Canary Islands (sec.64). That is why, although the data bank can be accessed on the Internet, it is only possible to consult it with permission. The situation is similar in the autonomous region of Valencia, where authorisation is required to access inventory data (Díaz Iglesias, 2002). However, in this case it is possible to make general searches and obtain lists of the registered archaeological entities.

Further information is available in Murcia, the Basque Country, Catalonia and Andalusia. In Murcia, there is a specific web site on Archaeological Heritage called ArqueoMurcia. On this site you can access the basic data of the listed archaeological entities: location, function, description and bibliography. In Catalonia, the data to which there is free-Internet access relates to the municipality where each archaeological entity is located, their time-function classification and their state of protection. The information provided by the Basque Country and Andalusia is more detailed. In 2002, the latter began to integrate the real estate databases (IAPH, 2007), *ARQUEOS* being one of them (Fernández Cacho, 2002a, 2002b). Here, the architectural, ethnological and archaeological real estate is managed via a single computing application. The basic information on these assets can be consulted on the Andalusian Historical Heritage Institute web site. Basic information on the archaeological sites protected as Cultural Heritage assets of other Spanish autonomous regions, such as Castile-Leon, Asturias and Cantabria, can also be obtained. As you can see in the chart taken from the 2007 report on sustainability in Spain (OSE, 2007: 462), the distribution of the Cultural Heritage assets in the different Spanish regions is not homogeneous (fig. 3.4).

Inventories and urban & territorial planning

In Spain, town-planning schemes must include a catalogue of protected sites, including the archaeological sites of each municipality. The catalogue is updated with each new scheme. When an archaeological site is included in such catalogue, it then has the maximum level of protection.

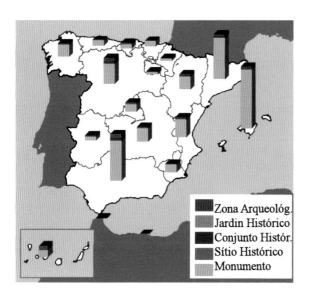

Fig. 3.4: The distrubution of the Cultural Heritage assets in the regions (OSE, 2007: 462).

Territorial planning is less developed and although archaeological sites that have the maximum protection level as cultural assets are usually included in territorial schemes, the rest (the majority) are added in a discretionary manner. The main problem with these planning documents is the limited treatment given to the archaeological information - so as to adapt it to the territorial scale - and the failure to integrate it within the different subsystems that make up the complex territorial and urban system. Generally speaking, archaeological sites are added to the territory as a series of obstacles that need to be overcome in processes like urbanization, expansion and improvement of the road systems, change of land use, etc. We can say that in Spain it is still necessary improve heritage policies with regard to urban and territorial planning, either by setting more explicit action criteria or by developing specific territorial planning for Cultural Heritage in general, and for the Archaeological Heritage in particular.

Some outstanding exceptions to this general picture are the territorial schemes of the Basque Cultural Heritage (PTSPCV, 2000), the town-planning schemes for Cultural Heritage included in the new legislation of the Spanish autonomous region of Murcia, and the program of local archaeological charts in Andalusia. The not yet approved PTSPCV (PTSPCV, 2000) focuses on the protection and promotion of the Basque Cultural Heritage outside the region (Izeta, 2001: 43). This plan implies a political commitment that goes beyond the integration of said heritage in the territorial plans of other administrations, even those that do not have direct competence in the field of culture. As it includes elements integrated in a comprehensive planning system, which can in turn be part of other schemes of territorial planning.

The PTSPCV base their archaeological heritage proposals on two basic aspects:
- The Archaeological Heritage requires a specific protection methodology.
- There are archaeological entities that are deemed not to merit preservation and therefore they must be documented and studied before they disappear in the course of works that entail land removal.

The scheme adheres to the classification categories applied to cultural real estate heritage by virtue of the Spanish act Ley 7/1990 of July 3 on the Basque Cultural Heritage (Ley 7/1990 de 3 de julio del Patrimonio Cultural Vasco): individual monuments, monument sites (groups of real estates), and cultural areas whose wide definition can be adapted to a great variety of situations. Also, the directions about the protection of the archaeological heritage seem only to include those that are already set by this act; those that are always mentioned are the measures regarding individual archaeological sites (either qualified or listed ones) and supposedly archaeological areas. The measures fall into three protection levels: archaeological reserve, strict preservation, maintenance, and no protection. This last level implies that, after carrying out archaeological actions to document the existing archaeological remains, they can disappear.

This document articulates the indiscriminate practice of destroying previously excavated archaeological sites, although preventive archaeology is still implicitly considered as an activity that liberates land. Moreover, the Spanish act Ley 4/2007 of March 16 on the Cultural

Heritage of the Spanish autonomous region of Murcia (Ley de Patrimonio Cultural de la Comunidad Autónoma de la Región de Murcia) has included a significant territorial element in the Cultural Heritage planning scheme (Section IV). This scheme is relevant to archaeological and paleontological parks, as well as cultural landscapes and will include the following aspects:
- Definition of their territorial scope.
- Description of the cultural features and values indicating their state of preservation.
- Setting the use limitations that must be respected according to their character, cultural value and state of preservation of the area, and if fitting, of the Cultural Heritage protection figures that must be declared pursuant to the present act.
- Definition of the use and management systems that are set and, if fitting, of the entities that are set up with regard to the area the scheme refers to.
- Setting of the criteria that guides the sectoral policies affecting the area and are compatible with the Cultural Heritage planning.

Finally, in the early 1990s, the Andalusian Ministry of Culture of the Andalusian government (Junta de Andalucía) promoted the drafting of hazard charts within the town archaeology scheme. In principle, the idea was not only to assess the hazards the archaeological heritage is subjected to in the current towns and cities but also to organise research teams that could channel the information obtained throughput the development of town archaeological activities (Temiño-Puya, 1993; Temiño, 2004: 214 y ss.). One hazard chart, for the town of Niebla (Huelva, Andalusia), has been published to date.

The town archaeology scheme and hazard charts soon ceased to be made. However, the latter were the source of the municipal archaeological charts. Although many of their objectives are similar to those of the old hazard charts, the change of name can be justified for two main reasons (Rodríguez de Guzmán – González-Campos, 2002). The objective was to extend the archaeological analysis to full municipalities so as to include their protection and preservation proposals in the local town planning scheme. Those semantic nuances suggesting that the archaeological heritage was a 'hazard' were eliminated. This comment results from the possibility that they are hazard charts 'of' the archaeological heritage instead of hazard charts 'for' or 'about' the archaeological heritage.

In order to make the municipal hazard charts, apart from gathering all the existing information on the archaeological heritage in each municipality, there were two requirements closely related to the hazard assessment on the archaeological heritage: the 'definition of positive and negative effects by means of the analysis of the currently in force rules and regulations' and the valuation of the 'state of preservation of the archaeological heritage so as to have a general view that channels punctual as well as general proposals' (Rodríguez de Guzmán – González-Campos, 2002: 82). Therefore there are three main variables that are taken into account in these studies with regard to the hazard analysis of the archaeological heritage: their potential preservation, their spatial distribution and the presence or probability of hazardous factors, which are still particularly relevant to town environments (Rodríguez de Guzmán – González-Campos, 2002; Rodríguez Temiño, 2004: 214 and ss.).

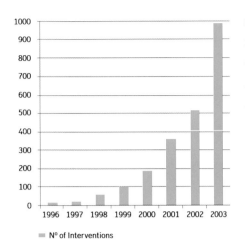

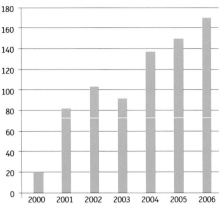

N° of Interventions

Fig. 3.5 (left): Growth pace of explorations and excavations in Galicia (Based on Cerdeño-Castillo-Sagardoy, 2005: 33).

Fig. 3.6 (right): Growth pace of explorations and excavations in Castile-La-Mancha (Tallón et al., 2005: 29).

Towards the protection of the historical landscapes

In the last twenty years, the expansion of the real estate sector in Spain, the changes of land use and the need for improving the transport infrastructure networks have caused the alteration of many areas, particularly along the coast, which has resulted in a drastic change in their appearance. The risk the Cultural and Natural Heritage has run throughout those years has been very high indeed and many (cultural and natural) environmentally-valuable territorial contexts have been irreparable damaged.

Together with the increasing number of intervention works in the territory, the number of archaeological activities has also significantly increased. A great part of such actions are made within an environmental impact assessment framework, as they legally have to include an archaeological impact study. Figures 3.5 and 3.6 show the growth pace of explorations and excavations in Galicia and Castile-La Mancha, as an example of this process. In Andalusia, this same trend can be traced with the increasing number of information requests from the companies assessing the environmental impact to the information services of the Andalusian Historical Heritage Institute (fig. 3.7).

Parallel to that, the authorised systematic archaeological activities (linked to pre-historical and historical research projects) have considerable decreased. You could say that the process of interventions with an impact in Andalusia and other Spanish autonomous regions has caused a change of trends. Today, the number of archaeological activities carried out as an 'emergency' is higher than that of the 'systematic' ones due to the need for documenting archaeological remains that interfere in infrastructure planning, urbanization and the expansion of intensive farming (fig. 3.8). In response to pressures on the archaeological heritage the Spanish government has signed the European Landscape Convention. It came into force on March 1, 2008.

It should be noted that some autonomous regions include measures in their Cultural Heritage legislation to protect large areas noted for their outstanding cultural and natural values. Examples are the protection envisaged for cultural landscapes in the legislation of Murcia and La Rioja, for cultural spaces in legislation of Castile-Leon and for the heritage areas recently defined in the Andalusian legislation. These instances are seen as positive influences for other areas. As we have previously said, the Spanish act *Ley 4/2007* of March 16 on the Cultural Heritage of the

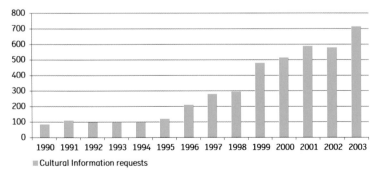

Cultural Information requests

Fig. 3.7: Number of request for information received at IAPH.

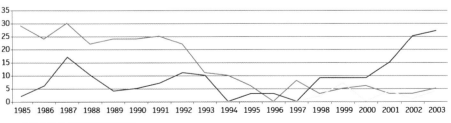

Archaeological Surveys/Research
Archaeological Surveys/Emergency
Archaeological Surveys/Specific

Fig. 3.8: The development of arcaheological fieldword (Fernández Cacho, 2008).

Spanish autonomous region of Murcia (*Ley del Patrimonio Cultural de la Comunidad Autónoma de la Región de Murcia*) included the obligation to draft Cultural Heritage plans for archaeological and paleontological parks and cultural landscapes. The latter are not included in the protective measures envisaged by the law but are deemed to have a special planning status and therefore must be identified and characterised, and any changes to them must be duly controlled. The cultural landscape can be defined as the 'part or rural, town or coastal territory where there are any goods that are part of the Cultural Heritage whose historical, artistic, aesthetical, ethnographical, anthropological, technical or industrial value and integration with the natural or cultural resources deserves a special planning' (Section 61). Moreover, according to the Act *Ley 7/2004 of October 18, 2004* on the Cultural Historical and Artistic Heritage of La Rioja (*Ley del Patrimonio Cultural, Histórico y Artístico de La Rioja*), cultural landscapes are considered as a category under Cultural Heritage goods, a classification within the real estate. By virtue of this act, a cultural landscape is the 'extension of land that represents the interaction of human work with nature' (Section 12). Special consideration is given to the cultural landscape of vineyards. The Act *Ley 12/2002* of July 11 on the Cultural Heritage of Castile-Leon *(Ley del Patrimonio Cultural de Castilla y León)* does not include measures for the cultural landscape but does include that of cultural space. Cultural spaces are made up by 'those real estate declared as Cultural Heritage that, due to their special cultural and natural values, require a preferential treatment for their management and spreading'. In other Spanish autonomous regions, like Castile-La Mancha or Aragon, these spaces have been called archaeological or cultural parks, although all of them refer to management tools to spread the cultural value of a territory or area whose natural resources or value can also be significant. So far, in Castile and Leon only the Sierra de Atapuerca mountain range (in Burgos) has been declared as a cultural space, declared as an archaeological area in 1991 and World Heritage in 2000. Finally, the Act *Ley 14/2007* of November 26 on the Historical Heritage of Andalusia (*Ley del Patrimonio Histórico de Andalucía)* includes the legal protection measure of 'heritage area'. Heritage areas are 'those territories or spaces that make up a diverse complementary archaeological site, made up by diachronic goods that represent human evolution, whose use is for the community, and, if fitting, have a landscape and environmental value' (Section 25). One or several heritage areas can be legally managed by being declared as cultural parks provided with a management body consisting of the administrations and sectors involved. (Section 81).

Appendix

Understanding the landscape as society's heritage gradually overcomes the dichotomy between Natural Heritage and Cultural Heritage, which strongly exists in the administrative practice and the university, due to the sectorization in knowledge with regard to natural sciences and human sciences. The primacy of space in the first one and time in the second one affects the management objectives of both kinds of heritage: whereas the aim of the Natural Heritage management is to maintain its balance of basic conditions, in the case of Cultural Heritage the idea is to try to conserve it due to its non-renewable nature and the need to guarantee its authenticity as an essential value.

Space and time, territory and historical processes become, nonetheless, essential dimensions for the analysis of landscapes with cultural values. Its protection as well as the management of its dynamics is one of the main future challenges in Spain, as they must play an important role in its territorial development (Sabaté, 2006). The progress achieved in the management of its Cultural Heritage are moving in this direction, although with different rhythms and results.

david.villalon@juntadeandalucia.es

References

Almagro Gorbea, M. & Benito López , J.E. 1993: Evaluación de rendimientos y optimización de resultados en prospección arqueológica: el Valle del Tajuña. In: Jimeno Martínez, A., del Val Recio J. & Fernández Moreno, J.J. (Edit.): *Actas Inventarios y Cartas Arqueológicas. Homenaje a Blas Taracena. Soria (1941-1991), Ca*stile-Leon Ministry of Culture and Tourism. Junta de Castilla y León, Valladolid, 151-158.

Amores Carredano, F., García Sanjuán, L., Hurtado Pérez, V., & Rodríguez Bobada, M.C. 1999: Geographic Information Systems and Archaeological Resource Management in Andalusia (Spain). In: Barceló, J.A., Briz, I. & Vila, A. (Edit.): *New Techniques for Old Times. Computer Applications in Archaeology 1998.* BAR International Series 757, Oxford. 351-358.

Antona del Val, V. 1993: Inventario y protección del Patrimonio Arqueológico de la Comunidad de Madrid, In Jimeno Martínez, A., del Val Recio, J.M. & Fernández Moreno, J.J. (Edit.)*: Actas Inventarios y Cartas Arqueológicas. Homenaje a Blas Taracena. Soria (1941-1991).* Castilla-León Ministry of Culture and Tourism. Junta de Castilla y León, Valladolid, 239-245.

Barreiro Martínez, D. 2006: La aureola perdida (Propuesta para una Arqueología Aplicada) *ArqueoWeb, 8(1).* Universidad Complutense de Madrid In [Consulted on 8/04/2008]

Blasco Bosqued, M.C. & Baena Preysler, J. 1999: Los SIG y algunos ejemplos de su aplicación para el estudio y gestión de cartas arqueológicas. *Los S.I.G. y el Análisis Espacial en Arqueología,* Universidad Autónoma de Madrid, Madrid, 81-91.

Burillo, F., Ibañez, J., Loscos, R.M., Martínez, M.R., Polo, C., Simón, J.M. & Sopena, M.C.1993: Prospección e informatización para la elaboración del Inventario Arqueológico de Aragón. In: Jimeno Martínez, A., del Val Recio, J.M. & Fernández Moreno, J.J. (Edits.)*: Actas Inventarios y Cartas Arqueológicas. Homenaje a Blas Taracena. Soria (1941-1991),* Castile-Leon Ministry of Culture and Tourism, Junta de Castilla y León, Valladolid, 99-116.

Burillo, F., Ibáñez, J. & Polo, C. 1994: El Patrimonio Arqueológico en el medio rural, *Conservación Arqueológica. Reflexión y debate sobre teoría y práctica. Cuadernos II.* Andalusian Historical Heritage Institute, Junta de Andalucía, Jerez, 3 6-49.

Cerdeño, M.L., Castillo, A. & Sagardoy, T. 2005: La Evaluación de Impacto Ambiental y su repercusión sobre el Patrimonio Arqueológico en España. *Trabajos de Prehistoria* 62, No. 2., 25-40.

Council of Europe 1999: *Core data standard for archaeological sites and monuments.* Council of Europe, Strasburg.

Criado Boado, F., González Méndez, M., Bonilla Rordíguez, A., Cerqueiro Landin, D. & Méndez Fernández, F. 1989: Resultados de la prospección intensiva en la Sierra de O Bocelo y en el Valle de Furelos (A Coruña). *Cuadernos de Estudios Gallegos, 103,* 25-50.

Del Val Recio, J., Fernández Moreno, J.J., Delibes, G., Fernández-Posse, M.D., Antona, V., Ruiz Zapatero, G. & Keay, S. 1993: Mesa redonda: Los inventarios al servicio de cdla Gestión e Investigación Arqueológicas: In: Jimeno Martínez, A., del Val Recio, J., & Fernández Moreno, J.J. (Edits.)*: Actas Inventarios y Cartas Arqueológicas. Homenaje a Blas Taracena. Soria (1941-1991),* Castile-Leon Ministry of Culture and Tourism. Junta de Castilla y León, Valladolid, 251-262.

Díaz Iglesias, J.M. 2002: Los productos de difusión de ARQUEOS. In: Fernández Cacho, S. (Ed.): *ARQUEOS. Sistema de Información del Patrimonio Arqueológico de Andalucía,* Andalusian Historical Heritage Institute, Junta de Andalucía, Granada, 168-183.

Fernández Cacho, S. (Ed.) 2002a: *ARQUEOS. Sistema de Información del Patrimonio Arqueológico de Andalucía.* Andalusian Historical Heritage Institute. Junta de Andalucía. Granada.

Fernández Cacho S. 2002b: *ARQUEOS. The Information System of the Andalusian Archaeological Heritage.* In: García Sanjuán, L. & y Wheatley, D.W. (Eds.): *Mapping the Future of the Past. Managing the Spatial Dimension of the European Archaeological Resource,* University of Sevile, University of Southampton, Andalusian Historical Heritage Institute, Seville, 27-36.

Fernández Cacho, S. 2008: *Patrimonio Arqueológico y Planificación Territorial. Estrategias de gestión para Andalucía.* Andalusian Historical Heritage Institute & University of Seville. Jerez.

Fernández Cacho, S., Mondéjar Fernández de Quincoces, P. & Díaz Iglesias, J.M. 2002: La información de Patrimonio Arqueológico de Andalucía: Valoración general. In: Fernández Cacho, S. (Ed.): *ARQUEOS. Sistema de Información del Patrimonio Arqueológico de Andalucía ,* Andalusian Historical Heritage Institute, Junta de Andalucía, Granada, 143-166.

Fernández Cacho, S., Navascués Fernández-Vitorio, R. & Blasco Aranda, E.M. 2000: Geo*ARQUEOS*: A System for the creation, updating and validation of the digital cartography of the Andalusian Archaeological Heritage. *Archeologia e Calcolatori* 11, 359-373.

Fernández-Posse, M.D. & Alvaro, E. 1993: Bases para un inventario de yacimientos arqueológicos. In: Jimeno Martínez, A., del Val Recio, J.M. & Fernández Moreno, J.J. (Eds.): *Actas Inventarios y Cartas Arqueológicas. Homenaje a Blas Taracena. Soria (1941-1991),* Junta de Castilla y León, Castile-Leon Ministry of Culture and Tourism, Valladolid, 65-72.

Fontes Blanco-Loizelier, F.L. 2001: Las aplicaciones de Bases de Datos y Sistemas de Información en Arqueología: Historia y perspectivas de futuro. *Boletín de la Asociación Española de Amigos de la Arqueología, 41* Asociación de Amigos de la Arqueología, 149-174.

García Sanjuán, L. 2004: La prospección arqueológica de superficie y los SIG. *Actas del I Encuentro Internacional de Informática aplicada a la Investigación y Gestión Arqueológicas. Córdoba, May 7-9, 2003,* University of Córdoba, Córdoba, 185-210.

García Sanjuán, L., Vargas Durán, M.A. & Wheatley, D. 2004: Prospecciones de superficie en la zona de afección del embalse de Los Melonares (Almadén de la Plata, El Pedroso y Castilblanco de los Arroyos, Sevilla). *Anuario Arqueológico de Andalucía, 2001. Tomo III. Actividades de Urgencia,* Andalusian Ministry of Culture, Junta de Andalucía, Seville, 969-972.

Giannotti García, C. (Coord.) 2005: *Desarrollo metodológico y aplicación de nuevas tecnologías para la gestión integral del Patrimonio Arqueológico en Uruguay. TAPA, 36.* Consejo Superior de Investigaciones Científicas, University of Santiago de Compostela, Santiago de Compostela.

González Pérez, C.A. & Bóveda López, M.M. 1999: Un modelo de clases para el registro arqueológico. In: González Pérez, C.A.: *Tecnologías de la Información y Patrimonio Cultural 1: El Paradigma Orientado a Objetos,* Laboratorio de Arqueoloxía e Formas Culturais. University of Santiago de Compostela, Santiago de Compostela, 13-16.

Hernández Núñez, J.C. 1998: *Los Instrumentos de Protección del Patrimonio Histórico EspaÑo.,* Sociedad y Bienes Culturales, Grupo Publicaciones del Sur, Cádiz, 1998.

Andalusian Historical Heritage Institute 1999: Base de Datos del Patrimonio Histórico de Andalucía. Área metropolitana de Sevilla. *Boletín PH, 27.* Andalusian Historical Heritage Institute, Junta de Andalucía, 212-217,

Muñoz Cruz, V. & Ladrón de Guevara, M.C. (Coords.) 2007: *El Sistema de Información del Patrimonio Histórico de Andalucía (SIPHA).* Andalusian Ministry of Culture, Junta de Andalucía, Seville, 2007.

Izeta, J. I. 2001: Ordenación del Territorio, Política Económica y Política Cultural: bases para el desarrollo local. In: Gómez De La Iglesia, R. (Dir.): *Cultura, desarrollo y territorio. III Jornadas sobre iniciativa privada y sector público en la gestión de la cultura,* Xabide, Gestión Cultural y Comunicación, Vitoria-Gasteiz, 41-46.

Martín Ruiz, J.A., Martín Ruiz, J.M. & Sánchez Bandera, P. 1999: Prospección arqueológica sistemática en el término municipal de El Valle de Abdalajís (Málaga). *Anuario Arqueológico de Andalucía, 1994. Tomo II. Actividades Sistemáticas,.* Andalusian Ministry of Culture. Junta de Andalucía, Seville, 154-160.

Molina González, F., Rodríguez Temiño, I., Contreras Cortés, F., Esquivel Guerrero, J.A. & Peña Ruano, J. 1996: Un Sistema de Información Arqueológica para Andalucía. *Catalogación del Patrimonio Histórico. Cuadernos VI,* Andalusian Historical Heritage Institute, Junta de Andalucía, Seville, 86-93.

Observatorio de la Sostenibilidad en España 2007: *Sostenibilidad en España 2007,* Spanish Ministry of the Environment , Madrid.

Pereda Alonso, A. 1981: Los Inventarios del Patrimonio Histórico-Artístico Español. *Análisis e Investigaciones 9,* 23-44.

Rodríguez De Guzmán Sánchez, S. & González-Campos Baeza, Y. 2002: La tutela del Patrimonio Histórico a través de las Cartas Arqueológicas Municipales. *Boletín del Instituto Andaluz del Patrimonio Histórico, 38,* Andalusian government Junta de Andalucía, Seville, 19-90.

Rodríguez Temiño, I. & Puya Garcia de Leániz, M. 1993: Zonas arqueológicas en ciudades actuales. In: Oliva Alonso, D. (Coord.): *Casa-palacio de Miguel Mañara,* Andalusian Ministry of Culture, Junta de Andalucía, Seville, 65-85.

Rodríguez Temiño, I. 2004: *Arqueología Urbana en España,* Ariel Patrimonio. Barcelona.

Ruiz Zapatero, G. 1996: La prospección de superficie en la arqueología española. *Quad. Preh. Arq. Cast. 17,* Catellón County Council, 7-20.

Ruiz Zapatero, G. & Jimeno Martínez, A. 1999: Archaeological inventories in Spain: problems and solutions in a decentralized country. In: Hansen, H.J. & Quine, G. (Eds.): *Our Fragile Heritage. Documenting the Past for the Future,* The National Museum of Denmark, Copenhagen, 35-50.

Sabaté Bel, J.1981: De la preservación del patrimonio a la ordenación del paisaje. In: *El paisaje y la gestión del territorio,* 1 ed. Barcelona: Barcelona County Council, 329-342.

Sánchez Palencia Ramos, F.J. 1981: El Inventario Arqueológico Español, *Caesaraugusta, 53-54,* CSIC, 101-114.

Sánchez Quirante, L. 1991: Prospección arqueológica superficial del río Bodurria-Gallego-Sierra de Baza. *Anuario Arqueológico de Andalucía, 1989. Tomo II. Actividades Sistemáticas,* Andalusian Ministry of Culture, Junta de Andalucía, Seville, 57-62.

San Nicolás del Toro, M. & Lacárcel García, E. 2003: Sistema de Información Arqueológica de Murcia. Dirección General de Cultura de Murcia. Unpublished document available on http://www.gisad.org/archivos/SIA-2003.pdf

4 | Le recensement des données archéologiques pour la reconstitution des paysages historiques et les conditions de leur intégration dans l'aménagement durable des territoires : l'approche française

Philippe Vergain

En préambule, il faut rappeler que cette question ressort en France de législations différentes et indépendantes relevant des trois codes du patrimoine, de l'urbanisme et de l'environnement, mais qui peuvent être mises en œuvre de manière concomitante – notamment sous l'influence de la réflexion européenne en la matière – par une volonté commune des services de l'État concernés dans les régions. C'est en effet à ce niveau d'organisation territoriale que s'effectue l'activité du service déconcentré de l'État qui a la responsabilité de l'archéologie : la Direction régionale des Affaires culturelles (DRAC).

La démarche qui consiste à proposer des reconstructions de paysages historiques à partir de données archéologiques renouvelées par l'activité archéologique de terrain est très récente même si le concept « d'inventaire archéologique », contemporain de celui de *musée*, est une création de la Révolution française et a été développé et précisé tout au long du XIXe siècle. Dès 1838, les premiers répertoires archéologiques vont recenser les principaux monuments qui documentent l'histoire et l'archéologie au sens originel c'est-à-dire surtout la Préhistoire.

La structuration de ce que l'on appelle encore la *carte archéologique nationale* (ensemble des données archéologiques connues) ne remonte qu'aux années 70 du XXe siècle et n'est donc que légèrement postérieure au développement du ministère de la Culture qui va en assurer la constitution au plan national. Le principe d'une base de données associée à un SIG et alimentant en informations les aménageurs du territoire a été acquis dans les années 90 avec un développement maximal à la fin du siècle dernier.

Depuis les années 1980 en effet, les services archéologiques de l'État dans les régions (Services régionaux de l'Archéologie au sein des Directions régionales des Affaires culturelles sous l'autorité du préfet de Région) fournissent à ceux qui en font la demande les données archéologiques disponibles à fins de conservation, études ou prise en compte dans l'aménagement des territoires. De ce point de vue, l'inventaire des sites archéologiques et des paysages historiques que l'on restitue à partir d'eux est étroitement lié au développement de l'archéologie préventive dans la mesure où les diagnostics livrent de nouvelles informations et les fouilles permettent de préciser les datations, les interprétations et les localisations.

Il ne faut pas oublier pour autant l'apport des dépouillements bibliographiques des archives de fouille et des publications anciennes ou plus récentes, des opérations de prospections de tous ordres ainsi que des opérations archéologiques programmées qui sont autorisées par l'État.

La « carte archéologique nationale » – telle que définie et inscrite dans le Code du patrimoine au L 522 – loin d'être une liste figée de sites sélectionnés correspond au recensement de données archéologiques critiquées et organisées. À ce titre, elle est en perpétuelle évolution compte tenu de l'activité archéologique de terrain et s'enrichit ainsi des résultats de toute nouvelle opération archéologique. Elle contribue par là-même à une meilleure connaissance des évolutions historiques des territoires à partir notamment de reconstitution de paysages culturels participant, selon des modalités que nous allons examiner, à l'aide à la décision en matière d'aménagement des territoires.

Le recensement des données archéologiques, vérifiées et localisées, contribue ainsi à la constitution de l'inventaire général du patrimoine culturel en matière d'archéologie

Le rôle pivot des archéologues des Services régionaux de l'Archéologie, en partenariat avec tous les acteurs archéologiques sur les territoires y compris les opérateurs de l'archéologie préventive
Il est de la responsabilité des SRA et du *Département de Recherche en Archéologie subaquatique et sous-Marine (DRASSM* qui est un service à compétence nationale) pour le Domaine public maritime de recenser les données archéologiques existantes, de les intégrer après validation, critique et localisation avec la meilleure précision possible, au sein de la base nationale baptisée actuellement « *Patriarche* » qui est un Système de Gestion de Bases de Données associé à un SIG. Celle-ci est ainsi alimentée par chaque service régional mais reste consultable par toutes les régions et par l'administration centrale. Le cadre juridique qui fonde l'action de l'État en ce domaine est le *Code du patrimoine* dans ses articles L 522–5 et L 522–6 (section 1 : rôle de l'État).

Ce sont les archéologues des SRA qui valident des données – couvrant un champ très large allant de l'information d'une découverte isolée signalée dans une revue locale du XIXe siècle à des vestiges urbains fouillés récemment, de manière exhaustive qui peuvent être fournies tant par les établissements publics spécialisés en archéologie (universités, Centre national de la Recherche scientifique...), que par les collectivités locales dotées de services patrimoniaux ou par tous les opérateurs en archéologie préventive (INRAP, opérateurs publics ou privés agréés). Ce travail est bien évidemment le fruit de collaborations inter institutionnelles et pluridisciplinaires à l'issue d'opérations archéologiques autorisées, décidées ou prescrites par l'État (ministère de la Culture ayant en charge l'archéologie) tant pour le recensement initial des données que pour les interprétations en terme d'entités archéologiques, de sites ou de paysages culturels historiques. La disponibilité des fonds géographiques à une échelle adaptée constitue un paramètre essentiel à la qualité de l'information disponible ce qui encourage le développement d'une collaboration étroite avec les collectivités territoriales qui bien souvent disposent des fonds numérisés proposant la meilleure précision.

Des collaborations de recherches associant les acteurs de l'archéologie partenaires responsables des opérations de prospections ou de travaux collectifs de recherches thématiques ou chronologiques qui permettent les réponses de l'État :
Des conventions particulières lient l'État aux différents intervenants archéologiques qui veulent concourir à l'établissement de cette « carte archéologique ». Ce travail pour être efficace nécessite des échanges réguliers et faciles entre les différents partenaires des opérations de recensement faisant suite aux conventions : universités ou *unités mixtes de recherche* avec le Centre national de la Recherche scientifique, services archéologiques de collectivités territoriales, Office national des Forêts, Parcs naturels nationaux ou régionaux...

Un projet informatique a été récemment lancé au niveau national pour faire évoluer le dispositif *Patriarche* actuel en fluidifiant la circulation des informations notamment par la création d'un système aisé d'import/export des données de *Patriarche* à destination des partenaires conventionnés, cela afin d'éviter des doubles saisies tout en permettant la nécessaire validation.

Les dépouillements par les archéologues des SRA de tous les rapports de diagnostic, des rapports de fouilles préventives, des résultats de prospections diverses ou d'études collectives alimentent et mettent ainsi à jour la base nationale : révisions en matière de chronologie, d'interprétation ou de localisation de données connues, nouvelles données, interprétations de paysages historiques qui permettent des créations de « zonages » en vue de mesures de conservation ou de préservation.

À partir du niveau minimal que constitue l'entité archéologique (EA), une nécessaire approche pluridisciplinaire multiscalaire et une mise en perspective transversale pour tenter d'aborder collectivement la restitution de « paysages historiques.
C'est à partir des données archéologiques recensées, critiquées et validées que peuvent se dégager des reconstitutions de nature historique : sites majeurs, ensembles urbains, paysages historiques... L'unité minimale retenue dans *Patriarche* est celle de l'*entité archéologique (EA)* qui associe au couple structure / datation, une géométrie figurée par un polygone, mais avec la possibilité d'émettre le doute sur un ou plusieurs des termes constituants (fig. 4.1). Ce travail préliminaire permet ensuite de proposer une reconstruction historique qui est généralement menée en collaboration avec les structures de recherches, essentiellement les universités et le Centre national de la Recherche scientifique très souvent dans le cadre des *unités mixtes de recherches (UMR)* dont près de 25 sont aidées par le ministère de la Culture. C'est ce dernier qui est à l'origine des crédits obtenus par les équipes d'archéologues pour réaliser tant les opérations de prospections (terrestres ou aériennes, subaquatiques, géophysiques...) que les reprises de documentations anciennes permettant de nouvelles datations ou interprétations (*Programmes collectifs de Recherche/PCR*...).

De telles démarches sont aussi portées – directement ou en collaboration – par les services archéologiques des collectivités territoriales associant plus étroitement encore les deux démarches de connaissance et de valorisation des territoires. C'est notamment dans le domaine urbain que les exemples sont les plus développés, mais des expériences en milieu rural sur des thématiques spécifiques sont également attestées : environnement des grottes

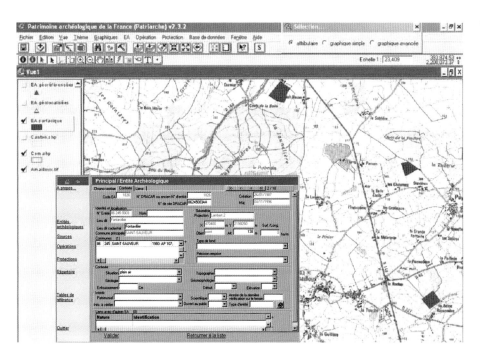

Fig. 4.1 : Copie d'un écran de Patriarche : entité archéologique décrite et SIG).

ornées, ensembles mégalithiques, maillage des territoires ruraux antiques et médiévaux, exploitations des matières premières comme dans les districts miniers...

La prise en compte du patrimoine archéologique et des paysages historiques dans la mise en valeur des territoires : des servitudes à la gestion durable des territoires

Une législation française très récente qui a bénéficié de l'évolution de la doctrine au niveau européen ainsi que de la prise en compte de l'environnement dans sa dimension culturelle

Nous insisterons en premier lieu sur des procédures qui intéressent directement la question de la prise en compte des paysages historiques dans le paysage et constituent des outils performants pour peu que les données archéologiques y soient intégrées, au moins dans la constitution des dossiers en amont de la décision :

- les servitudes liées aux protections au titre des monuments historiques ou des sites ,
- les servitudes liées aux dispositifs originaux que sont ceux des espaces protégés.

Au préalable, rappelons que le *Code du patrimoine* a consacré la notion de conservation par l'étude pour le patrimoine archéologique (définition empruntée à la Convention de Malte ratifiée par la France) et que les services de l'État en région proposent donc au préfet des zones de présomption de prescription de diagnostics archéologiques à partir desquelles se développe l'archéologie préventive : diagnostics suivis ou non de fouilles préventives. Ces zones de saisine des dossiers d'aménagement du territoire sont le résultat de la connaissance par les SRA des enjeux scientifiques dans une logique de conciliation des intérêts patrimoniaux et économiques. Des stratégies régionales s'appuyant sur des bilans d'activité établis par les SRA en collaboration avec leurs partenaires sont proposées aux instances de contrôle scientifique de l'archéologie française (*Commissions interrégionales de la Recherche archéologique : CIRA*) et justifient de tels choix qui n'excluent aucunement des interventions d'archéologie préventive hors zonages. Les paysages historiques identifiés peuvent donc être concernés par les mesures de l'archéologie préventive comme ils peuvent bénéficier, ponctuellement, des servitudes proposées par les diverses protections existantes. Cela reste du ressort de la stratégie des DRAC à partir du dialogue instauré entre leurs services patrimoniaux et dans le cadre des échanges avec les collectivités territoriales et avec les propriétaires. Aucune hiérarchie entre sites ou paysages ne peut être dégagée à ce jour au niveau national qui justifierait tel ou tel choix régional de protections. La mise en place de diagnostics d'archéologie préventive reste pour tous la règle.

La création de servitudes archéologiques par les protections au titre des monuments historiques ou des sites naturels, historiques et paysagers

La politique de protection des sites et paysages archéologiques et historiques s'appuie aussi sur les mesures plus classiques de protection au titre des Monuments historiques depuis 1913 ou des Sites naturels, historiques ou paysagers depuis 1930. Un site archéologique peut ainsi être protégé, après avis de la *Commission régionale du patrimoine et des sites* (CRPS), au titre des Monuments historiques et donc *classé* Monument

historique ou *inscrit* à l'Inventaire supplémentaire des Monuments historiques de la même manière qu'il peut être protégé au titre des Sites naturels, historiques et paysagers qui prend pleinement en compte la dimension historique des paysages (avec la même hiérarchie de protection : classé ou inscrit). Il faut, dans les deux cas, obtenir l'accord du ou des propriétaires (qui peuvent s'avérer très nombreux pour un site archéologique) et surtout veiller à la bonne gestion des abords qui sont automatiquement générés par la protection lorsque le site est en élévation : périmètres de covisibilité dits aussi de 500 m.

Les servitudes alors créées peuvent être très pénalisantes pour la commune sur lequel le site est positionné et cela explique qu'il n'y ait pas de systématicité de ce type de protection, y compris pour des sites archéologiques considérés comme majeurs. La réflexion, sur initiative de la DRAC, est menée autant que possible avec les communes en tenant compte de l'ensemble des contraintes pesant sur le territoire concerné et de tous les enjeux archéologiques. Le choix peut être fait de privilégier l'acquisition par la collectivité territoriale (avec l'aide de l'État ou non) des terrains contenant des vestiges pour la constitution de «réserve archéologique». La notion de réserve archéologique ne peut se concrétiser de manière pérenne et donc avec le plus de garantie possible que si une servitude d'occupation du sol est alors créée.

La création de servitudes archéologiques au sein des espaces protégés (PSMV et ZPPAUP)

Les « Espaces protégés » sont, quant à eux, des outils transdisciplinaires et une bonne base de dialogue avec les collectivités territoriales pour permettre une politique urbanistique et architecturale visant un cadre de vie de qualité et de « haute qualité environnementale» (voir encadrés). Ces deux dispositifs réglementaires et opérationnels, *PSMV* (*Plans de Sauvegarde et de Mises en Valeur*) des secteurs sauvegardés et *ZPPAUP* (*Zones de Protection du Patrimoine architectural, urbain et paysager*), montrent comment la prise en compte dynamique du patrimoine et de la qualité architecturale et urbaine, conçues comme des agents qualitatifs du cadre de la vie en société, se placent au cœur même de la logique du développement durable dont elle sert les dimensions environnementale, économique, sociale mais aussi culturelle.

Des données de la «carte archéologique» aux «portés à connaissance» des documents de planification : critères de sélection et impact de la diffusion de l'information sur la conservation.

Les services de l'État dans les régions (SRA au sein des DRAC pour l'archéologie) participent depuis longtemps au «porté à connaissance» pour les différents documents d'urbanisme et contribuent donc à la réflexion sur la prise en compte des données archéologiques dans la planification des aménagements des territoires. Ils répondent également aux études d'impact qui leur sont adressées, comme ils assurent les réponses à des demandes spécifiques de collectivités territoriales, d'aménageurs et de propriétaires des sols.

Trois législations, modifiées récemment, permettent désormais, d'un point de vue réglementaire, une meilleure prise en compte de l'archéologie dans l'aménagement des territoires :

- L 121.2 du *Code de l'urbanisme* : [études techniques pour l'Inventaire général du patrimoine culturel : archéologie et ethnologie],
- article 79 du *Code minier* : [respects des intérêts de l'archéologie dans les travaux de recherche ou d'exploitation d'une mine],
- L 511.1 du *Code de l'environnement* : [prise en compte en amont de l'archéologie dans les études d'impact].

La prise en compte de l'archéologie, qui est inscrite désormais dans ces trois codes concernant directement l'aménagement du territoire, peut ainsi être facilitée, sous réserve de la capacité des services à traiter l'information, d'une réflexion nationale sur sa mise en forme harmonisée et adaptée aux attentes des services instructeurs et de la mise à disposition d'outils assurant une large diffusion des informations attendues. Ce travail, qui nécessite une importante formalisation critique des

Zonage N et Nm pour le porter à connaissance

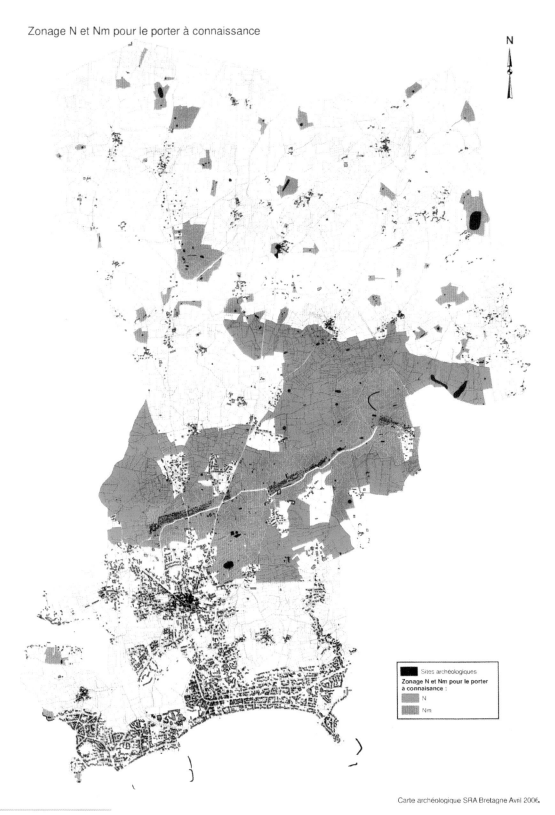

Carte archéologique SRA Bretagne Avril 2006.

Fig. 4.2 : L'exemple de la réponse de l'archéologie au sein du Plan Local d'Urbanisme de la commune de Carnac.

informations archéologiques (au-delà des « extraits de la carte archéologique » tels que prévus par le *Code du patrimoine*), est aujourd'hui très inégalement exercé sur le territoire national. Il a fait l'objet d'un premier séminaire professionnel à Bibracte à l'automne 2007 dont les actes sont en cours de préparation (sous la direction de Hannois, Négri et Vergain, 2009, à paraître). Des exemples choisis de ces contributions exemplaires alimentent cependant la présente réflexion européenne dont un petit nombre sélectionné illustre ce texte (fig. 4.2).

Une réflexion sur la qualité et la forme de l'information archéologique à transmettre dans le cadre des documents de planification du territoire est désormais en germe au niveau national. La réponse variera selon la nature du document et les attentes des services instructeurs ou des demandeurs : cartes communales, *Plan local d'Urbanisme (PLU)*, *Schéma de Cohérence territoriale (ScoT)* ou *Directives territoriales d'Aménagement (DTA)* ; réponses aux Études d'impact ; participation à la *Gestion intégrée des Zones côtières (GIZC)*... Dans tous les cas, elle tiendra compte aussi des avancées de la recherche archéologique et devra justifier une démarche de connaissance évolutive, ce qui interdit l'idée d'un document opposable aux tiers.

Des travaux spécifiques portent déjà ou vont porter sur des milieux considérés comme plus fragiles ou reposant sur des thématiques scientifiques mieux maîtrisées et des territoires explorés. On notera ainsi, sans que la liste soit exhaustive, les thèmes suivants, objets d'études avancées :

- Les grottes ornées avec la prise en compte de leur environnement hydrogéologique amont,
- les *oppida* du centre de la Gaule autour de la réflexion paysagère menée à Bibracte,
- les ensembles mégalithiques de Bretagne (Carnac), Lozère, Aveyron et de Corse,
- les littoraux atlantique et méditerranéen au sens de la Loi Littoral (communes littoral),
- l'inventaire des sites archéologiques des lacs alpins (patrimoine mondial Unesco),
- les agglomérations secondaires antiques sur le modèle du parc européen de Bliesbrück-Reinheim,
- la reconnaissance des paysages historiques montagnards des Alpes comme des Pyrénées.

Les enjeux de la restitution publique des données archéologiques et de leur mise en valeur autour de la mise en ligne de *l'Atlas de l'architecture et du patrimoine en* 2008

Une meilleure synergie entre historiens, géographes, environnementalistes, archéologues et architectes, indispensable tant pour le passage des données archéologiques à la reconstitution des paysages historiques que pour la prise en compte de leur protection, devrait se confirmer avec la mise à disposition sur Internet des travaux interprétatifs dans le cadre du volet « géoportail » de *l'Atlas de l'architecture et du patrimoine*. Dès 2008, seront ainsi valorisées tant les pratiques, que les suggestions de formalisations à partir des expérimentations mais surtout seront mises à disposition du plus grand nombre toutes ces informations d'ordre archéologique qui sont attendues, tant par les producteurs de données avides de confronter leurs approches que par les publics tant dans un souci de protection par la connaissance que de prise en compte dans le développement durable des territoires.

La sélection des données transmises : des bases de données aux restitutions qui seront diffusées par l'Atlas de l'architecture et du patrimoine.

Le projet *Atlas de l'architecture et du patrimoine* a été initié par la *Direction de l'architecture et du patrimoine* pour répondre au besoin d'une restitution de la connaissance des patrimoines ethnologique et ethnographique, archéologique, architectural, urbain et paysager. Cette restitution est commandée soit par des obligations réglementaires de publication comme pour les *zones de protection du patrimoine architectural, urbain et paysager (ZPPAUP)* ou les zones de présomption de prescription archéologique prévues dans le *Code du patrimoine*, soit nécessaire pour servir aux intérêts de la protection, de la gestion et de la valorisation du patrimoine, mais aussi de la recherche scientifique notamment en archéologie.

L'objectif prioritaire de l'*Atlas de l'architecture et du patrimoine* est de partager entre services patrimoniaux et établissement publics de l'État, services archéologiques des collectivités territoriales et opérateurs en archéologie, les données élaborées par chacun d'entre eux, mais utiles dans l'exercice de leurs missions spécifiques. Il s'agit donc, dans un premier temps, d'optimiser l'exploitation des données spatiales existantes et d'améliorer leur accessibilité et leur interopérabilité.

L'*Atlas* contribuera ainsi à l'information du public, des gestionnaires du sol et des aménageurs publics ou privés dans le cadre du développement durable des territoires. Ce projet contribue aussi à la « modernisation de l'État » par l'utilisation de l'information géographique, telle que préconisée par la décision interministérielle du 19 janvier 2001. Il s'inscrit dans la proposition d'une directive du parlement européen (INSPIRE) et du conseil de l'Europe établissant une infrastructure d'information spatiale commune à tous les États membres.

La place des paysages historiques dans l'Atlas de l'architecture et du patrimoine en cours.

Si la réflexion en matière d'archéologie urbaine est déjà ancienne en France à partir d'exemples locaux souvent relayés par le *Centre national d'Archéologie urbaine* (Tours, Saint-Denis, Chartres, Arles ou Marseille pour ne citer que certains parmi les plus exemplaires), le cheminement est souvent incomplet jusqu'à la notion de « paysage historique », y compris en matière urbaine. Un certain cloisonnement au sein du ministère de la Culture entre les archéologues, les historiens de l'architecture et les architectes comme la faible visibilité d'expériences associant les trois domaines expliquent en partie le faible nombre de restitutions satisfaisantes d'approches complémentaires pour proposer des paysages historiques. Les collectivités territoriales ont pour certaines d'entre elles tenté de rompre ces cloisonnements en particulier sous la pression des contraintes de l'aménagement de leurs territoires.

En contre exemple, le département de la Seine-Saint-Denis, dans une préfiguration grandeur nature de ce que pourrait être l'*Atlas de l'architecture et du patrimoine*, offre un des exemples les plus aboutis sur un tel sujet : son travail d'inventaire du patrimoine culturel notamment archéologique sur les communes du département est déjà présent sur la maquette actuelle (accès Internet) (fig. 4.3). En ce qui concerne le monde rural, les expériences sont multiples mais encore trop peu mises en évidence

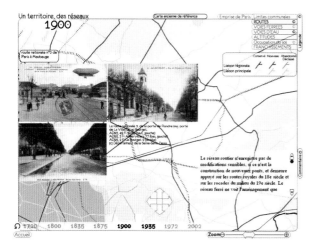

Fig. 4.3 : Un exemple de restitution d'un paysage historique.

de communes) qui doivent pouvoir s'investir dans ces structures mixtes de recherche en pleine restructuration. Les bases d'un clair partenariat entre l'État et les collectivités territoriales ont été posées avec la mission d'*Inventaire général du Patrimoine culturel* confiée aux Conseils régionaux et avec la volonté du ministère de la Culture suivant en cela la représentation nationale de développer les services archéologiques de collectivités territoriales agréés pour l'archéologie préventive, pan complémentaire à l'INRAP du dispositif public en ce domaine pour la réalisation des diagnostics comme pour la candidature aux chantiers de fouille préventive au niveau national.

Restera ensuite à garantir les conditions de la meilleure constitution et surtout de la pérennité des « Archives du sol », c'est-à-dire à la fois toutes les données archéologiques recueillies, critiquées et formalisées et toutes les reconstitutions ou interprétations qui en sont issues, permettant la réflexion collective en matière de paysages culturels par exemple. Cette volonté politique doit permettre de garantir à tous la possibilité d'un retour aux sources premières par la conservation tant des mobiliers que des archives constituées durant la fouille mais aussi pendant toutes les études et analyses au moyen du développement sur le territoire national d'un réseau de « centres de conservation et d'étude » présentant les mêmes exigences que celles réservées aux «°archives nationales » et assurant le lien avec la médiation par les Musées de France.

Encadrés concernant les « espaces protégés »

Les « plans de sauvegarde et de mise en valeur » (PSMV) des secteurs sauvegardés
Leur objectif est de conserver, restaurer et mettre en valeur des ensembles urbains présentant un caractère historique et/ou esthétique remarquable. Ils composent un ensemble de règles particulières applicables dans un périmètre déterminé constituant un « secteur sauvegardé ». Les démarches entreprises à cet effet conjuguent différents moyens d'analyse fine de l'existant pour dégager ses potentialités et ainsi favoriser sa mise en valeur. Dans ce cadre, le tissu et la forme urbaine sont considérés comme essentiels dans l'appréciation de ce qui doit être « transmis aux générations futures ». Une synergie est recherchée pour les moyens nécessaires à la mise en œuvre des objectifs, au contrôle de la réhabilitation et à la re-dynamisation de l'occupation des quartiers anciens.

Les problématiques alors abordées et concernant le « développement durable » sont très diverses, par exemple :
- pour les centres anciens : rechercher une mise en valeur de ceux-ci en revitalisant les activités et en recherchant des nouvelles fonctions qui soient adaptées à leur cadre bâti,
- pour les quartiers plus récents, qu'il s'agisse d'habitat ou d'activités artisanales voire industrielles : révéler et faire connaître leur valeur particulière et chercher les moyens de les qualifier pour le futur, tout en les protégeant de destructions intempestives (fig. 4.4).

avec quelques tentatives associant les approches ethnologiques et environnementales, véritables ponts autour des questions touchant à la relation Nature/Culture : ainsi sur le littoral (Parc naturel régional de Narbonnaise en Languedoc), en montagne (paysages intermédiaires des Pyrénées), en milieu forestier notamment en Haute-Normandie avec l'ONF ou dans le cadre des « cœurs de Parc » avec l'exemple récent de l'atlas archéologique du Parc naturel national des Cévennes.

Les liens avec les autres disciplines scientifiques, notamment autour de la question des évolutions climatiques, des études de matériaux et des datations mais aussi avec les sciences sociales restent encore trop distants malgré des collaborations exemplaires sur les questions des cortèges fauniques et des évolutions des paysages naturels anthropisés depuis le Néolithique, sur l'environnement des grottes ornées paléolithiques et plus globalement des manifestations de l'art rupestre préhistorique ou des évolutions des paysages ruraux du nord de la France.

En guise de postface...
Il faut espérer que la mise en ligne de l'*Atlas de l'Architecture et du Patrimoine* constituera un formidable appel d'air favorisant la restitution la plus large possible de travaux encore trop isolés, forçant ainsi des échanges et permettant une relance de la réflexion sur le modèle wallon du *Historical Landscape Characterisation* adapté à la francophonie (voir *thésaurus en cours de construction à la table-ronde de Toulouse en novembre 2008*).

Les cadres pour une collaboration renforcée notamment avec les ethnologues, autour des projets scientifiques et culturels des musées de territoire, sont en place pour assurer le développement d'une démarche réellement anthropologique pour l'archéologie au sein des sciences sociales et humaines. Il reste à s'appuyer autant que faire se peut sur le réseau des *unités mixtes de recherche* (universités, Centre national de la Recherche scientifique, ministère de la Culture avec l'INRAP) sous réserve de trouver les moyens d'associer complètement les Écoles d'Architecture et les géographes et environnementalistes des équipes de recherche trop peu impliqués jusqu'alors, sauf exceptions.

Les collectivités territoriales et, parmi elles, les Régions seront les premières demandeuses de telles réponses cohérentes avec leurs services patrimoniaux (surtout présents pour l'archéologie au niveau des départements et des agglomérations, voire aujourd'hui dans les communautés

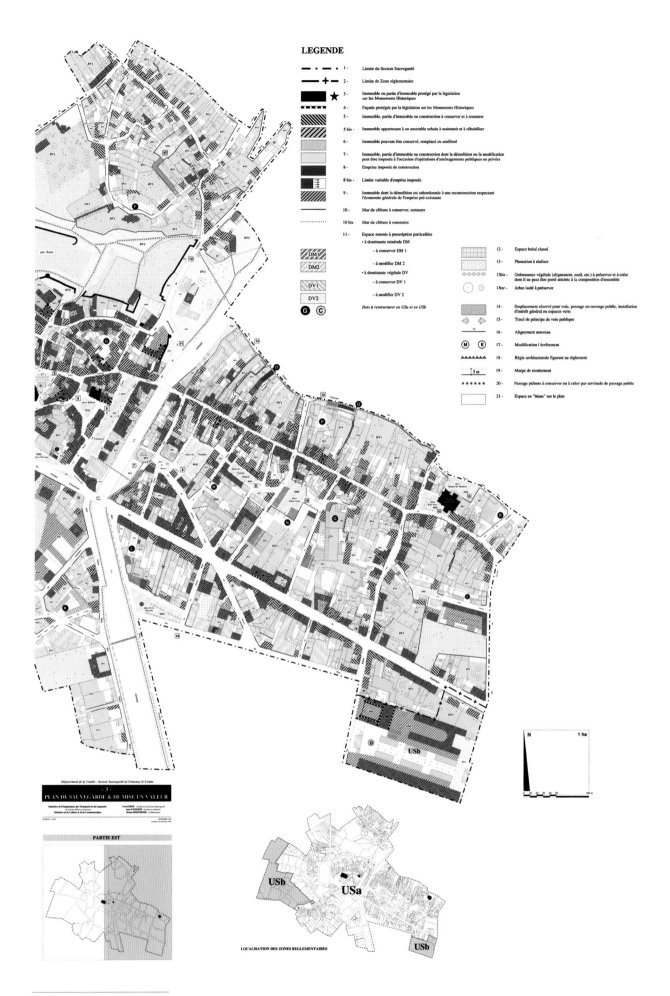

Fig. 4.4

Fig. 4.5

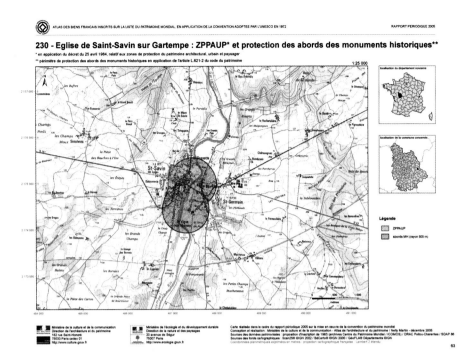

Les zones de protection du patrimoine architectural, urbain et paysager (ZPPAUP)

Il s'agit de servitudes annexées au document d'urbanisme qui doit reprendre leur prescriptions. Les zones de protection ainsi définies ont un double objectif :

- elles permettent d'assurer, pour le territoire qu'elles couvrent, une meilleure gestion du patrimoine historique, architectural et urbain en adaptant plus précisément le type de protection aux sites et à leurs enjeux. En particulier, leurs dispositions réglementaires peuvent être ajustées pour traiter des relations particulières entre des paysages et des sites construits ou à construire et d'éviter ainsi l'édification de bâtiments en contradiction avec les critères du « développement durable »,
- pour les zones rurales, villages, bourgs ou constructions isolées, la question de la réutilisation du patrimoine existant est actuellement la plus préoccupante : pose tout particulièrement problème la construction de lotissements à la périphérie des noyaux anciens de qualité mais sous-habités, tout comme l'abandon progressif des bâtiments agricoles de qualité architecturale reconnue mais inadaptés aux techniques et normes en vigueur. La solution relève autant dans le changement des mentalités en ce qui concerne l'habitat que de la recherche d'autres modes de productions agricoles plus proches de la qualité que de la productivité (fig. 4.5).

vergain.philippe@culture.gouv.fr

5 | Listing of archaeological sites – the Icelandic case

Kristín Huld Sigurðardóttir and Sólborg Una Pálsdóttir

In Iceland the systematic listing of archaeological sites started in 1907. Before then, in 1817 when Iceland was still under Danish rule, ten sites were listed by the *Royal Danish Commission for the protection of archaeological remains.* The Icelander Finnur Magnusson, a professor and archivist in Copenhagen, was a member of the Royal Commission. He had a great influence on deciding what kind of remains were listed in Iceland. Most of them were runic inscriptions, Finnur being Scandinavia's main rune specialist at that time. Other remains which were protected in 1817 were a *þing*-site on Snæfellsnes in western Iceland, a fort (Borgarvirki) in north-western Iceland and a bath at Reykholt in western Iceland (Rafnsson 1983, ix-xix).

In 1907 the first legislation governing the protection of the archaeological heritage of Iceland was adopted by the Parliament. According to the Heritage Act of 1907, one of the roles of the then newly-appointed State Antiquarian was to list all archaeological sites which he considered worthy of protection (Heritage Act 1907 Art. 5-6).

In the following decades, over 400 archaeological sites, most of them with a few remains, were listed, covering approximately 800 remains. Most (84%) of the sites were listed between 1926 and 1930. The listing was mainly based on scholars' attempts to locate places mentioned in the Icelandic Sagas. The selection was seldom founded upon archaeolgical research and the sites were rarely visited prior to listing. Instead, the listing relied heavily on written documents. Often, the only information preserved regarding the sites was a written description, without any drawings or photos. In 1969 a new Heritage Act was approved, but it was not until yet another revision of the act, adopted in 1989, that this procedure was changed. Under the 1989 Act, all archaeological sites in Iceland over one hundred years old were automatically to be protected by law. Thus, a two-tier system of protection

Fig. 5.1: Snorri Sturluson's bath in Reykholt, thought to date from the 12ᵗʰ-13ᵗʰ centuries. One of the sites protected by royal decree in 1817. *Photo: Fornleifavernd ríkisins/Kristín Huld Sigurðardóttir 2006.*

of archaeological sites was established: firstly the 800 or so listed remains and secondly all sites which are over one hundred years old of which there are believed to be about 200,000. As a result of this "100-year principle" very few new sites have been listed during the last two decades. The term "*cultural landscape*" was not included in Iceland's heritage legislation until the 2001 Heritage Act was passed (Heritage Act 2001 Art. 9).

Monitoring of sites was not effective until with the establishment of District Antiquarians in about 2000. Prior to that, in 1981, the National Museum of Iceland, which was at that time in charge of Iceland's archaeological heritage, made a condition survey of the listed sites by sending questionnaires to the residents of 408 properites with listed sites. The response rate was only 37.7%. The results of this survey caused concern that respondents were only aware of the existence of 151 listed sites. Of these 151 sites, 27 were in danger, 42 had been disturbed, 17 had disappeared and the location of 8 was not known (Georgsson 1984, 15-20). This called for a new policy and a re-evaluation of the listed sites which is currently one of the main tasks of the Archaeological Heritage Agency of Iceland (Fornleifavernd ríkisins). The agency was established by the adoption of the current Heritage Act, No. 107/2001, and became the central authority for the protection and management of archaeological monuments and sites. It is a governmental agency under the Ministry of Education, Science and Culture.

Under Article 11 of the Heritage Act of 2001, the director-general of the Archaeological Heritage Agency of Iceland decides which remains are to be listed. Items listed may consist of individual archaological remains, a cluster of

remains or a cultural landscape. Protection granted by listing extends 20 metres beyond the outer edge of the visible remains. The listing must be announced in the Official Gazette (Stjórnartíðindi). The owners of listed sites are eligible for financial compensation if they can prove that the use of their land has been reduced by to the listing (Heritage Act No. 107/2001, Article 25.) However, it must be remembered that all sites over 100 years of age are protected under the Heritage Act (Article 9) and if the landowners want to build on land containing archaeological remains they have to pay for an archaeological study (Article 14). Under Article 27, those who damage sites can be fined or even imprisoned. Under Article 17, the cost of measures necessary for the conservation of listed sites is borne by the state. Due to increased demands from the tourist industry, some of the sites will be used in cultural tourism. In such cases, parties wishing to make use of the archaeological remains have to meet the cost of their restoration and pay for access paths and information signs. These provisions are interpreted as meaning that the state only pays for the protection necessary to keep the remains as they were when they were listed, while those who want to make use of a site have to pay for everything else, including extra protective measures to meet increased environmental pressure.

Generally speaking, when a site has been listed it is supposed to be protected for future generations. In 2000 the Icelandic parliament decided to allocate a large sum to archaeological excavations in the period 2002-2006. A political decision was made by the Parliament that some sites associated with the conversion of Iceland to Christianity in 1000 AD should be excavated. These included Þingvellir, which in 2004 became the first World Heritage site in Iceland, and the bishoprics Hólar and Skálholt. All these sites were listed. According to Iceland's national archaeological strategy, drawn up by the Heritage Agency in 2005, no listed sites will be excavated in the immediate future, apart from the minor research projects which the Archaeological Heritage Agency itself is undertaking. The demand for space is not really threatening the listed sites. On the other hand, many of the sites protected by the "100-year principle" are threatened by the demand for space. By law, no development is allowed at listed sites. There is an inconsistency between various statutory provisions regarding the extent of protection against development at listed sites. Under the Antiquities Act, it is forbidden to disturb the ground within 20 metres from the outermost visible edge of the site; under the Environmental Assessment Act, No.106/2000, (Appendix 3 iii (d)) this distance is 100 metres.

Whether or not listed sites are freely accessible to the public varies from site to site. Some of them are in the middle of farmers' meadows, so it is difficult to have them assessible to the public. Most are accessible, however, and admission to all is free.

The re-evaluation of listed sites started in 2007 and is expected to last until 2010. During this time every site will be accurately surveyed, photographed and registered.

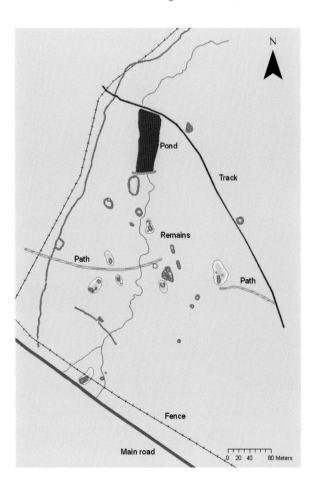

Fig. 5.2: An example of a drawing of a listed site, Hálskot in Dalvíkurbyggð. *Drawing: Fornleifavernd ríkisins/Sólborg Una Pálsdóttir, 2007*

Table 5.1

Criteria	Explanation
Rarity	Is the site unique, or is it typical for the country as a whole, or for a special area in the country?
Research value	All sites have research value, but some are more likely to yield new information and knowledge in the future.
Visibility	This value is based on both the visibility and educational factor. Is the site highly visible in the landscape? Is the form and extent of the site easy to see? Will people find it easy to imagine the situation and environment of the site when it was created or in use?
Authenticity	Is the site really what it was thought to be, in respect to age, space and type?
Contextual value	The value of the site may increase greatly if the site has been preserved as a part of a larger context, both in relation to contemporary remains and the historic landscape.
Symbolic/ Historical value	Sites with definite historical significance or those which are associated with a notable event a person of historical significance shall be highlighted.
Accessibility	Listed sites are "national treasures". It is thus important that they be made accessible.
Condition	The condition of the site is an important factor in the evaluation. Listed sites should preferably be in good condition in respect of their age, type and surroundings.

GPS locations of sites will also be established and the condition and value of the sites will be assessed. In some cases, the sites undergoing re-evaluation consist of single remains; in other cases they consist of larger areas or cultural landscapes, like the one illustrated in Fig. 5.2. What is special about Icelandic archaeological sites is that most of the original structures were made of turf and stone, with some wooden frames in the case of the houses. Changes in land use and population spread in Iceland, with the growth of towns and the decline in the rural population, meant that large regions were deserted before the introduction of mechanised farm equipment. As a result, some fairly ancient sites are still visible on the ground.

The listed sites must include examples forming a cross-section of all types of sites found in Iceland. They must include examples of what is special and typical for the country as a whole, and also what is typical and special for each area. The criteria used to assess eligibility for preservation are presented in table 5.1.

Fig. 5.3: Surveying a listed site, Hávarðarstaðir in Þorvaldsdal. *Photo: Fornleifavernd ríkisins/ Sigurður Bergsteinsson 2007.*

Icelandic archaeology falls mainly under the term historical archaeology. The re-evaluation is thus based both on historical and archaeological data. In some cases, information relating to the use and even age of the remains can be found in the historical sources. Archaeological studies of listed sites concentrates on the comparison of the field surveys and thus the different types of remains. In order to date and/or determine the type of the site some small excavations are undertaken at the sites.

The Agency's strategy places great emphasis on increasing the information available for sites through multimedia presentations of various kinds in the coming years. Indeed, some information is already to be found on the web.

The definition of a cultural landscape in Article 9 of the Heritage Act of 2001 is very broad. The Heritage Act authorises the Agency to protect large areas and not merely man-made structures and their surroundings. Under Article 11 of the Act, if the Agency wishes to protect an area extending further than 20 metres from the listed remains, this must be done by agreement with the owner of the site. However, no site or place where the cultural landscape itself is the main reason for the protection has yet been listed.

The Heritage Act of 2001 provides for the registration of all remains over 100 years old. In an ideal world, the selection of sites to be listed would be based on such an overall registration of all archaeological sites; this would ensure the diversity of the sites to be protected for future generations. In reality, however, only 30% of the sites have been registered. Under Article 11 of the Heritage Act of 2001 local authorities are obliged to register archaeological remains in areas subject to planning. This provision was first introduced in the Heritage Act of 1989. According to Article 11 of the Heritage Act 2001, the location of all the listed sites must be shown on planning maps.

Very slowly but surely, we will obtain the necessary perspective of all sites and monuments in Iceland. This registration work is being done both by private firms owned by Icelandic archaeologists and by archaeologists employed by the museums. The Archaeological Heritage Agency is not handling registration of sites other than the listed ones. So far, the information has been stored in five or six different databases owned by the firms. In order to standardise the information for storage in the central database owned by the Archaeological Heritage Agency, the Agency has developed standards to be used by all archaeologists in Iceland.

Apart from the work on the re-evaluation of listed sites, a task to be tackled in the coming years is the registration of all archaeological sites in the country and the collection and protection of the information in a central database.

kristinhuld@fornleifaverdn.is

References

(Environmental Assessment Act) Lög *um mat á umhverfisáhrifum nr. 106 frá 25. maí 2000.*

Georgsson, Ágúst,Ó. 1984. *Könnun um friðlýstar fornleifar.* Ljóri 5.árg. 1. tbl. 1984. Reykjavík. p. 15-20.

(Heritage Act 1907). *Lög um verndun fornmenja dags. 16. nóv. 1907.*

(Heritage Act 1969). *Þjóðminjalög nr. 52 19.maí 1969.*

(Heritage Act 1989). *Þjóðminjalög nr. 88 29.maí 1989.*

(Heritage Act 2001). *Þjóðminjalög nr. 107/2001.*

Rafnsson, S. 1983. *Frásögur um Fornaldarleifar I.* Reykjavík: Stofnun Árna Magnússonar.

6 | Listing – precondition of protection?

Katalin Wollák

Abstract: For seven years in Hungary two forms of protection have existed; the constitutive and declarative protections. As the 2001 legislation declared, every known site is protected by the force of law. This protection comes into force through the registration, which is an administrative process done by the National Office of Cultural Heritage. The present number of the registered sites is almost 60,000. The scheduling of the sites and territories of outstanding historic and cultural values is a different procedure which concludes with a decree from the ministry of culture; there are about 1000 scheduled items.

The previous strategy for scheduling was to protect sites in danger, but recently the function of the protection has changed. It is due to the wider heritage management opportunities, as the necessary provisions in the interest of archaeological heritage can be defined already in the planning phase of different spatial developments. The recently adopted Landscape Convention establishes a cooperative relationship with authorities responsible for nature conservation with an aim to preserve the whole historic environment.

The Historical Background

The law on the protection of monuments of 1881 can be considered the first milestone in the history of archaeological heritage management in Hungary, although from the middle of the 19th century we start to see regulations on declaration commitment. In the case of a chance find it had to be reported to the Hungarian Academy of Science, the information on findings went in to the Hungarian National Museum. All of antiquities: remains of a church, a castle, other old buildings, stone, wooden, or metal objects, goldsmith's work, armour, paintings, furniture, jewellery – any that were created before the first half of the 18th century – should be reported (fig. 6.1). The data was recorded in a register in order to obtain an overall view of the antiquities in the country. The law called attention to the preservation of the archaeological finds which came to light, for example during railway-building, but it prescribed measures only for the protection and maintenance of historical monuments (Wollák, K. 1999, p. 469; Nagy, M 2003, p 34).

After the Second World War the 1949 decree established a new institution, the National Centre of Museums and Monuments, chance finds had to be reported either to this Centre, or to the local authorities. The legal status of the

Fig. 6.1: Milestones of the heritage management.

1802	Hungarian National Museum
1841	Society of Doctors & Investigators of Nature (1846: Archaeological section)
19th century	museum societies, county museums
1847	Hungarian Academy of Science – appeal to report on historical remains (1858 Archaeological Committee)
1872	Temporary Committee for Historic Monuments
1881	**1st law: On the protection of monuments (Act XXXIX. 1881.)**
1881	National Committee for Monuments
1929	Law on the settlement of some questions on museum, library and archive affairs
1949	**Law: On the Museums and Monuments (Decree 13. with Force of a Law 1949.)**
1949	National Centre of Museums and Monuments
1952	Archaeological Archive in the Hungarian National Museum
1957	National (and Budapest) Inspectorate of Monuments
1958	Archaeological Institute of the Hungarian Academy of Science
1963	chain of county museums
1992	National Board for the Protection of Monuments
1997	Law on the protection of monuments (Act LIV. 1997.)
1997	**Law: On the protection of cultural assets (Act CXL. 1997.)**
1998	Cultural Heritage Directorate
2001	**Law: On the protection of cultural heritage (Act LXIV. 2001.)**
2001	National Office of Cultural Heritage

| **important regulations** | establishment of basic institutions |

findings changed, they became state-property, the Centre could offer financial reward to the finder and the owner of the land. The decree introduced a new definition: the archaeological protected area, sites and archaeological monuments with outstanding values, and endangered important sites - mainly under the earth - were protected by administrative measures. The Centre advised which territories of archaeological or historical importance (monuments and sites) should get protected status. The aim of this protection was to preserve these archaeological remains in their undisturbed position, due to this legal status the different developments could not endanger these (a few hundred) protected sites In 1952 the central archaeological archival department was established within the Hungarian National Museum, since then all archaeological interventions have to be reported to the national museum and also to the local museum where the finds were kept. The later regulations defined what the precise content of these reports should be (called documentation): the excavation diary, the drawings, the photo documentation, the mapping and a short summary of the archaeological activity (Wollák, K. – Zsidi, P. 1998. p. 309). This archive contains the numerous available records on excavations from the 19th and early 20th centuries as well (Rezi-Kato, G. 2003. p. 431).

New Regulation with a European Perspective
The regulations of 1997 brought about basic changes. The aim of the new legislation was to transform the legal background, to redefine the role of the state authorities in reference to cultural (archaeological) heritage. Another aim was to build in the basic principles of La Valletta Convention on the Protection of Archaeological Heritage (Council of Europe 1992) to the new law (Wollák, K – Zsidi, P 2003. p. 243). The legislation separated the duties of the professional organisations authorised to carry out excavations (such as museums and other institutions) from the tasks of the heritage management organisations. The newly founded state agency, the Cultural Heritage Directorate (fig. 6.1), became responsible for licensing and supervising excavations, preparing the surveys for sites to be protected making proposals to the minister, and maintaining an advising scientific committee. Its task was to create a new, central database of archaeological sites as well (Jankovich, B. D. 2000. pp 13; Wollák, K 2007. pp 73). The introduction of the preventive/investment led archaeology system (now financed by the investor) meant that the budget for the archaeology has to cover the costs of the excavation, the documentation, the primary conservation of the findings, the primary finds processing and the extra expenses of housing the finds.

The basic elements of the 1997 legislation have been incorporated into the current 2001 law without major changes. The law articulated the complete separation of professional and administrative tasks. This new regulation "On the protection of cultural heritage" (Act LXVI. 2001) - which came into force in October 2001 - intended to cover the total immovable heritage (built and archaeological heritage) and certain part of the movable heritage (cultural goods) based on integrated approach. The law determined the definition of archaeological heritage as: all detectable signs of human life originating before 1711 above ground, below ground or water and in natural or artificial cavities which help to reconstruct the history of humankind and its relationship with the environment. The legislation also introduced a new notion: areas with archaeological interest or archaeologically sensitive areas. This category covers territories where – due to their geophysical or geomorphologic conditions or due to the existence of known sites nearby – archaeological remains have the potential to be found or assumed to exist.

Institutions Participating in Heritage Management
To describe the present situation of archaeological heritage management in Hungary we have to enumerate the basic elements of the present law. All types of archaeological interventions (those using destructive or non-destructive methods) can be done only with a licence (with the exception of rescue excavation in case of chance findings). The lower-level decree on the implementation of the law declares that only responsible organisations, such as county and national museums with an archaeological competence, archaeological departments at universities, the Institute of Archaeology of the Hungarian Academy of Sciences and national heritage organisations (among them the recently founded Field Service for Cultural Heritage) have the right to conduct excavations. The leader of the excavation can only be an archaeologist with a professional degree who is employed by (or has a temporary contract with) one of the above organisations. The valid legal system does not allow either commercial or amateur archaeology. As the volume of the archaeological activity is constantly growing (fig. 6.2) and the total number of the active archaeologists is approximately 400 (The Association of Hungarian Archaeologists has presently 324 members); approximately half of these people are in permanent employment, therefore a few small private archaeological firms appeared as not license capable subcontractors.

Since 2001 as a consequence of the law on the protection of cultural heritage certain restructuring has been taken place in Hungary. A new organisation was constructed through merging the 3 year old Directorate responsible for archaeology and movable heritage and the National

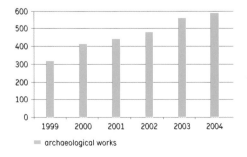

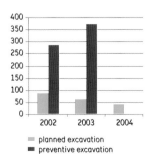

Fig. 6.2: Number of excavations in Hungary (from Bozóki-Ernyey, K 2007. p. 112).

Board for the Protection of Monuments (which had 43 years direct responsibility and almost 130 years indirect responsibility). The new organisation, the National Office of Cultural Heritage (which inherited all tasks of the antecedent institutions) has primary authority functions. In the field of heritage management the basic task was to embed the archaeological sites into the planning processes. In order to fulfil these tasks several regulations have been modified and an efficiently working mechanism had been created in the frame of the administrative licensing process of different development (this could be any type of building activity, road/railway construction, pipeline-laying [gas, electricity, telecommunication], mining activity, mineral extraction, water supply, etc.) At any development – to which field work is necessary – the competent licensing authorities must procure the professional statement of the statutory archaeological authority (granted by the office) and the archaeological requirement will become part of the licence also. This statement (expert opinion) defines the obligatory measures of how the archaeological heritage should be managed from the strictest objection (e.g. the investment must not be realised) ranging through archaeological mitigation to simple monitoring/observation (Wollák, K 2007. p 81).

Hungary became an EU member state in 2004, and with this the beneficiary of the 2007-2013 EU budget; the Hungarian government began an ambitious public road development programme. In the frame of the programme the Hungarian government was planning to build till 2015 a highway system almost 2500 km long (including the improvement of certain other public roads fig. 6.3). As a result of this programme, railway trunk lines, ports of public interest, central and regional airports, logistic centres on the domestic sections of the Pan-European corridors are planned to be modernised. Hungary became part of the Schengen system in 2007, because of this certain developments had to be executed on the border stations as well. There are other national projects which should be noted; the Vásárhelyi project (The flood management and control of the Tisza River, based on traditional flood prevention like dikes, flood bed clearing, water reservoirs, while also taking into consideration environmental protection and nature conservation), the construction of waste deposit units, modernising of various pipelines and other cable systems. Meanwhile several large scale private investments took the form of new shopping malls, residential areas, regeneration of different city quarters (Bozóki-Ernyey, K 2007.pp.113).

Carrying out the relative archaeological tasks creates enormous duties not only for the excavating organisations but also for the heritage agency. Since 2001 the National Office of Cultural Heritage has functioned on a regional level, presently in seven regional offices, where the inspectors of archaeology carry out the specialist tasks (defining the level of the necessary archaeological intervention, licensing excavations, supervising the sites and excavations. etc). In quality controlling and licensing an advisory scientific body, the Excavation Committee gives special expertise.

Origins of the Registry

Another basic task of the office was to develop the official central registration of Hungarian archaeological sites (a national inventory including the archaeological map of the country). This task was already formulated in the analysis of the state of Hungarian archaeology prepared in 1995 by the Archaeological Committee of the Hungarian Academy of Science (Jankovich, B. D 1996. pp. 3). The author drew attention to the lack of a standardised inventory of archaeological sites. It was also noted that exploration of the sites was executed by the Archaeological (Research) Institute of the Hungarian Academy of Science and the county museums, while the protection and the small scale authority tasks were divided between the Hungarian National Museum (which kept the records), the ministry and county museums; these practices were quite inefficient.

In spite of the fact that the Central Archaeological Archive of the Hungarian National Museum collects the documentation nationwide, the information available was not suitable per se for building a database. The museum provided an annual overview of all excavations in Seria I. of the "Régészeti Füzetek" (Archaeological Reviews, since 1958), the series was continued in renewed form: "Régészeti Kutatások Magyarországon / Archaeological Investigations in Hungary" with an issue on the excavations of the year 1998, as a joint publication of the Hungarian National Museum and the Directorate of Cultural Heritage. In addition to the brief excavation reports, the new publication contains short papers in Hungarian and other languages on the given year's major excavations and finds (Rezi-Kato, G. 2003. p. 431). As the National Museum had been responsible until 1998 for the protection process and the maintenance of the inventory of the protected sites as well, it prepared a small computerised database at the beginning of the 1990s which contained

Fig. 6.3: Listed and excavated new sites along the track of road no 67.

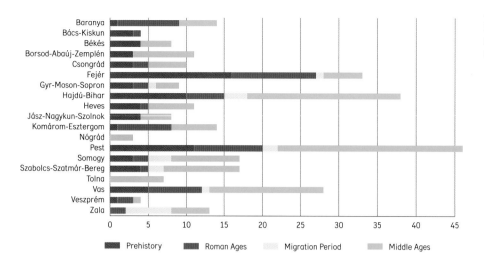

Fig. 6.4 Distribution of scheduled archaeological sites in the 19 countries.

data of approximately 700 protected sites throughout the country (Wollák, K. 1999. pp 473; Wollák, K. 2001. pp. 343) (fig. 6.4). The database incorporated the basic professional information of the sites and site-complexes including the land register data.

The task to develop a complex national database was not only a legal requirement. During the logical framework analysis of the Hungarian archaeology in 1999, it became obvious that from the lack of a comprehensive, unified inventory system (one which expands to the classification of the sites as well) the archaeological heritage management cannot supply appropriate data for the development plans. This means the validation of the heritage issues is unsolved in the process of economic planning and the representation of archaeological interest is very low (Nagy, M. 2000. p. 32). Although the comprehensive study, "Felmérés a régészet helyzetéről 1989-1999" (Survey on the state of archaeology) did not touch upon especially the situation of the archaeological archives in the examined period, but it referred already to the measure of the archaeological heritage, counting with around 100.000 sites (Jankovich, B. D. – Nagy, M. 2002. p. 98).

Different Approaches to Archaeological Heritage

While developing an official central registration of the Hungarian archaeological heritage, we faced another interpretational problem. To understand the roots of this problem we have to observe the differences between the professional and the legal approach on archaeological evidence (Raczky, P. 2006. p. 246). The professional methodology on recording archaeological phenomena has been explored in Hungary , defining the adequate core data, the minimum level of the survey or the required criteria system. There are certain elements which can have slightly different roles in the identification process of the different countries, as e.g. the reliability of the field walk survey, the certifying function of the aerial survey, but all these methods have a solid scientific background the outcome of which is the professional inventory.

The Hungarian legal approach is different. Legally only such territories can be considered as sites which are registered, and this fact is known by the owners, developers etc. therefore the legal consequences and the further duties are connected to this status. This diverse approach can be observed in the legal text of the 2001 law, although it defined the archaeological heritage comprehensively – based on the scientific standards – , the archaeological authority is allowed to formulate prescriptions in the interest of a site, only in the instance of it being a registered site. This limited right for intervention originates from the legal definition: *Archaeological site: clearly defined geographical areas on which the elements of archaeological heritage can be found in their primary relations and which have been registered by the Office* (detail from 2001. law). These professional and legal interpretations are significantly divergent, while it is evident that sufficient information about the "real" size of a site can be procured either by different (expensive) prospection methods, or after total excavation of sites which happens very rarely. We apply predictive modelling seldom in Hungary, but this method could not help on the merit. Due to these legal requirements in the administrative processes only the known and registered sites can be designated as archaeological sites, which is contradictory to the archaeological approach.

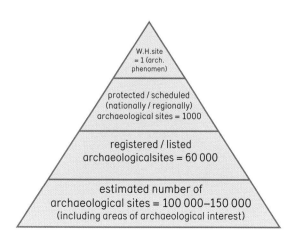

Fig. 6.5 Number of archaeological sites in Hungary.

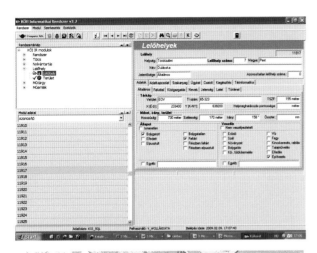

Fig. 6.6 Database sheet of the inventory.

Fig. 6.7 GIS map created from the database.

Levels of protection in Hungary

To understand the scale of this problem we must briefly review the different elements of the Hungarian archaeological heritage. We differentiate between three levels of protection:

- general (ex lege) protection, by law, executed by listing process,
- enhanced protection on two levels (national and regional) by scheduling process (on both level we can find territorial protection: "landscape-type" ensemble of sites),
- world heritage sites (due to its archaeological phenomena).

As well as the above mentioned categories there is the significant set of the non-listed / non-registered phenomena: the archaeologically sensitive areas (areas of archaeological interest). Since 2001 the law declares ex *lege* protection for the known sites. They are protected by law. This protection comes into force through the registration, which is an administrative process, done by the national office. To follow the phrases of the Hungarian system I used the thesaurus of the European Heritage Network prepared under the auspices of the Council of Europe (http://european-heritage.coe.int/sdx/herein/thesaurus/consult.xsp) and I also applied the selected version from our website (http://www.koh.hu/index.php). For the general registration of a site into an inventory (database) I found the English expression: "schedule of monuments" (in French: "carte archéologique") and for the protected sites – "protected archaeological sites"/"scheduled monument" (in French: "sites archéologique").

Content of the Site Inventory, Estimations and Accessibility

The digitalised inventory of scheduled sites and archaeological monuments of the National Office of Cultural Heritage contains almost 60,000 registered sites (fig. 6.5). The antecedent of the present database was created by the Directorate of Cultural Heritage. The basic conception was to create a digitalised inventory lifting all available data in a standardised system which can serve, not only for the authority, but also for professional/scientific purposes (Jankovich, B. D. (2003) pp. 6) (fig. 6.6). The preparatory works began in 1999, and the information technology development started in 2000. The structure of the SQL-based database can handle information on sites, on protected cultural goods, and later on historic monuments/listed buildings. The database was completed with an Arc View base GIS system (fig. 6.7), presently about 1/4 of the registered sites has a GIS map, the loading of the database has been happening since 2001 (Bozóki-Ernyey, K 2007. p. 107).

The basic source of the database was the Archaeological Topography of Hungary, a large-scale project of the Hungarian Academy of Sciences that began in the 1960s. The volumes of the series were based on information contained in local (museum) archives, the re-examination of old find assemblages and documentation (preparation of new photographs, drawings and maps) which were completed on each site with field surveys (fig 6.8). The volumes had been written in co-operation with archaeologists from the regional museums (Bálint, Cs. 2003. p. 428). Between 1966-1998 ten volumes were published (Veszprém county 4, Békés county 3, Komárom-Esztergom county 1 and Pest county 2) (fig. 6.9). Although some

Fig. 6.8: Detail of the microregional topography in Békés county (from Hungarian Archaeology at the turn of the Millenium 2003, p. 40).

other volumes are still under preparation, the continuation of this series is quite problematic. The other source of the database came from the archives of the Hungarian National Museum, The Budapest Historical Museum and the county museums (Rezi, K. G. (2003). p. 16).

As I referred before, the estimated number of the archaeological sites in Hungary is between 100,000 – 150,000. This calculation is based on the published volumes of the topography. During the preparation of the volumes 396 settlements of the mentioned four counties were surveyed (out of nearly 3200 existing settlements). The total amount of the reviewed territory was 10,950 km², this equates to 11,7 % of the country. The final result was the identification of 9952 archaeological sites. Using a rough calculation from these numbers; more than 1/10 of the country's territory was surveyed and around 10.000 sites were identified. We can therefore calculate that there is approximately 100.000 sites in Hungary, among which less then 60 % is registered up till now (Wollák, K 2007. p. 78).

The database functions via the intranet, the general public can retrieve information from the website of the office (www.koh.hu) assissted by a simple search engine. Only the basic data is available: the system shows which plots are registered as archaeological sites (on the queried settlement). The system indicates the level of protection (world heritage sites; enhanced protection on national or regional level; general=ex lege protection). When someone requires detailed information, he/she can request it from the office for a certain charge. Since 2001 during the preparation of the master plans of the settlements it is obligatory to prepare a heritage impact assessment which contains the information on archaeological sites as well. On those settlements which have to renew, or wanted to modify their master plans, these public plans contain the textual and geographical data of the archaeological sites. For the professionals and the other authorities the office supplies the required information free of charge, the local governments get the information officially of *ex lege* protected and the scheduled sites. From the homepage of the office anyone can download a leaflet with general information, the description of the scheduling process,

also the list of scheduled sites since 2001, and the list of proposals for scheduling. There is an ongoing debate on the accessibility of this information; neither valid legal background allows full publicity, the professionals would also not support full access because of the great scale of the treasure hunting.

The GIS module of the system is able to depict sites at a national scale through visualising the geographical, hydrogeological layers of a site, to depict individual archaeological phenomena. The database is continues to be populated with recent archaeological interventions and surveys, microregional research, university theses and heritage impact assessments. The obligation to prepare assessment exists not only in the main planning processes, but also in the case of certain large scale investments. The essential task of each assessment is to explore, and define the existing elements of the cultural (meaning built and archaeological) heritage by identifying the known sites, and also by examining the sites of archaeological interest through field walking. Although the regulation states the requirements precisely, the quality of the assessments are quite different (e.g. the poorer local governments cannot finance all of the field surveys) but more than one hundred assessments are prepared each year. This has helped, not only in exploration of new archaeological heritage elements, but also in refining the existing data.

One of the biggest problems of the central inventory is the lack of the cadastral (lot) numbers from the files. This data is important, as in administrative processes the relevant authorities use the cadastral numbers as the basic identification element of any given investment to be licensed. The office has to give its expert opinion on the territory of the investment defined by cadastral numbers. The professional registers of the museums and the archaeological topography – which compose the basis of the inventory – contained data of the geographical location of the sites defined by coordinates. It is therefore an ongoing task to convert the original data in to the required form – this is a long process, as currently only about 1/4 of the registered sited contains the cadastral numbers. The registration of new sites is now an administrative process. The clients

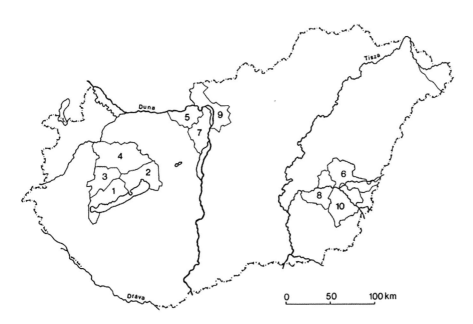

Fig. 6.9: The 10 published
volumes of the Archaeological
Topography of Hungary.

may appeal against it, and we already have our first cases before court. Although our legal system is different from the anglo-saxon one (based on precedents), but the decision in the first case will be still determinative.

Present Problems, Future Challenges

As well as the known sites (having general/ex lege protection) the inventory contains in a separate module the date of the scheduled sites and territories which have enhanced protection. The 2001 legislation differentiated two levels of protection: the enhanced protection (national level) and the highly protected sites and territories (regional level) having outstanding historic and cultural value. The possibility of protection by scheduling has been existed since 1949, the previous strategy was to protect sites in danger (Wollák, K. 1999. pp. 473). In the 1950s, a vigorous campaign was begun to register the endangered sites and as a result of this, several hundred sites came under protection, but were not processed correctly. The review of scheduled sites and defining the terms of their protection has begun in recent years only. The majority of the protected sites and territories lie in Transdanubia; over thirty sites are listed in Pest, Fejér and Hajdú-Bihar counties. (fig 6.4). Most of these sites lie on the outskirts, rather than in the centres of settlements, and the number of listed medieval monuments is by far the highest. Among them are; open-air museums, archaeological parks, national memorial places and conserved or partially reconstructed historic monuments.Others, such as hill forts, tumuli, fortifications and caves, can be found in their natural environment (Wollák, K. 2003. p. 428). Currently the first step of the process can be a proposal from anyone, which is then evaluated by the office; but in most cases the heritage agency starts the protection process itself by preparing a scientific document. When necessary, a conciliation is organised on the spot; owners and all effected stakeholders are invited. The office compiles the complex documentation including the social and economic effects of the protection status, and finally the minister of cultural affairs decides on scheduling. It is executed by a ministerial decree, therefore it cannot be appealed. Since 2001 about 120 new items have obtained the protected status by this scheduling process therefore

the number of the scheduled sites is presently around 1000. There has been a recent development of 2008, the advisory Scientific Committee which gives expertise in licensing the excavations are now involved in the preparation process as well.

As a result of this institutional and legal restructuring after 2001, the tasks of the different institutions were clarified (Visy 2000. p. 30). The National Office of Cultural Heritage takes care of the central nationwide site register. All institutions that conduct archaeological activity have to send reports to the office (in a summary form within 30 days, and as a full document within a year). Concerning the archaeological investigations of the previous year the office publishes the issues of the "Archaeological Investigations in Hungary" (the short reports are written in Hungarian) annually. The research institutions (University programmes of micro-regional research, aerial and field surveys, heritage impact assessments) obtain comprehensive knowledge on the archaeological heritage of any given territory; while the museums (which conduct the most excavations) develop their professional registers of their regions, the national museum preserved its function being the central archaeological archive. In April 2007, the new state archaeological service (Field Service for Cultural Heritage) was established. This service is responsible for any archaeological intervention of state financed infrastructural projects, flood-prevention projects and certain large scale projects above a given amount of the invested money. This means that the new institution took over responsibility for a large amount of tasks and budget of the county museums. These developments have divided the archaeologists' community. The Service began to develop different protocols including those on the documentation of excavations; this institution also became data-supplier for the central inventory as well.

To judge precisely the output of the recent changes is quite difficult, but it is necessary to stabilise the functions of the excavating institutions in the near future. This stabilisation could also help in developing mechanisms for managing the backlogs; those final depositions of the excavated archaeological finds or those scientific publications. This will be one of the greatest challenges over the next few years.

In the recent years the function of the protection by scheduling process has changed, due to the new legislation which introduced the *ex lege* protection. Since 2001 the heritage office has, already in the planning phase of different developments, the right to define the necessary provisions in the interest of archaeological heritage (referring to the registered/listed sites). There are not too much further tools for protecting-preserving scheduled sites, therefore we have to evaluate the future position of scheduling, thinking rather on classification, characterisation of archaeological heritage.

Nowadays archaeological issues have certain negative connotations in Hungary, (in the business community specifically) as they can block development, lengthen the investment processes or make them more cost-dependent. In order to regain the support of the general public and the decision makers everyone involved in heritage management must transfer knowledge of the archaeological heritage to a broader scale. We should not only rethink our protection strategy, but efficient measures of a more proper site-management should be elaborated in order to slow down the decrease the number of sites. Certain positive elements can be taken forward; the cooperation with nature conservation, during their inspection work the guards should have got the right to supervise archaeological sites and report on any disturbance. Another measure could be the recently adopted Landscape Convention (February 2008);resulting from the cooperation with authorities responsible for nature conservation we hope the public's perception of the historic landscape will bring them closer to the different elements of their own past and environment.

wollak2000@yahoo.com

References

Bálint, Cs. 2003: Archaeology and the Hungarian Academy of Sciences In: Visy, Zs & Nagy, M. (ed.): Hun*garian Archaeology at the Turn of the Millennium Mi*nistry of National Cultural Heritage - Teleki László Foundation, Budapest, 426-428.

Bozóki-Ernyey, K. 2007: Preventive Archaeology in Hungary One Step Behind In: Bozóki-Ernyey, K (ed.): European Preventive Archaeology. Papers of the EPAC Meeting 2004, Vilnius, National Office of Cultural Heritage, Hungary – Council of Europe. Budapest, 105-121.

Jankovich, B. D 1996: A magyar régészet helyzete. Henszlmann-Lapok, No 5, 1–13.

Jankovich, B. D. 2000: Jelentés a KÖI 1999 évi munkájáról – Report about the activity of the Cultural Heritage Directorate in 1999. Jelentés-Report 2000. A Kulturális Örökség Igazgatóságának évkönyve Budapest, 9-26.

Jankovich, B. D. – Nagy, M. 2002: Felmérés a régészet helyzetéről 1989-1999, NKÖM-KÖH Budapest.

Jankovich, B. D. (2003). Régészeti lelőhelyek nyilvántartása. In: Visy, Zs.(ed): *Régészeti műemlékek kutatása és gondozása a 3. évezred küszöbén.* Pécs, 5–13.

Nagy, M 2003: The protection of the archaeological heritage in Hungary In: Visy, Zs, & Nagy, M. (ed.): *Hungarian Archaeology at the Turn of the Millennium* Ministry of National Cultural Heritage - Teleki László Foundation, Budapest, 30-38.

Nagy, M. 2000: A magyar régészet helyzetének elemzése - Logical framework analysis of the Hungarian. In: Marton, E (ed.): Jelentés-Report 2000. A Kulturális Örökség Igazgatóságának évkönyve Budapest, 27-39.

Raczky, P. 2006: A régészeti lelőhely fogalmának tudományfilozófiai alapon történő axiomatikus meghatározása, Archaeologiai Értesitö 131, 246-248.

Rezi, K. G. 2003. A régészeti műemlékek központi adattárától a régészeti műemlékek egységes adatbázisáig. In: Visy, Zs. (ed): *Régészeti műemlékek kutatása és gondozása a 3. évezred küszöbén.* Pécs, 15–19.

Rezi-Kato, G. 2003: Registration and databases In: Visy, Zs; Nagy, M. (ed.): *Hungarian Archaeology at the Turn of the Millennium* Ministry of National Cultural Heritage - Teleki László Foundation, Budapest, 430-432.

Visy, Zs. 2000: The role and significance of the archaeology in the integrated Europe of the 21st century, In: Willems, W.J.H.(ed.): Challenges for European archaeology, Zoetermeer, 27-31.

Wollák, K. – Zsidi, P. 1998: Archaeological Heritage Management in Hungary - Wengry: zarzadzanie dziedzictwem Arceologicznym, in Z. Kobyliński (ed.): *Ochrona dziedzictwa archeologicznego w Europie*, Warszawa, 308-312.

Wollák, K. 1999: Methods of heritage protection in Hungary - the setting of archaeological parks, In: E Jerem & I Poroszlay (ed.): Archaeology of the Bronze age and Iron age. Experimental Archaeology, Environmental Archaeology, Archaeological Parks, Budapest, 467-476.

Wollák, K. 2001: Helyzetkép védett régészeti
  lelőhelyeinkről. Műemlékvédelem XLV/6, 342-349.
Wollák, K. 2003: Listed archaeological sites – volunteers
  and amateurs in archaeology In: Visy, Zs & Nagy,
  M. (ed.): Hungarian Archaeology at the Turn of the
  Millennium Ministry of National Cultural Heritage -
  Teleki László Foundation, Budapest , 428-430.
Wollák, K. & Zsidi, P. 2003: A régészeti örökség
  védelmének jogi háttere és fővárosi gyakorlata,
  In: Viga, Gy.- Holló, Sz.A. & Schwalm, Cs. E. (eds.):
  Vándorutak Múzeumi örökség Tanulmánykötet
  Bodó Sándor tiszteletére 60. születésnapja
  alkalmából Budapest, 241-255.
Wollák, K. 2007: The Protection of Cultural Heritage
  by Legislative Methods in Hungary, In Edited by
  Erzsébet Jerem, E., Mester, Zs. & Benczes, R (eds.):
  Archaeological and Cultural Heritage Preservation
  Within the Light of new Technologies, Budapest,
  73-82.

7 | Listing archaeological sites, protecting the historical landscape. The situation in the Republic of Ireland

Eamon Cody

Abstract: This paper, which opens with an introduction to the development of state archaeology in Ireland, outlines the legal background to the care of monuments in the Republic of Ireland. It looks at the roles of both monuments legislation and planning legislation and stresses the importance of the Record of Monuments and Places, the state's official record of monuments, in managing the archaeological resource. It deals with issues relating to the maintenance of the record, describes the survey and research that underpins the record, and outlines how the results of the survey and research are made available.

Introduction

Management of the archaeological resource in the Republic of Ireland is governed in the main by the legislative provisions of the National Monuments Acts and also to an important extent by the provisions of planning law. Within the state responsibility for the care and protection of archaeological monuments rests with the National Monuments Service (NMS), part of the Department of the Environment, Heritage and Local Government. Issues relating to the care and protection of archaeological objects, also governed in the main by the National Monuments Acts, lies with the National Museum of Ireland.

The state service archaeology in Ireland has its origin in 19th century political and social change. The Church of Ireland, the church of one-eighth of the population, was the established state church governed by the English monarch from 1537 to 1870. The *Irish Church Act* of 1869 disestablished the Church of Ireland and it became a self-governing voluntary body (Ford and Milne, 1998, 90-3; Milne 1998, 149). With the loss of its endowments the Church of Ireland could no longer maintain its extensive

properties and the Church Temporalities Commission was given the task of disposing of these. Churches still in use with their graveyards were vested in the Representative Body of the Church of Ireland and others were taken over by local authorities. A category of 'National Monuments' was created to care for ecclesiastical buildings that had fallen out of use and this task was assigned to a state body, the Board of Works (now the Office of Public Works) though it was not until 1882 with the passing of the *Ancient Monuments Protection Act* that provision was made for the care of archaeological monuments by the state (Sweetman 2000, 527). Under the 1869 act the Church Temporalities Commission was empowered to vest ecclesiastical buildings in the Board of Works. The state acquired other monuments as a result of changes in land tenure. A series of land acts passed over a period of some 50 years from 1870 transformed landholding in Ireland from a system of territorial landlordism to one of owner occupancy. This change was effected by the Land Commission, one of the main tasks of which was to purchase estates with a view to transferring ownership to the tenants (Comerford 1998, 295; Comerford 1998, 296). Under the 1903 and 1923 *Land Acts* it became possible for the Land Commission to vest any monuments of historic, traditional, artistic or archaeological interest on lands it had purchased in the Board of Works (Sweetman 2000, 528). The state acquired a range of monument types in this way. In 1875 the Board of Works appointed its first inspector of national monuments, a post filled on a part-time basis until 1930, when the first full-time inspector of national monuments was appointed. The role of the inspectors, who were always architects, was to oversee works of preservation, and occasionally restoration, of national monuments.

Fig. 7.1: Megalithic tomb at Kernanststown, County Carlow. The enormous roof-stone is the largest of all Irish tomb roof-stones.

In the 1950s archaeologists joined the NMS for the first time and over the next three decades, in conjunction with the architectural staff, took part in major programmes of excavation, conservation and presentation at important sites. In addition, in the 1960s, the NMS began a survey of the state's archaeological monuments (the Archaeological Survey of Ireland). From the late 1980s, first slowly and then from the early 1990s that saw a rapid increase in the pace of economic activity the role of the NMS began to change. Hitherto active on the ground in survey and excavation, the accelerated scale of archaeological activity meant that the NMS had to devote more and more time to its regulatory role. Developer-funded excavation facilitated the rapid growth of a commercial archaeological sector to carry out the vastly increased number of excavations. The role of the NMS is now, substantially, a regulatory one concerned with the licensing of excavation, provision of archaeological advice to planning authorities, and management and updating of a central Sites and Monuments database. The scale of the economic boom has placed great pressure on the capacity of the NMS to deal with increased archaeological activity. Adjustment to two episodes of institutional re-organisation in the last dozen years has also contributed to the pressure. The NMS, for long part of the Board of Works (Office of Public Works), was in 1996 combined with other cultural and heritage bodies in a single Department of Arts and Culture. This situation obtained until 2002 when the Department of Arts and Culture was abolished and its functions assigned to different departments. At this time the NMS was assigned to the Department of the Environment, Heritage and Local Government while responsibility for the management of some 750 national monuments in legal ownership or guardianship of the Minister for the Environment, Heritage and Local Government, was returned to the Office of Public Works.

The NMS, with an archaeological staff of about 40, has a wide range of responsibilities. Its main areas of work include the conduct of a survey of archaeological monuments; the maintenance of records of monuments and of shipwrecks; the provision of archaeological advice and expertise in relation to the care of some 750 monuments in the ownership or guardianship of the State; the licensing of a variety of archaeological works such as excavation (in consultation with the Director of the National Museum of Ireland), the use of detection devices for archaeological purposes and diving on known protected wreck sites; the provision of input and advice in relation to the protection of the archaeological heritage to planning and other authorities in respect of individual planning and other development applications, projects and plans; the maintenance of an archive consisting of the records of the survey of archaeological monuments, reports of licensed excavations, and a large collection of photographic images; provision of advice to government on legislative and policy issues relating to the archaeological heritage; provision of advice to individuals and local groups on archaeological issues that may arise from proposals to carry out works to historic graveyards and other heritage sites and on archaeological matters generally.

Care of monuments – the role of monuments legislation

Since 1994, legislation in the Republic of Ireland affords a limited measure of protection to all known archaeological monuments. The move to the concept of universal protection was a gradual one over a period of almost 70 years. In the early days of the state the focus was on providing a relatively high level of protection for a limited number of monuments. Over time there was a move towards providing lesser forms of protection to greater numbers of monuments. The various levels of protection are still in place; today while all known monuments are accorded a basic level of protection a small proportion are also subject to one or other higher levels of protection.

The earliest monuments legislation of the independent Irish state is the *National Monuments Act* of 1930. It deals with issues relating to the care of archaeological monuments and archaeological objects and with archaeological excavation. It also provides definitions of the elements of the archaeological heritage. This act defines a 'monument' as any artificial or partly artificial structure or building above or below the ground, any cave or stone that has been artificially altered or put or arranged in position and any prehistoric or ancient tomb, grave or burial deposit.

Fig. 7.2: Earthwork complex at Tara, County Meath. One of Ireland's premier archaeological sites with monuments dating from the Neolithic, Bronze Age, Iron Age and Medieval periods.

The act goes on to define a 'national monument' as any monument or the remains of a monument the preservation of which is a matter of national importance by reason of the archaeological, historical, architectural, traditional or artistic interest attached thereto.

In regard to the care of monuments the main focus of the act is on the care and maintenance of national monuments including provision for the acquisition by the state of such monuments. The act provided that anyone proposing to carry out works at or in proximity to a monument in state care must seek the consent of the state heritage office. Some 750 monuments are in state care and these include some of Ireland's premier archaeological sites (figs. 7.1 – 5).

The act also provides for the placing of a preservation order on any monument deemed to be of national importance which is in danger of destruction, thus entrusting its preservation to the state.

While the 1930 act takes a somewhat restricted approach to monument protection in that it focuses almost exclusively on monuments that would meet the definition of a national monument, it takes a more universalist approach in regard to archaeological excavation and archaeological objects; under the act anyone proposing to carry out an excavation for archaeological purposes must obtain a licence and anyone finding an archaeological object is obliged to report the discovery to the authorities.

An amendment to the National Monuments Act in 1954 provided for publication of lists of monuments the preservation of which was deemed to be of national importance. In addition the amendment also provided for the listing of such other monuments as the heritage authorities thought fit. A landowner proposing to carry out works to a monument so listed was obliged to give two months notice of his intention to do so.

The scope of monument protection was widened in 1987 by the *National Monuments (Amendment) Act* of that year which provided for the establishment of a Register of Historic Monuments. An historic monument is defined as any monument in existence before 1700 AD and such other monuments of later date as the heritage minister might designate as such. However qualification for entry to the register does not imply automatic entry. Each monument has to be individually registered, a procedure which takes time and entails publication in *Iris Oifigiúil* (the official government gazette). To date some 3000 monuments have been entered in the register.

The 1987 amendment act also addressed the issue of underwater archaeology. The main provision in this area was to grant automatic protection to all wrecks over 100 years old. In addition, the act also decreed that all diving on known protected wreck sites for the purpose of looking for archaeology or for wrecks would require a licence under the act. This amendment also prohibited the use of detection devices at an archaeological site, unless licensed to do so.

During the 1970s and 1980s, in a response to increasing impacts on monuments through EU-sponsored land reclamation schemes and increasing economic activity it became evident that there was a need to establish a list of all known monuments. It was decided to establish a 'Sites and Monuments Record' (SMR) along the lines of the model used in England. Accordingly a Sites and Monuments Record was compiled between 1985 and 1992 based on a search of the archaeological literature, of cartographic sources and on the available fieldwork in the NMS archives. As part of the process an archive file was created for each entry in the SMR.

With the issuing of the SMR there was, for the first time, a list of all known monuments. It was designed primarily to be used by planning authorities and agencies responsible for development works that might impact on the archaeological heritage. With the production of the SMR there was now in place a record of all known monuments in the state. It was now possible to see if a proposed development was likely to impact on a monument. However the SMR had no statutory basis.

Fig. 7.3: Dún Aonghasa, a dramatic cliff-top fort on Inis Mór island off the west coast of Ireland. Defended by stone ramparts and outside these a 30 metre wide band of *chevaux-de-frise*.

This was remedied in the 1994 *National Monuments (Amendment) Act* that provides for the establishment of the Record of Monuments and Places (RMP). The Record of Monuments and Places is a statutory list of known monuments in the Republic of Ireland. It should be explained that the word 'Places' in the term 'Record of Monuments and Places' refers to places where monuments are believed to exist. The RMP is a sub-set of the earlier non-statutory SMR. The SMR is a listing of all known monuments whether surviving or destroyed. It also lists possible or potential monuments and includes many which are mentioned in the archaeological literature but have not been located. The RMP is a list of all monuments that have been located and of places where a monument is believed to exist. The term 'places' generally refers to monuments which no longer survive above ground but whose existence can be reliably demonstrated by cartographic or other evidence. In other words, if a monument is levelled and has no surface expression its sub-surface remains are still legally a monument. All monuments listed in the statutory RMP have been located. Monuments mentioned in the archaeological literature but that have not been located are not entered in the RMP but remain in the non-statutory SMR and if in time a monument listed there is located and meets the definition of a monument in the legislation then it qualifies for inclusion in the RMP. The non-statutory term 'Sites and Monuments Record' is still retained to describe the overall set of monuments, supposed monuments that have not been located and also includes supposed monuments that on inspection did not prove to be so.

The RMP was issued in hard copy format on a county basis between 1995 and 1998 and lists some 120,000 monuments. Like the earlier and non-statutory SMR, it consists of a set of large-scale maps for each county on which the known monuments are circled and numbered. Every set of county maps is accompanied by a printed manual which records each monument by its unique map number, provides locational details about it, and records its classification, e.g., stone circle, barrow, church etc.

The issue of the RMP was governed by a Statutory Instrument that stipulated how it should be made public. The legal instrument provided that it should be issued in hard-copy format on a county by county basis, that its issue should be advertised in the local newspapers in each county, and that copies should be available for inspection by all in local libraries. With the issue of the RMP for each county there was a publicly-available document detailing the location of all known monuments.

The RMP gives a measure of protection to all known monuments; under the terms of the legislation anyone proposing to carry out works at or close to a monument in the RMP is obliged by law to give two months notice in writing to the NMS. This interval gives the NMS time to deal with the issue in the best interests of the monument. In effect, the RMP gives a measure of protection to all known and located monuments in that it places an obligation on a landowner or anyone else to notify the NMS of any proposals to carry out works that might impact on a site in the record. As a comment on this measure it should be noted that the system in place is not so much a protection system as a notification system as the legal obligation is to notify the heritage authorities of any proposed works that might impact on a monument.

To sum up, the levels of protection currently available under National Monuments legislation are as follows. The basic level of protection provided to the very great majority of monuments derives from inclusion in the RMP. As noted, this requires a landowner to lodge two months notice of proposed works with the NMS. The onus is on landowners, or anyone acting on their behalf, to make themselves aware of the existence of monuments on their properties. A higher level of protection is accorded to monuments entered in Register of Historic Monuments. In such cases landowners are informed in writing and provided with a map of any monument on their property that is so entered. As in the case of a monument entered in the RMP, any works proposed for a monument entered in the Register of Historic Monuments must be notified in writing to the NMS two months in advance of the proposed works. The highest level of protection is accorded to national monuments that are protected by a Preservation Order or are in the guardianship or ownership of the Minister for the Environment, Heritage and Local Government or in the guardianship or ownership of a local authority. Anyone proposing to carry out works at or in proximity to such monuments must seek the consent of the minister to do so. Under the *National Monuments (Amendment) Act* of 2004, the minister, in adjudicating on

Fig. 7. 4: High cross at the ecclesiastical centre, Monasterboice, County Louth. In the background is a round tower and ruined medieval church.

such applications, is obliged to consult with the Director of the National Museum of Ireland. The 2004 amendment stipulates that the minister in arriving at a decision may take into account not only archaeological but also public interest considerations. The 2004 amendment also provided that archaeological works on approved road developments (in effect motorway construction) would be carried out under 'directions of the Minister' following consultation with the Director of the National Museum of Ireland.

Care of monuments – the role of planning legislation

The greatest impacts on the archaeological resource arise from development projects, be they large or small in scale. Monuments legislation, a function of central government in Ireland, on its own could never hope to deal with these impacts given that planning decisions are made, primarily, by some eighty planning authorities at local level within tight time-frames. Archaeological provisions in planning law play a vital role in the management of the archaeological resource.

Since 1994, under planning regulations, the NMS has been a statutory consultee in the planning process. The *Planning and Development Act* of 2000 (consolidating all previous planning legislation) and associated Regulations (issued in 2001) relating to the Act include provisions for protection of the archaeological heritage in the planning process. All proposed developments that would affect or be unduly close to 'a cave, site, feature or object of archaeological interest' or of a monument in the RMP, in the Register of Historic Monuments or a national monument in state ownership or guardianship must be referred to the NMS, acting on behalf of the Minister for the Environment, Heritage and Local Government, for comment. The NMS can recommend that an archaeological assessment be carried out which in turn may result in more detailed archaeological works. Archaeological assessment may lead to a project redesign. Where there may be a direct negative impact on an archaeological monument the NMS may recommend that the planning authority refuse permission for a development at that location. Every effort is made to ensure archaeological remains are preserved *in situ*. Where this is not possible the archaeological remains are preserved by record, i.e., the developer is required to fund an excavation. The *Planning and Development Act* of 2000, mentioned above, gives statutory recognition to both preservation *in situ* and by record.

The *Planning and Development Act* of 2000 also states that any developments requiring an Environmental Impact Assessment must be referred to the Minister for the Environment, Heritage and Local Government so that their archaeological implications can be assessed by the NMS, and if deemed appropriate suitable mitigation measures recommended. Many of the major projects requiring Environmental Impact Assessment are carried out by state bodies such as the National Roads Authority and Bord Gáis Éireann (gas supply). It is worth noting that the NMS has agreed Codes of Practice with these and some other large developer bodies the purpose of which is to provide a framework within existing legislation and policies to enable the developer body proceed with its programme while ensuring appropriate management of the archaeological resource. The codes are based on an agreed set of principles and actions including the appointment by the developer body of an archaeologist to oversee the archaeological components of the entire process (Gleeson 2007, 142-3).

Under planning legislation local authorities are obliged, every six years, to draw up development plans for their own areas. These plans set out an overall strategy for the proper planning and sustainable development of the area and include objectives for the zoning of land. Under the legislation these plans must also include mandatory objectives for archaeological heritage. Inclusion of archaeological objectives in development plans is particularly useful as these objectives carry considerable weight if it is found necessary to object to individual development proposals that are archaeologically undesirable.

As noted, the NMS may make recommendations to the planning authorities in relation to relevant archaeological issues. It must be stressed that the comments forwarded

Fig. 7.5: One of the churches at the ecclesiastical centre, Clonmacnoise, County Offaly. A notice (to the viewer's left) identifies it as being in state care.

by the NMS in relation to the archaeological implications of a planning proposal to local authorities are recommendations and that local authorities are not obliged to take them on board. However the experience is that, in general, local authorities do have regard to the archaeological recommendations of the NMS. It is hoped, in the near future, that a digital tracking system to streamline heritage-related planning referrals currently being rolled out will generate statistics relating to the operation of the referral system; it will enable the level of adherence by each local authority to the NMS recommendations be monitored. Like any citizen, the NMS may appeal any grant of permission or any conditions attaching to that permission. Where the NMS considers that it is in the interests of the archaeological heritage to do so it may decide to appeal a grant of permission. This is done under planning legislation to an independent planning board (*An Bord Pleanála*) whose decision is binding. Though seldom resorted to, the NMS has usually been successful in its appeals to this board.

As is clear, planning law caters for the archaeological heritage and it is used by the NMS to mitigate developmental impacts on the archaeological resource. However and for whatever reason, be it late referral of a planning application or non-referral, if it is not possible to use planning law to mitigate archaeological impacts, then the NMS may invoke the provisions of the National Monuments legislation to protect archaeology. As already noted, in the case of monuments with the highest level of protection any works proposed at or in proximity to such monuments require the consent of the Minister under National Monuments legislation, irrespective of a grant of planning permission.

Maintaining the archaeological record

The RMP is the essential element in the protection of archaeological monuments whether using planning law or monuments legislation. All referrals from local authorities are based on examination of the RMP maps. Such referrals are treated as de *facto no*tifications of an intention to carry out works that may affect a monument in the RMP. The NMS may then make recommendations to the planning authority to mitigate the impact of a proposed development on the monument.

A limitation of the RMP is that, essentially, it is a site based monuments protection mechanism and cannot adequately cater for threats to unknown archaeology, i.e., it does not cater for the spaces between the monuments. Large scale developments requiring an Environmental Impact Assessment are, as noted, required to be referred to the NMS. However, so as to ensure that developments that may fall below the threshold that would trigger an Environmental Impact Statement are also assessed as to their archaeological potential, planning authorities are advised to bring to the attention of the NMS developments in areas where there are no known monuments if such developments are 0.5 hectare or more in area or 1 kilometre or more in length.

The importance of the RMP in the protection of archaeological monuments, whether using planning law or monuments legislation, has been mentioned. The 1994 legislation that led to the establishment of the RMP also includes an obligation on the state to maintain it. This implies that the RMP should be managed, updated and re-issued. To this end the SMR database on which the RMP is based is under constant update. Newly-discovered monuments are added to the database as information about them becomes available.

The format of a revised RMP is currently the subject of internal discussion and study. The revised RMP will take advantage of the availability of updated base mapping. The aim is to put in place an updated and readily updatable RMP using digital technology. As noted above, the RMP is a site-based, more specifically a class-based system. The possibility of combining a class-based system with a spatial one, in line with the PLANARCH model is being explored. Final decisions must await a review of the state's archaeological policy and practice to be carried out in 2008.

Publicising the archaeological record

The RMP is underpinned by survey and research on each monument. The non-statutory SMR and the statutory RMP are products of an ongoing national archaeological survey, mentioned above, being conducted by the Archaeological Survey of Ireland. The role of the Archaeological Survey of Ireland is to visit all monuments in the state and compile a descriptive record of each. This survey has focused principally on recording all certain or possible archaeological monuments dating to before 1700 AD but also has included a selection of monuments dating to succeeding centuries according to their interest or merit. The national survey has been completed for the great majority of known monuments. An Urban Archaeology Survey, comprising reports on 240 towns, was completed in 1995. Additionally, extensive surveys of disappearing peat-land are underway since 1991.The hardcopy and computerised fieldwork and related records of these surveys form the SMR archive which contains information on some 140,000 sites. The archive records are open to the public by appointment and form the basic source data for decisions relating to the care and protection of the archaeological resource.

Fig. 7.6: Selection of Archaeological Inventory series for various counties.

The NMS is committed to making information about the archaeological heritage available to all. Since its inception, the Archaeological Survey of Ireland has been linked to a publication project which envisaged the publication of short descriptive accounts of all monuments. Publication is in the form of a hard-copy Archaeological Inventory series arranged on a county basis with individual chapters arranged by monument class. Each chapter has a short introduction that refers to aspects of the morphology, dating and function of each monument type. Some 20 hard-cover volumes dealing with 15 counties have been published and work is ongoing (fig. 7.6). This series is aimed at a general readership as well as those involved in heritage management and also scholars involved in research.

The development in 2008 of a dedicated web-site www.archaeology.ie has enabled the NMS to improve its delivery of information to the public. A download facility and interactive mapping element enables access to SMR data. Work is in hand to place the descriptive accounts in the published inventory series on the web-site. Web availability will enable regular updating of the records.

Comment

The legislative system for the protection of archaeological monuments is quite good. However because it has developed piecemeal over time it is now somewhat complex and would benefit from some rationalisation. For instance, there are now four ways of protecting a monument in monuments legislation – by inclusion in the RMP, in the Register of Historic Monuments, it may be made subject to a preservation order, or may be in the care of the state or a local authority as a national monument. A 2002 discussion document proposed introducing a two-level Register of Monuments. This is one of the matters being addressed in a review of archaeological policy and practice currently underway.

Some strengthening of the basic protection afforded monuments listed in the RMP would seem to be desirable. At present, as noted, the legal requirement on anyone proposing works that may impact on a monument is to notify the NMS in writing two months in advance. There would be merit in adding to this a specific prohibition on damaging a monument.

The existing RMP, a paper document, is now some ten years old and there is a need to re-issue an updated version. As noted, work is underway on this project with the aim of putting in place an updated version using digital technology. The aim is to put in place a system that can be updated on a regular basis. For reasons outlined above, final decisions on the format of an updated RMP are yet to be finalised. It is important to note that information on newly-discovered monuments continues to be added to the parent set of monument data, the SMR. Roll-out of SMR data on the website www.archaeology.ie means that all monument data for the state will be available via the internet in the near future.

The issue of the RMP in the 1990s was primarily for the purpose of affording a measure of protection to the known monuments in the state. This was mainly achieved by providing planning authorities with the necessary information to enable them to identify developmental impacts on archaeological heritage. When allied to the provisions of

the *Planning and Development Act* of 2000 that requires the notification to the NMS of developments that would impact on archaeological remains, the result is a reasonably thorough mechanism to mitigate archaeological impacts in the planning process. However the volume of referrals to the NMS (13,000 in 2007), the inherent delay in referring papers, combined with the requirement to adhere to the tight deadlines that operate in the planning system poses considerable pressure on resources. A better response would be for local authorities to hire county archaeologists to comment on planning issues. With an archaeologist as part of the local authority planning team a more timely and stream-lined response could be made to planning applications with an archaeological relevance. A small number of local authorities do employ archaeologists and this has proved successful to the extent that the Department of the Environment, Heritage and Local Government is actively encouraging such appointments.

The value of the RMP, a list of all known monuments, cannot be overstated. Its importance in mitigating impacts on the archaeological heritage has been outlined above. It is also a great boon to archaeological research. Until its issue and that of its non-statutory precursor the SMR there was limited knowledge of the extent of the state's monumental inheritance. Now there is the scope to list and map the distribution of the various monument types, thus facilitating research. In making available the SMR data, i.e., the overall set of monument data, on the website www.archaeology.ie there is scope for local communities, local heritage organisations, schools etc to inform themselves of the monumental heritage in their locality. This can only lead to a greater appreciation of the nation's archaeological heritage.

eamonn_cody@environ.ie

References

Comerford, R. V. 1998: Land Acts, in Connolly, S.J. (ed.): The *Oxford Companion to Irish History*, Oxford University Press, Oxford, 295.

Comerford, R. V. 1998: Land Commission, in Connolly, S.J. (ed.): *The Oxford Companion to Irish History*, Oxford University Press, Oxford, 296.

Ford, A. & Milne, K. 1998: Church of Ireland, in Connolly, S.J. (ed.): *The Oxford Companion to Irish History*, Oxford University Press, Oxford, 90-3.

Gleeson, P. 2007: Rescue Excavation in Ireland, Roads and Codes, in Bozóki-Erneyey, K. (ed.): *European Preventive Archaeology*, Papers of the EPAC Meeting, Vilnius 2004, National Office of Cultural Heritage, Hungary and Council of Europe, Directorate of Culture and Cultural and Natural Heritage, 137-45.

Milne, K. 1998: Disestablishment, in Connolly, S.J. (ed.): *The Oxford Companion to Irish History*, Oxford University Press, Oxford, 149.

Sweetman, D. 2000: The Man-Made Heritage: The Legislative and Institutional Framework, in Buttimer, N., Rynne, C. & Guerin, H. (ed.): *The Heritage of Ireland*, The Collins Press, Cork, 527-33.

8 | Seven years after Seville: Recent progress in managing the archaeological heritage in Poland

Andrzej Prinke

Abstract: The organizers of the present Symposium referred in their introduction to the Seville Conference (RAPHAEL Project, 2000), which dealt mainly with the IT applications in archaeology (namely: computer inventory systems, including GIS). Our present meeting tries to cover a much broader scope: how to introduce and integrate several new approaches to the field of archaeological heritage management. Therefore, our symposium may be an opportunity to look for ways towards an unified system of: archaeological theory + legal acts + practical research methods + management system aided by specialized tools including IT products.

In the seven years since Seville, several radical changes have occurred in Poland in this field, including:

- A new law on the protection of historical monuments (2003), which also covers the entire archaeological heritage (http://www.muzarp.poznan.pl/archweb/archweb_pol/przepisy/ustawa.pdf; in Polish),
- The radical reorganization of the central and regional institutions which form the National System for Protection of Historical Monuments: (a) the creation of a new central institution called KOBiDZ (Krajowy Ośrodek Badań i Dokumentacji Zabytków or: National Heritage Board of Poland), established in Warsaw in 2007; (b) the establishment of sixteen regional Voivodship (provincial) Inspectors of Monuments with their Offices and Branches – reformed in 2003,

- e-Archeo: the on-line national database on archaeological sites (SMR), launched in 2004.

In the following I would like to present brief information on the above as well as some other topics, starting with the key issue of this meeting.

Listing archaeological sites

Poland enjoyed a good starting point for this task long before the era of the computer-based SMRs (Sites and Monuments Records) of the 1980s and 1990s. Already in 1978, we joined just a few other European countries carrying out the "total" version of the National Archaeological Survey (AZP), which combines extensive fieldwalking of the whole accessible area of the country with complete archive survey.

The AZP Project is based upon a number of simple rules: The whole territory of Poland is divided into ca 8,500 AZP Working Areas (fig. 8.1) of 35 km2 each, i.e. 5 x 7 km in size (fig. 8.3), according to the National Archaeological Grid, specially prepared for this task. Such an arbitrary working unit originated from the A4 format sheet of a 1:25,000 scale map. The grid provides a standard location background, independent of the map type or of the detailed location

Fig. 8.1: Polish Archaeological Record (PAR): territorial division scheme.

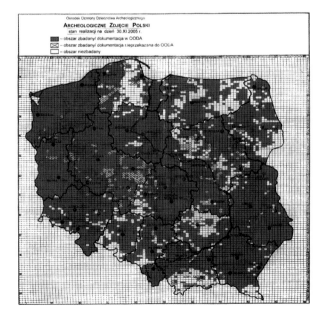

Fig. 8.2: PAR inventory map 1:25.000 (single working area).

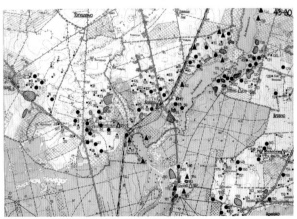

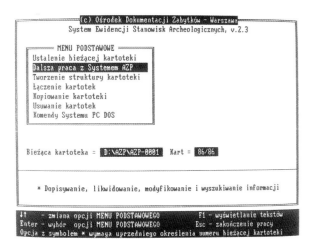

Fig. 8.3: First Polish database on archaeological
sites: *SYSTEM_AZP* (1986).

heritage, including first of all opinions on locations of the
developers' projects and the conservator's requirements
concerning the archaeological heritage protection. The
methodological transition from the "single site mental-
ity" to the modern holistic idea of the historical landscape
occurred – thanks to AZP - in a very natural way. Simply,
the results of the systematic fieldwalking of the extensive
areas let us identify entire microregions of early human
occupation instead of single, isolated sites. The new legislation introduced the lists of protected historical monuments (including archaeological sites) as obligatory to
all three levels of the national administration: central
(Ministry of Culture), regional (Voivodships / provinces)
and local (municipalities).

Upscaling and integration

In the late 80s, the development of the digital version of
the Polish SMR started, when the Poznan Archaeological
Museum launched the first version of its regional database
on archaeological sites in 1986 (SYS*TEM_AZP*; fig. 8.3) -
an application which was later modified, upgraded and
enhanced several times: AZP_*Fox* and AZP_Max, and also
adopted in other regions of Poland. The next enhance-
ments of the system were: a GIS module (mAZe*Pa*), based
on the MapInfo system and a database on aerial photographs (APh_*Max*; fig. 8.4), as the method of the aerial
archaeological reconnaissance in Poland has experienced
an upsurge in the last few years, which results now in ever
richer regional photographic archives.

mAZePa (or: AZP map) constitutes the GIS module of
the programming system facilitating access to the AZP
cartographic documentation. The newest release of this
application performs, among others, the following basic
functions:Choice of any part of a topographical map in
one of five ways: after AZP work sheets, index of topographic map sheets in scale 1:10.000, locality name or
extended user-defined cartographic index.It reads text
data files, previously created by the aid of *AZP_Max* programme and automatically locates the described sites.
The above set of data and programmes enables the automatic generation of a complete standardized Archaeological Site Register Form, including the site situation sketch
at 1:10.000 scale.It creates the user-defined archaeological site maps, based upon the records previously retrieved
in the *AZP_Max* programme according to chosen criteria. The user can choose between 59 traits, according to
which each site is described in the database. This enables
the creation of a wide range of single and multi-aspect
problem oriented maps and also the addition of supplementary elements such as vector drawings.http://www.
muzarp.poznan.pl/archweb/archweb_pol/Publikacje/
publo1/full_6.htmlt enables the simultaneous work with
maps and text databases by using basic GIS tools (statistic, visualisation, buffer retrieve method etc.).The facility
for the automatic performance of many complex routine
functions by definition of so-called *projects*.Possibility of
presenting aerial photos inserted into a map, containing

methods. The AZP Working Area number used together
with the site number within the AZP Working Area constitutes a *unique identifier* of a single site, independent
of the changing administrative borders etc. Each site also
has its second, more traditional address, which consists
of a locality name and a site number within the locality.
Based on the specific nationwide documentation standard (archaeological site register form, 1:10,000 maps and
1:25,000 maps (fig. 8.2), etc.) as much as 270,000 km², i.e.
87% of the area of Poland, has been surveyed so far with
over 435,000 sites registered. Approximately 60% of them
belong to the category of the so-called traces of human
occupation - very poor in archaeological materials while
the others include more distinct remains of settlements
and cemeteries, production and cult centres as well as
early towns. Site register form: The form's structure is
highly formalised which made a subsequent conversion of
its contents into the computer database structure much
easier. It is based upon the Polish core data standard for
archaeological sites. The site register form consists of
48 fields, divided into 13 groups which describe all main
aspects of a single archaeological site, i.e.: its administrative and geographical location, present use of the
site area, chrono-cultural classification of archaeological materials, soil type, site area, distribution pattern of
archaeological materials on the site surface, threats to
the site, survey authors, museum collections and other
data (research history of the site, archives, bibliography,
map sheet no., cartographic coordinates of the site etc.).

The results of AZP are the major source of information
necessary for all kinds of management of archaeological

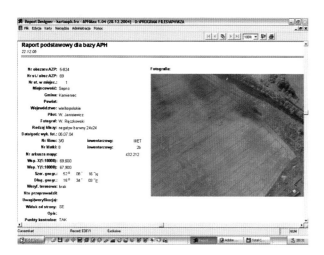

Fig. 8.4: *APh_Max*: database on aerial
photos for archaeology (2000).

Fig. 8.5: Archaeological air reconnaissance: Stare Szamotuły –
a previously unknown mediaeval town (2006): an interpretation.

controlled vocabularies. Its logical model consists of four levels of generality; the user, moving from the uppermost level 1 (describing a site) to the most detailed level 4 (that of a single find), follows, in a way, a typical sequence of the archaeological research procedures.

Basic procedures of the National Archaeological Survey (AZP), i.e. fieldwalking and archival query, have been enhanced, wherever possible, by the broad range of non-destructive methods (i.e.: aerial photos; fig. 8.5), DC / direct current resistivity method), including phosphate (original: phosphor) test.

Protection of Historical Landscape

Landscape Parks are a specific form of protection of the landscape that has been introduced in Poland. Unlike for the National Parks, there are no restrictive bans for the inhabitants and visitors. The only prohibitions are the introduction of industrial and urban developments or intensive forms of farming (fig. 8.6).

The project presented here is an example of team work involving land planners from the Provincial Office for Land Planning in Poznan, local authorities (City and County Councils), and academic experts from several disciplines (botany, biology, geography, geomorphology, archaeology, ethnology, history). Their aim was to work out a modern, i.e. integrated (inter-disciplinary) and dynamic model of an area, protected for its natural and cultural values, well researched and easily accessed by the general public. Unlike traditional 'National Parks' or 'nature reserves', the Landscape Parks should break down the old, isolated formulas of "one-discipline-attitude" by integrating at least two main categories of values that have so far been mostly isolated: those of nature and culture.

The reasons for such a fusion are numerous and obvious:
- It creates richer and more differentiated, and therefore more attractive offer for the public.
- It makes archaeological explanation much easier by presenting prehistoric monuments and problems in a close environmental context (the evolution of cultural phenomena can then be presented parallel with the development of the natural environment).
- It enables the combination of the financial and organizational resources of all the partners.
- In addition to the above, such a solution follows the current tendency in archaeology and ecological sciences to draw closer to one another, including common practical action (this tendency is even reflected in a common ministry for protection of the environment and cultural heritage in some countries).

The general objectives of the project are:
- Protection of the main values of the area by proclaiming it a Landscape Park; such an act then helps to limit any future industrialization and urbanization of the area. Protection can comprise many different values and can be defined in several steps, according to the individual needs. It is then executed by local law.

discernable traces of archaeological relics, due to which their precise location is possible.Use of orthophotomaps.

APh_Max programme is an application to launch and manage databases of aerial photos for archaeological research; it creates unique file for each photograph, containing a full description of the photographed location (archaeological site) as well as technical data of the photo (film description, conditions of conducting the aerial reconnaissance, pilot's and photographer's names, date of taking the photo, inventory number of film and frames, archive etc.).

At the same time, another, related type of a database, called *MuzArP*, allowed to integrate the information on the archaeological sites with the museum collections (including their rich context in the form of archives, bibliography, results of expert's evaluations, etc.).

The data structure of the *MuzArP* system includes 351 fields. Data control is executed with the help of 55

Fig. 8.6: Lednica Landscape Park: Lednica Lake with
Ostrów Lednicki Island (early mediaeval stronghold).

- Education of the visitors in different aspects of regional geography, biology, history (including prehistory, history of culture, etc.), based upon the most spectacular and instructive examples to be found in the field. At the same time, it is an opportunity to convince the visitor of the very necessity to protect nature and monuments. The project includes numerous ways of presenting natural and cultural values, such as: written information in the field (plates with maps and texts, sign-posts) and printed information for tourists (guides, folders, maps).
- Weekend tourism. One of the presumptions in favour of creating Landscape Parks was to choose areas located within the reach of mass weekend tourism of large urban agglomerations. According to the definition of a Landscape Park, its interior should be accessible by general public in many different ways: on foot (the project includes proposals of tourist walking routes, marked in the field) and by bicycle (special cycle routes). It also includes the possibility of short-term lodging within the park area.

The Law

The new law on historical monuments protection follows the basic EU directive concerning the long unsolved problems: who pays for archaeological rescue research? The new law answers this acute question in a very clear and rigorous way: the destroyer does. However, at the end of 2007, the Polish Commissioner for Human Rights Protection (Ombudsman) referred the law to the Constitutional Court, which sustained his argumentation. As a result, some financial and legal mechanisms need to be created within the next 18 months, i.e. by spring 2009 that

will render it possible for the country to participate in the expenses incurred in relation to the archaeological rescue research. It must be noted here that in 1996 Poland ratified the La Valetta European Convention from 1992.

Interests of the archaeological heritage protection are well safeguarded also in a few related legal acts adopted in the recent years. They include:
- Town and Country Planning Act (2003),
- Toll Motorways Act (1997),
- "Environmental Protection Law" Act (2001). In today's practice, all sites and areas integrated within the local development plans are protected by law. It is the regional Office of the Archaeological Heritage Service that formulates the lists of sites to be protected. Without their approval, the local plan cannot become valid.

System of the protection of monuments

National Heritage Board of Poland:
- The institution of culture called into being by the Minister of Culture. Its formal status is that "it functions as the main substantial background and the coordinator of measures undertaken concerning the protection of culture heritage in Poland. Its goals and objectives are implemented through the cooperation with Voivodship Inspectors of Monuments and directors of representatives of Voivodship Offices for the Protection of Monuments as well as with other institutions specialized with the protection of monuments, including universities." (http://www.kobidz.pl/app/site.php5/Show/11.html).
- General Inspector of Monuments:
  - Creates national program of the protection of monuments,
  - Enhances regional development plans within the sphere of the protection of monuments,
  - Administrative activity (II instance),
  - Organizes and conducts controls,
  - Oversees Voivodship Inspectors of Monuments,
  - Carries out the national evidence of monuments, as well as the list of stolen monuments.
- Voivodship Inspector of Monuments:
  - Implements tasks of the national program of the protection of monuments,
  - Administrative activity (I instance),
  - Organizes and conducts controls,
  - Manages the register and voivodship evidence of monuments,
  - Supervises the works carried out on monuments,
  - Elaborates the voivodship plans for the protection of monuments in the event of armed conflict and contingency,
  - Popularizes the knowledge on cultural heritage.
- Director of the Representation of Voivodship Office for the Protection of Monuments:
  - activity (I instance),
  - Organizes and conducts controls,
  - Supervises the correctness of works carried out on monuments,
  - Popularises knowledge of monuments.

Fig. 8.7: TransEuropean gas pipeline: archaeological trench (length: 1.8 km).

e-Archeo: the on-line national database on archaeological sites

From the end of the 1990s, the development and upgrading of the entire system for historical monuments protection and rescue research methodology have been boosted by two major investment projects: the construction of the Polish section in the Trans-European gas pipeline from Siberia to Western Europe (500 km; fig. 8.7) and the construction of a motorway system (2.300 km; fig. 8.8). Never before has Polish archaeology faced a similar challenge. Within a few years it was necessary to solve many problems all at once, including arrangements for the method of financing such extensive research, organizing numerous research teams, developing unified documentation standards (using IT that has now been made available, but is still neither fully nor universally implemented), preparing premises for the storage of archaeological materials that have been acquired in the course of research, etc.

e-Archeo is one of the most important and innovative tools that supports the entire range of archaeological rescue work: it is an on-line national database on archaeological sites (SMR), launched in 2004. It is used for developing and storing data on archaeological sources originating both from current excavations and from those discovered and published before. The system permits the registration of all the elements of an archaeological site (settlement phases, facilities, layers and movable artefacts). The content of the majority of fields is controlled by means of glossaries. It has been constructed in php computer language, based on a PostgreSQL database server, visible for standard internet browsers, in the manner which enables digital record as well as the analysis of particular elements of archaeological sources. A specific feature of this system is the possibility of not only receiving information, but also of correlating, elaborating and eventually obtaining definite results in the form of both graphic (charts, maps), statistic and text files. Due to e-Archeo one can access the information regarding particular elements of a single file (sites, features, layers, moveable artefacts, bibliography, outcomes of physical-chemical research etc.). It is also possible to compare files, i.e. to point out both common and preclusive features. The main unit of *e-Archeo* structure is the archaeological site. Multicultural complexes are described as separate units within a single unit – site, recognized on the basis of settlement stage. Each holder of the (obligatory) permission for carrying out archaeological field research is obliged to enter the basic data on the examined site(s) to the system. *e-Archeo* has three levels of data availability depending on the user's access rights: guest (browsing general data), researcher (browsing the whole database) and manager (entering data).

The main drawbacks

Two main drawbacks of the present Polish situation are:
- Lack of predictive modelling,
- No legal ground for any requirements based on theoretical predictions; in each case, empiric data (artefacts, archaeological features) have to be presented.

To sum up: the present short list of major problems to be solved includes:
- the fast growing endanger of archaeological sites (construction boom, great development projects, highly industrialized agriculture, illegal use of metal detectors etc.),
- the need for better integration of archaeological professional milieu (incl. definition of basic common tasks and code of ethics),
- the necessary compromise between research-oriented and commercial archaeology,
- prevention of misuse of archaeological knowledge for political or commercial aims (Z. Kobylinski, Archeologia wobec wyzwan współczesności (Archaeology against the Actual Challenges) http://blog.snap.org.pl/?p=1 (in Polish).

aprinke@man.poznan.pl

References

Jaskanis, D. 1987: La carte archeologique polonaise: theorie et pratique, Nou*velles de l'Archeologie 28*, 42-52.

Jaskanis, D. 1992: Polish National Record of Archaeological Sites: A computerization, in: Larsen, C.U. (ed.), *Sites & Monuments. National Archaeological Records*, Copenhagen, 81-87.

Prinke, A. 1992: Polish National Record of Archaeological Sites: A computerization, in: Larsen, C.U. (ed.), *Sites & Monuments. National Archaeological Records*, Copenhagen, 89-93.

Prinke, A. 1994: Protection and salvage archaeology in Poland. An example from the historical region of Wielkopolska (Greater Poland), in: Koschik, H. (ed.), *Aspekte europaeischer Bodendenkmalpflege*, Materialien zur Bodendenkmalpflege im Rheinland 3, 29-31.

Prinke, A. 1994: Can developing countries afford National Archaeological Record? The Polish Answer, in: *Theme papers. Cultural property, Conservation &. Public Awareness*, World Archaeological Congress - 3, New Delhi, December 4-11, 1994, New Delhi.

Prinke, A. 1995 (in press): AZP_Fox, ver. 1.73. A computer database management system on archaeological sites. User's guide, *Poznanskie Zeszyty Archeologiczno-Konserwatorskie*. 4, Poznan.

Fig. 8.8: TransEuropean gas pipeline and national motorway system.

9 | Listing and scheduling archaeological sites. Recent developments in the Netherlands

Peter Schut and Nathalie Vossen

Abstract: Over the past 10 years, the archaeological system in the Netherlands has changed in response to a number of developments, some of which are interconnected. Key among these have been the implementation of the Valletta convention in Dutch legislation, decentralisation, the introduction of commercial archaeology and the rapid growth in archaeological research. Partly as a result of these developments, and of the more landscape-oriented approach now being taken, thinking as to how sites should be listed and scheduled has changed.

Developments in legislation

National legislation on archaeological heritage management is a fairly recent thing. Although the first provincial ordinance for the protection of the *hunebedden* megalithic tombs was passed in Drenthe in 1734, it was not until 1946 that national regulations were put in place. And it would take a further 15 years for the first Monuments and Historic Buildings Act to be passed (Bakker 1979; Van Es 1972; Willems 1997; Eickhoff 2003). This legislation, which was revised in 1988 (Monuments and Historic Buildings Act 1988) regulates, among other things, the scheduling of archaeological monuments, the permit system for changes to scheduled monuments, authorisation to perform excavations and the ownership of finds. In the latest review of the Monuments and Historic Buildings Act in 2007 (Archaeological Heritage Management Act), several essential points in the legislation were amended to bring it into line with the Valletta Convention.

The key principles underlying the new legislation are:
- The aim should be to preserve archaeological values *in situ*. The soil is after all the best preserver of archaeological remains and features.
- The presence of archaeological values must be identified at the earliest possible stage of the spatial planning process so that they can be taken into account in the further development of plans.
- The developer must pay for the investigation and documentation of archaeological values if preservation *in situ* is not an option.

The Archaeological Heritage Management Act amends existing legislation, affecting not only the Monuments and Historic Buildings Act 1988, but also the Earth Removal Act, the Environmental Management Act and the Housing Act. As such, it incorporates archaeological interests into the regulations governing land use planning and development and their implementation.

Though, in practice, archaeology in the Netherlands is visible mainly in the form of excavations, the new legislation does not exclusively regulate excavations. Under the Monuments and Historic Buildings Act, a licence was needed to perform excavations, and only universities, local authorities and the former ROB were eligible for such a licence. Under the new Archaeological Heritage Management, on the other hand, anyone may apply for an excavation licence. Until recently, archaeological agencies performed excavations under the auspices of the National Herigate Agency. Now, they are free to apply for a licence themselves. Applicants must meet certain requirements. In March 2008, the Ministry of Education, Culture and Science (OCW) issued an excavation licence to 25 commercial agencies. A number of local authorities and universities will also have their own excavation licence in the near future. The number of excavations (including the digging of test trenches) has increased in recent years, from 175 in 1990 to over 500 in 2007. Unlike 15 years ago, a report must be published on every archaeological excavation, to ensure that the information generated is available to the profession within two years of an excavation being completed. Commercial archaeology of this kind has existed in the Netherlands since the late 1990s.

Under the Monuments and Historic Buildings Act 1988, the Minister must have an up-to-date central archaeological information system. ARCHIS, as the system is known, is administered by the the Cultural Heritage Agency. It consists of a database containing information on 75,000 archaeological findspots and 13,000 sites (fig. 9.1). Holders of an excavation licence are obliged to enter the results of all archaeological investigations in the system.

The National Museum of Antiquities in Leiden had kept a register of finds since the nineteenth century, but this task was transferred to the State Service for Archaeological Investigations (ROB) when it was set up in 1947. The automated system ARCHIS, which was developed in the 1990s as a successor to the STAIRS system established in 1974, plays an important role in Dutch archaeology (Zoetbrood et al. 1997). ARCHIS II is accessible online to all archaeological agencies and government archaeologists (local and provincial). In combination with the Indicative Map of Archaeological Values (IKAW), a third revised edition of which was published in 2008, the system forms the basis of policy on archaeology and land use planning.

One product of ARCHIS has been incorporated into a special cultural heritage resources website for non-archaeologists, including planners, policymakers, designers and other interested parties (Kennis Infrastructuur Cultuurhistorie, www.kich.nl). The site combines information on archaeological monuments, historic buildings and historic landscapes with a GIS system, to create an information platform that serves as an example of collaboration and integration between the different cultural heritage disciplines. The many advantages of making information on archaeological sites accessible include ensuring that the heritage is considered from the outset in spatial planning processes and increasing the involvement of the local population.

New legislation: new role for central, provincial and local government in archaeological heritage management

There are three levels of administration in the Netherlands: central, provincial and local, each with its own powers and responsibilities. This division is also reflected in the new legislation, under which local authorities, in particular, have a greater role in archaeological heritage management. The role of the different authorities is described briefly below, along with the government's policy for producing a representative list of legally protected monuments.

Central government

The role of central government in respect of registered sites has changed over the past 20 years. The ROB was initially responsible for all sites, including those that enjoyed statutory protection. The ROB's successor, the Cultural Heritage Agency, is now only responsible for scheduled monuments: selected sites of (inter)national importance, which represent important elements of the history of the Netherlands. These sites are evaluated by means of a preservation assessment in the field. This is examined further below.

Until the mid-1990s provincial archaeologists were employed by the ROB, and each province had its own monuments map showing all known, evaluated archaeological sites. In other words, all sites for which at least one documented observation is available. Often, a field survey including a number of boreholes will also have been made to assess the physical quality and size of the site. The provincial Archaeological Monuments Maps (AMKs) are dynamic maps to which new sites are continually added. Besides demand for information on known archaeological values, the need for information on predicted archaeological values began to grow. The ROB therefore decided, in the late 1990s, to produce a nationwide Indicative Map of Archaeological Values (IKAW), which shows the likelihood of archaeological remains being found in a particular area. However, the scale of the underlying maps (soil maps) means the map can be used only on a scale of 1: 50 000. Furthermore, the IKAW refers chiefly to archaeological remains lying within 1.2 m of the surface, which represents a major limitation in some parts of the Netherlands. Nevertheless, these two instruments – the AMK and IKAW – have come to play a key role in the spatial planning process.

Provincial authorities

In the mid-1990s the provincial archaeologists employed by the ROB were moved to the twelve provincial authorities. The way in which the archaeologists fulfil their new role differs from one province to another, but the focus will be on devising archaeology policy.

All provincial authorities have a role in assessing local authority land use plans to ensure they comply with provincial policy, including policy on archaeology. As a result, regional plans produced by the provinces were already 'Malta-compliant' before the Archaeological Heritage Management Act entered into force, since local authorities were obliged to include a section on archaeology in every new land use plan. Most provinces have issued their own instructions for archaeological investigations, preliminary or otherwise, tailored to the local situation. Some have even produced their own research agenda.

Under the new legislation, provincial authorities are able to designate archaeological 'attention areas'. Though attention areas do not have the same status as a provincial monument, they indicate to local authorities that they may exercise their own powers there provided they meet certain conditions set by the provincial authority. In the worst-case scenario, a local authority might even be compelled to produce a new land use plan.The provinces are also managing the archives where all the finds and documentation of the excavations of their regions are stored.

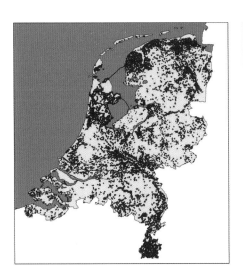
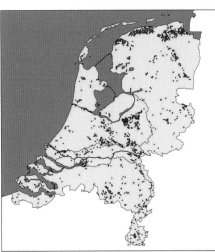

Fig. 9.1: The distribution of archaeological sites (left) and scheduled monuments (right) in the Netherlands (Cultural Heritage Agency).

Local authorities

The Archaeological Monuments Map (AMK) forms the basis of many local authority archaeological values maps and policy maps. However, it has legal force only once it has been incorporated into local authority land use plans. Under the new Archaeological Heritage Management Act, local authorities are obliged to take account of known archaeological sites and of predicted archaeological values. This gives the sites on the archaeological monuments map a certain legal status. Over the coming years, all local authority land use plans will have to include a section on archaeology, thus putting into practice the objectives of the new legislation. Archaeology has already been included in many of the plans drawn up over the past few years.

In response to the new legislation, more and more local authorities, some working in partnership, have appointed municipal or regional archaeologists to give them in-house expertise on archaeology. Over a hundred of the 442 local authorities in the country now have access to in-house archaeological expertise. The other authorities hire in experts from commercial agencies. In-house expertise has helped enhance support for archaeological interests.Although the Archaeological Heritage Management Act is based on the principle of preservation *in situ*, in practice, *ex situ* preservation occurs in many cases where excavation is the less costly option. As a result, over the past few years many local authorities have commissioned archaeological investigations (2300 surveys in 2007). Thanks to these investigations, the number of known sites has increased, though the number of sites being preserved has not risen proportionately. The sites are generally incorporated into plans, and in some cases can be preserved *in situ*, though often they are excavated.

All parties in the rapidly changing field of archaeology are investing more and more in informing the public and in projects designed to engender support for archaeology. Media attention, walking and cycling tours of sites of archaeological interest, popular publications, information panels and the like have made archaeology a product that attracts interest from many quarters, bringing knowledge directly to a larger audience.

Towards a representative list of monuments

The *Archeologie Balans* (Lauwerier & Lotte 2002; Van Dockum et al. 2006) presents a baseline measurement of the archaeological resource, as well as discussing other matters such as developments in society and questions concerning our heritage. As such, the report plays a key role in the management of the archaeological heritage (fig. 9.2). 2009 will see the publication of an integrated heritage review encompassing archaeology, the cultural landscape and the built heritage.

In response to the first Archaeology Report, in 2006 Zoetbrood et al. produced a report analysing the current list of legally protected monuments (*Uit Balans*). They argued that the list is not representative of the entire stock of known archaeological sites. It was found, for example, that, while 30% of all visible monuments are scheduled, only 10% of non-visible sites enjoy this status, despite the fact that the non-visible resource may be assumed to be greater.

Uit Balans provides a basis for scheduling policy over the coming years. The key aim is to devise a selection policy that will produce a representative list of scheduled monuments, with a greater focus on the contextual setting of the landscape. Several years ago, the minister decided to institute a temporary moratorium on the registering of monuments, with the aim of developing a new selection policy. In late 2007 this moratorium was lifted.

However, given the capacity available and the legal implications of designation, the number of new listings in the Netherlands has been restricted. An analysis of the sites already registered has shown that a number of complex types are over-represented, while others are under-represented. Over the next few years, the focus is shifted to the following types of monument:

Fig. 9. 2: Simplified overview of the known archaeological resource in the Netherlands (Cultural Heritage Agency).

PERIOD	Celtic fields	places of sacrifice	burial mounds	extraction of raw materials	houseterps	Industry	Infrastructure	castles	churches and monastries	agriculture	earthworks	castella/castra etc.	Megaliths	settlements	burials/cemetries	villae	city/village	Terps	Urnfields	stronghold	Total
Paleolithic														440							**440**
Mesolithic						10								820							**830**
Neolithic			2050	30		30				20			80	710	60						**2980**
Bronze age			600				10			10				260	10				20		**910**
Iron Age	180		320		110		10			20				1240	40				1100	80	**3100**
Roman Period		10	10		30	20	90			10		70		660	100	130		100			**1230**
Early Middleages				10	200		10	30	30	50				383			100	140			**953**
High Middleages				20	2650	40	270	530	510		80			1460	90		590	290		860	**7390**
	180	10	2980	60	2990	100	390	560	540	110	80	70	80	5973	300	130	690	530	1120	940	**17833**

- Visible archaeological landscape elements
- Stone Age settlements (Palaeolithic – Mesolithic – Neolithic)
- Iron Age – Early Roman field complexes (celtic fields)
- Late Roman – Early Medieval settlements
- Early and Late Medieval rural settlements
- Shipwrecks
- Late Medieval – Early Modern Period archaeological complexes
- Archaeological complexes which, due to their unique character, do not belong to one of the categories above

In 2008, the focus has been on Roman period sites, and sites identified for scheduling include the aqueduct in Nijmegen, the temple at Elst, parts of the Limes road, the castella in Woerden and Utrecht, a Roman ship and part of the Corbulo canal including part of a vicus. Clearly, these will be protected at site level. Protection at landscape level requires a different approach, for which other instruments are available, with scheduling being used mainly in support of the landscape approach (Werkgroep Skrédiek 2003).

However, scheduling is only protection on paper. It does not guarantee physical preservation. Thus far, no financial support or compensation has been available to recompense owners for the restrictions associated with statutory protection and for changing the use of their property to make it archaeology-friendly. The issue of degradation also has implications for physical preservation. Though we know that the underground archaeological resource is slowly but surely deteriorating, as revealed in excavations, we know relatively little about the underlying processes, let alone possible solutions. Fortunately, this issue has also been tackled in recent years, resulting in studies of the degradation of botanical remains, bone and bronze, among other things, and also of the visibility of soil features (Kars & Smit 2003; Huisman, in prep.). The opportunities and difficulties associated with

archaeology-'friendly' construction mean we must constantly expand our knowledge of foundation techniques, settling and the impact of pile-driving, future accessibility, among other things. This knowledge is of course important for all archaeological sites, not just scheduled sites.

From site-based to landscape approach

The Netherlands is an entirely man-made cultural landscape, the most extreme example of which is the reclaimed land in the West of the country. The country's history of land reclamation, which in some cases extends back 800 years, can still be seen in the present land parcelling structure (fig. 9.3).

In the densely populated landscape of the Netherlands, the pressure on space is enormous. Furthermore, climate change means we will have to make radical changes to the landscape. The rivers need to be given more room, and the idea of returning some polders to the water is even being considered, sometimes for the sake of nature development, or to cope with rising water levels. These developments will have a major impact not only on the landscape, but also on the underground archaeological resource and the cultural heritage. Besides, the trend has been to develop new wildlife areas which, while bringing new opportunities, also has implications for the country's buried history. The call to adopt a multidisciplinary landscape-based approach has grown in various quarters in recent years, fed partly by the research tradition (Bloemers 1999; 2002) and by developments under the Belvedere project, including the designation of a number of key areas based on a combination (fig. 9.4) of archaeological, historical geographical and built heritage factors (Hallewas 2002). The aim of the Belvedere project was to support the cultural heritage as a driver and source of inspiration for new developments. The project is now drawing to a close, and national heritage landscapes are currently being defined, overlapping to some extent with the key areas, where

Fig. 9.3: Langbroekerwetering (province of Utrecht) in the 19th century. The parcelling, which is still preserved, dates from the 13th century.

Fig. 9.4: The Olthof in the municipality of Deventer. In the foreground, one of the forerunners of the historic farm seen in the background is being excavated.
Photo: Archeologie Deventer

the cultural heritage will be the main driver of developments (Linssen & Van Marrewijk 2005). The focus has been on selecting areas where future developments will be restricted and which have unique historical landscape value (Beusekom 2002). Comparison with the 'archaeo-regions' – areas displaying consistent landscape development and landscape-related settlement history – shows that many of them include national heritage landscapes. However, not all the selected landscapes are by definition archaeological hotspots, though archaeology may play a key role in telling their story. At this point in time, however, it is not entirely clear what additional role archaeology will be required to play, though there will certainly be opportunities to work closely with other disciplines to produce detailed histories of the areas. It is certainly worth investing in the national heritage landscapes from the point of view of engendering support and gaining experience of an interdisciplinary or multidisciplinary approach.

The Netherlands has a long tradition of taking an area-based approach (Bloemers 1999). In recent years, the focus has shifted more and more to multidisciplinary and, to some extent, interdisciplinary research programmes (Hidding et al. 2001; Spek et al. 2006; Van Beek & Keunen 2006). One new development in cultural heritage projects has been the involvement of local heritage groups and residents, bringing in local knowledge and interests, and making them relevant to a broader section of society (fig. 9.5). Local parties are more likely to become involved if they can see evidence of their own past. They provide a key support base for the cultural heritage in general, and archaeology in particular.

p.schut@cultureelerfgoed.nl

Fig. 9.5: Reconstruction, by the local community of Zelhem (province Gelderland), of what is believed to be a chapel built by Liudger in 800. The remains were found in 1946 underneath the church on the background.
Photo: P.A.C. Schut

References

Bakker, J.A. 1979: Protection, Acquisition, Restoration and Maintenance of the Dutch Hunebeds since 1734: An Active and Often Exemplary Policy in Drenthe (I), BRO*B 29*, 143-184.

Beek, R. van &. Keunen, L.J. 2006: A Cultural Biography of the Coversand Landscapes in the Salland and Achterhoek Regions. The Aims and Methods of the Eastern Netherlands Project, *BROB 46*, 355-382.

Beusekom, E. van 2002: Historic Landscapes in the Netherlands, in Fairclough, G. & Rippon, S. (eds.) *Europe's Cultural Landscape: archaeologists and the management of change*, EAC Occasional Paper 2, 49-54.

Bloemers, J.H.F. 1999: Regional Research Approach since the Early 70s in the Netherlands. A fundamental Decision with Long-term Effects, in: Sarfaij, H., Verwers, W.J.H. & Woltering, P.J. (eds.), *In Discussion with the past*, Archaeological studies presented to W.A. van Es, Zwolle, 317-327.

Bloemers, J.H.F. 2002: Past- and future-oriented archaeology: protecting and developing the archaeological-historical landscape in the Netherlands, in: Fairclough, G. & Rippon, S. (eds.) *Europe's Cultural Landscape: archaeologists and the management of change,* EAC Occasional Paper 2, 89-96.

Dockum, S.G. van,. Lauwerier,R.C.G.M. & Zoetbrood, P.A.M. 2006; Archeologiebalans (Archaeology Report). The National Review and Outlook, *BROB* 46, 41-52.

Eickhoff, M. 2003: *De oorsprong van het 'eigene' Nederlands vroegste verleden, archeologie en nationaal socialisme*, Amsterdam.

Es, W.A. van 1972: The Origins and Development of the State Service for Archaeological Investigations in the Netherlands, *BROB* 22, 17-71.

Hallewas, D. 2002: The Belvedere Project: an integrated approach in the Netherlands, in: Fairclough, G. & Rippon, S. (eds.) *Europe's Cultural Landscape: archaeologists and the management of change*, EAC Occasional Paper 2, 55-59.

Hidding, M., Kolen, J. & Spek, Th. 2001: De biographie van het landschap, in: Bloemers, J.H.F. & Wijnen, M.H. (eds.), *Bodemarchief in Behoud en Ontwikkeling. De conceptuele grondslagen*, Den Haag, 7-109.

Huisman, D.J. in press: *Degradation of archaeological materials*, Den Haag.

Kars, H. & Smit, A. (eds.) 2003: Handleiding fysiek behoud archeologisch erfgoed degradatiemechanismen in sporen en materialen. Monitoring van de conditie van het bodemarchief. Geoarchaeological and bioarchaeological Studies 1, Amsterdam.

Lauwerier, R.C.G.M. & Lotte, R.M. 2002: *Archeologiebalans 2002*, Amersfoort.

Linssen, M. & Marrewijk, D. van 2005: *Landschappen met toekomstwaarde. Cultuurhistorische karakteristiek van de nationale landschappen*, Utrecht.

Spek, Th., Brinkkemper, O. & Speleers, B.P. 2006: Archaeological Heritage Management and Nature Conservation, *BROB* 46, 331-354.

Werkgroep Skrédyk (LNV / RDMZ / ROB) 2003: *Historische geografie en monumentenzorg een notitie over de mogelijkheden voor een wettelijke bescherming van historisch-geografische elementen en patronen op basis van de Monumentenwet 1988*, Amersfoort.

Willems, W.J.H. 1997: Archaeological Heritage Management in the Netherlands: Past, Present and Future, in: Willems, W.J.H., Kars, H. & Hallewas, D.P. (eds.) *Archaeological Heritage Management in the Netherlands. Fifty Years State Service for Archaeological Investigations*, Assen/Amersfoort, 3-57.

Zoetbrood, P.A.M., Montforts, M.J.G., Roorda, I.M. & Wiemer, R. 1997: Documenting the Archaeological Heritage, in: Willems, W.J.H., Kars, H. & Hallewas, D.P. (eds.) *Archaeological Heritage Management in the Netherlands. Fifty Years State Service for Archaeological Investigations*, Assen/Amersfoort, 330-345.

Zoetbrood, P.A.M., Rooijen, C.A.M. van, Lauwerier, R.C.G.M., Haaff, G. van & As, E. van 2006: *Uit Balans, Wordingsgeschiedenis en analyse van het bestand van wettelijk beschermde archeologische monumenten*, Amersfoort.

10 | ASIS – more than a register of ancient monuments

Peter Norman and Rikard Sohlenius

Abstract: The perspective of the landscape that dominates the Swedish cultural heritage management of today is very much the result of spatial planners. To a large extent it originates in debate in the 1960s, against a background of the clash between the growing environmental movement and the development of a modern society expressed in large scale-projects. Examples of these include the expansion of water power when vast areas of land were laid under water and the building of one million new dwellings within a period of ten years from the mid sixties. This debate forced society to develop new tools for spatial planning. The old strategy of heritage protection focused too much on separate sites and monuments only. The need for a more spatial/or 'area-based' and contextual perspective was acute. One example of a new planning instrument is the Environmental Code which protects the natural and historic environment, including approximately 1.700 national heritage areas. The contextual perspective is however built on the knowledge of separate sites and monuments. Registers containing information of separate sites, monuments, historic buildings and churches have always been of central importance for the cultural heritage management.

ASIS – Ancient Sites Information System

The Swedish digital sites and monuments record is called ASIS (abbreviation for Ancient Sites Information System). It consists of among other things a geographical database with an application for on-line search (http://www.fmis. raa.se/cocoon/fornsok/search.html). While the application is publicly available for everyone, some of the information is restricted, for instance the position of some sites is not shown. This is due to the risk of looting and vandalism. However, professionals in cultural heritage management, spatial planning, research and education can log in and access all the information in the database.

The on-line search application presents the information about the sites and monuments together with geographical data from the National Land Survey. It is also possible to switch the background map to nautical charts from the Swedish Maritime Administration or to geological maps from the Geological Survey of Sweden.

The application has approximately 2500 professional users, mainly within Municipalities, County Administration Boards, Government Agencies and Museums. There are a growing number of organisations working with data extracts from ASIS in their own systems and GIS-programs. Most of the professional users are spatial planners or architects and not archaeologists.

ASIS contains information on over 1.5 million individual sites and monuments in approximately 570.000 different localities both on land and in maritime settings from the Stone Age to the Industrial Age (fig. 10.1). It is the Heritage Conservation Act that sets the framework for which site types are recorded, but not all of the sites and monuments in ASIS are protected by the Act as the system also includes other historically interesting sites. Out of 570 000 localities approximately 260 000 are protected.

Sites and monuments are defined as traces of human activity in past ages, having resulted from use in previous times and having been permanently abandoned. This definition also includes natural formations associated with ancient customs, legends or noteworthy historic events, as well as traces of ancient popular cults. Examples of sites and monuments are abandoned graves, cemeteries, settlements, rock art, boundary markings, harbour facilities, different kinds of ruins and cultivated land (figs 10.2 & 10.3).

The records in ASIS are made according to the standards of the National Heritage Board. A grave mound in the south of Sweden is documented in the same way as a grave mound in the north. The geographical position and extent of every object in the database is recorded to an accuracy of +/- 10 m. There are also different kinds of attribute information about the objects, among other things classification such as type of site, legal status and descriptions in full text. Every object has information about why the site was recorded, by whom and when it was done. Images and references (to articles, excavation reports etc.) can be connected to the relevant record in ASIS.

ASIS in an historic perspective

Sweden has a long tradition of surveying ancient sites and monuments. The first records, which focused on rune stones, were made at the end of the 16th century.

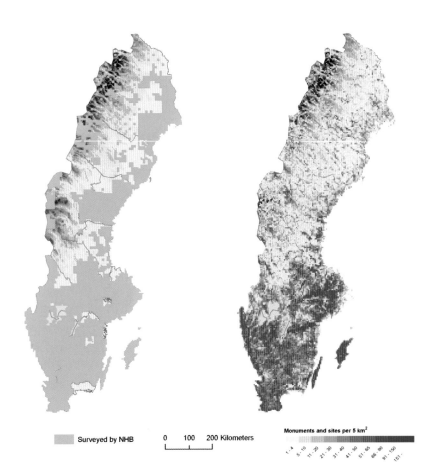

Fig. 10.1: The green areas in the left map show surveys of modern standard and the right map shows the density of known sites and monuments. Notice the correlation between the surveys and the presence of sites and monuments.
Illustration: Rikard Sohlenius, National Heritage Board

Surveyed by NHB   0   100   200 Kilometers

Monuments and sites per 5 km²

1-4   5-10   11-20   21-30   31-40   41-50   51-65   66-90   91-150   151-

A large-scale survey, which focused on monumental antiquities such as large chiefly burial mounds and rune stones, began in the second part of the 17th century. These surveys were a part of Sweden's ambition to manifest itself as a great nation-state. In the early twentieth century more systematic surveys began, and in pace with the growing knowledge of Swedish prehistory and improved legislation, the work found its shape in the mid-1940s. Since 1938 the National Heritage Board has surveyed ancient monuments over much of Sweden. Until 1995 the work was planned according to the publication of the National land Survey's Economic Map, which was supposed to display all known ancient sites and monuments. One important reason for the survey was that the Heritage Conservation Act gives general protection to all monuments whether they are known or not. This is also the reason why Sweden does not have any priority lists of ancient monuments and sites (fig. 10.1).

As a result of the surveys, our knowledge of the early history of Sweden has increased considerably. In the first decades of the survey the focus was above all on prehistoric graves, cemeteries, rock carvings, rune stones, and the like. Over the years the survey has also included types of archaeological remains and categories of ancient sites and monuments which previously received little attention, such as Stone Age settlement sites, prehistoric cultivated land, ruins of small scale industries and the remains of outlying land resources. This has led to a need for new surveys in parts of the country where the surveys are out of date because remains of this type were not previously recorded.

Field surveys today

During the field surveys performed by the National Heritage Board sites and monuments were recorded on maps (aerial photos) and in notebooks. The records were gathered in a register at the National Heritage Board.
The register was updated constantly with the results from surveys and excavations. Between 2003 and 2006 the register was replaced by ASIS.

As a result of ASIS and of new technology the field surveys changed, but the change was also caused by a different aim and direction of the Nation Heritage Board.

The National Heritage Board does not perform any field surveys today. They are instead done by local museums

Fig. 10.2: Stone Age settlements in the north of Sweden are often indicated by fire cracked stones and tools of quartz. Sorsele Parish, Västerbotten County.
Photo: Rikard Sohlenius, National Heritage Board

Fig. 10.3: A reindeer pen is a restricted area where domestic reindeers were gathered mainly for milking. They appear as areas of luxuriant grass and herb-rich vegetation that stands out against the surrounding landscape. Intensive reindeer herding was abounded in the 1950s, but nobody knows how old the pens are. Arjeplog Parish, Norrbotten County.
Photo: Rikard Sohlenius, National Heritage Board

or other local interests. The surveys are often guided by the need for better information. For instance during the last years there have been several surveys in the forests of Sweden, prompted by the fact that many sites in wood land are unknown and that sites are damaged by forestry.

The National Heritage Board supervises the field surveys and sets the standards for documentation. It is important that the sites and monuments are recorded in a similar way all over the country. Furthermore a high quality of the recordings is important. An object that is recorded as a rune stone in the database must in reality be a rune stone and it must be located where the digital record specifies. Therefore only experienced archaeologists are permitted to enter data in ASIS. These archaeologists have worked for several years in field survey and they are well aware of the importance of correct information. Every site that is discovered during a field survey must be checked by one of these experienced archaeologists. The National Heritage Board offers free education for entering data in ASIS to archaeologists who have the necessary qualifications. It is the National Heritage Board that defines the qualifications and gives authorization to enter data. Beyond this, however, there is no official certification system for archaeologists in Sweden.

An updated database is central, otherwise the information will lose value and be impossible to use in an efficient way, both for professionals and the public. But it is not only important that the updating is carried out, it must also be done within a reasonable time. The need for rapid high quality updating of ASIS has led the National Heritage Board to develop a method for field survey which includes a digital tool for documentation. This method is called Field-GIS. During the surveys a PDA (pocket PC) with a GPS is used. The PDA is prepared with information about the area of survey, mainly different kinds of geographical information (aerial photos, historical maps etc.). The geographical character of the monument is captured with the support of the GPS and the attributes are recorded in a special form. This is done with both scroll lists and free texts. The form is built on XML, which gives the option of unlimited text strings and the possibility to create relations between objects. The recordings are then entered in ASIS over the internet.

Field-GIS makes it possible to perform a complete digital recording in field. One advantage of the method is that the same person who undertakes the recording in the field also enters the information in ASIS. Before this development, there were several persons involved in making the information digital, with consequent risk of quality loss. Another advantage is the rapidity as the same day a record is made in the field it can be accessed in ASIS.

ASIS and the cultural heritage administration
The Swedish archaeological heritage administration is today an integrated part of the cultural heritage administration as a whole. The municipalities are the primary authorities for cultural-environmental protection.
They have the economic resources and the main responsibility for spatial planning. Several municipalities also have expert knowledge in the form of municipal museums

Fig. 10.4: An example when the planning system does not work. Even though the grave field was known and registered in ASIS it has been damaged by forestry. Rimbo Parish, Stockholm County.
Photo: Rikard Sohlenius, National Heritage Board

or municipal antiquarians (not always archaeologists). Important planning instruments are the Planning and Building Act and the Environmental Code.

The main responsibility for the legal supervision of cultural-environmental questions lies with the county administrative boards, which deal with most matters covered by the Heritage Conservation Act. This act is the core legislation for preservation of Sweden's historic environment. It gives a general protection to sites and monuments which means that all permanent ancient remains defined by the law, whether they are known or not, are protected. The act also regulates the handling of archaeological finds and procedures for obtaining a permit to remove such remains. For example, if the construction of a new industrial complex is proposed and there is a grave field recorded in ASIS within the area, it is the County administrative board which decides whether the grave field has a higher value than the planned complex or if it can be removed. The removal of an ancient monument implies an archaeological excavation, which is paid for by the company which is planning the exploitation. If an unknown archaeological monument is discovered during development the work must be stopped immediately and the County administrative board contacted for a decision on what must be done (usually an archaeological excavation).

The internal organization of the County Administrative Boards varies, but there are experts in various fields, which make it possible for them to weigh different interests against each other. An unusual construction is the informal responsibility for the cultural environment and cultural monuments borne by the County Museums. They receive some state grants for their work in assisting the County Administration Boards in these matters.

The overall supervision of cultural-environmental protection is the responsibility of the National Heritage Board, which also cooperates with other central authorities and boards. The National Heritage Board is responsible for innovations and looks after the interests of the sector in general. Examples of responsibilities in the archaeological field are writing hand-books and excercising quality control for archaeological reports. The National Heritage Board also has the overall responsibility for ASIS.

The number of people (or full time services) involved in the archaeological administration at the County Administrative Boards and at the National Heritage Board are about one hundred. Together with the people working in field archaeology (mostly rescue excavations) there are about five hundred practicing archaeologists in Sweden.

ASIS is a well integrated instrument in spatial planning, and because of ASIS planners can get important information about the historic landscape and where ancient monuments are situated. The County Administrative Boards use ASIS regularly in different matters, such as planning for roads, industrial complexes and buildings. For the archaeologists ASIS is necessary in preparation for an excavation, whether this is a rescue excavation or scientific research.

In some situations however, the sophisticated planning system does not work. One example is the forestry that damages an ancient monument situated in felling areas, even if these ancient monuments are registered in ASIS. The reason for this is probably a mix of carelessness by the forestry and a complicated administrative authority system (fig. 10.4).

Although ASIS is well integrated in spatial planning there is still much work to be done. ASIS is to a large extent the result of over 60 years of field surveys by the National Heritage Board. The information is created by archaeologists for archaeologists. This makes it difficult for spatial planners at municipalities and others to understand ASIS and see the historic landscape beyond the spots on the map. A big challenge for the National Heritage Board is therefore to develop tools to interpret the information. It is important that ASIS is easy to use and understand for everyone. We must remember that protection begins with the citizen who lives in the landscape. If we do not learn to communicate with society as a whole our voices in the end will be unheard and our demands will be unrecognized.

peter.norman@raa.se

References

Génetay-Lindholm, C. & Blomqvist, M. 2000. Developing an Information System for Ancient Sites and Monuments. In: Flodin, L. & Modig, A. (ed): Pro*jects and Progress in Archaeology at the National Heritage Board, R*iksantikvarieämbetet, Stockholm, 12-13

Jensen, R. 1997: *Fornminnesinventeringen – nuläge och kompletteringsbehov. En riksöversikt.* Riksantikvarieämbetet. Stockholm.

Nilsson, H. 2000: Surveys of Ancient Sites and Monuments. In: Flodin, L. & Modig, A. (ed): *Projects and Progress in Archaeology at the National Heritage Board*, Riksantikvarieämbetet, Stockholm, 9-11.

11 | Listing archaeological sites – integrating heritage: the case of Slovenia

Bojan Djurić, Phil Mason, Barbara Mlakar, Ksenija Kovaćec Naglić and Brigita Petek

Abstract: In the field of archaeology the compilation of various types of lists and data bases is one of the oldest and most widespread activities, which has received an additional, even enormous impetus with the development of information technology. Users were formerly drawn largely from the ranks of academic researchers, but for some time now they have been joined by various administrators, planners and many other interested parties, in isolated cases even by looters.

The Beginnings

Lists of sites as spatial entities, defined in some cases as a find spot, a structured artefact assemblage or an area of specific topographic characteristics, in other cases as an area with a characteristic toponym or an area connected with a particular oral tradition, were largely compiled in the form of archaeological maps in the Austro-Hungarian monarchy (including what is now Slovenia) from at least the middle of the 19th century (cf. Radics 1862). Lists of this type multiplied and were improved for exclusively academic and research purposes until at least and including the 1960's (e.g. Klemenc, Saria 1936; Saria 1939; Pahič 1962; ANSl 1975). After this point in time they were used as the support for monument lists, which was first specifically required for the territory of Slovenia (within Yugoslavia) by the Act of cultural monuments and sites of natural interest in People's Republic of Slovenia in 1948 (UL 23/1948; Petru 1962). Listing or scheduling as defined by English Heritage – "a short-hand term used for

the process which nationally important sites and monuments are given legal protection by being placed on a list or "schedule"" – practically began with this Act in 1948, because obligatory for the proprietor, landowner, or manager to be served with a written order, which restricted rights of ownership or management. Inclusion on this list was decided by the minister of Education on the basis of a list compiled by the Institute for the protection and scientific study of cultural monuments and sites of natural importance of Slovenia. The starting-point for the allocation of monument status was rested on its importance to the field of research.

However, the main work of the systematic inventorisation of archaeological sites in Slovenia was still led by the academic sphere and museums, because the numbers of archaeologists were extremely limited in the heritage protection service until the 1980's. The Protection of cultural monuments and sites of natural interest act in

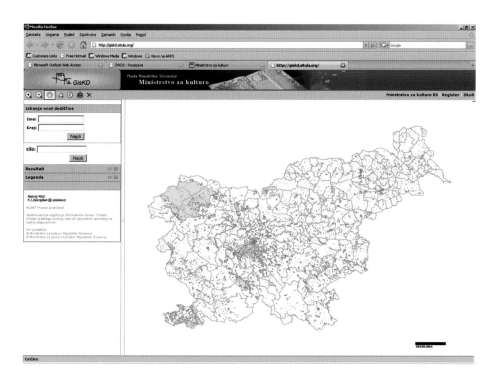

Fig. 11.1: The interactive entry screen map for Heritage unit search in the online GIS Heritage Register (http://rkd.situla.org) (© Ministrstvo za kulturo Republike Slovenije; © Ministrstvo za okolje in prostor Republike Slovenije).

1958 (UL 22/1958) led to the organisation of the heritage protection service into dispersed and mutually independent regional centres that eventually amounted to seven in total, each with its own regional list of sites, and the central state Institute of the Republic of Slovenia for the protection of natural and cultural heritage, which kept a cumulative list of monuments. This situation lasted until the merging of all the regional institutes into the Institute for the protection of cultural heritage of Slovenia in 2000 (UL 7/1999).

The Act passed in 1961 (UL 26/1961), defined for the first time the idea of a register and the registration of monuments, as well as defining those responsible for this. A specific Regulation for the registration of cultural monuments in the People's Republic of Slovenia (UL 29/1962) defined the extent of the data in the register (the registration sheet form), the form of the register (the register books, records and directories) and the mode of entry in the register.

This was the period of the formation of the heritage protection service and the conceptual apparatus of the profession. A typology of monuments and the criteria for their evaluation was established (Vestnik 1962):
- The degree of complexity of the locality.
- The European significance of the locality.
- The size of the locality, for which reason it has not been completely known.
- The importance of the locality in Slovenia.

This was particularly the case during the creation of the list of "Protected Archaeological areas in Slovenia" for the purposes of the Regional spatial plan of the Socialist Republic of Slovenia (UL 13/1967; Petru 1968-9), passed in 1967, with which the protection of an estimated 3000 archaeological sites was first put into effect in spatial planning. Three orders or evaluation categories were formed on the basis of the criteria for evaluation (Mikl Curk 1969; 1981), the most important of which were the value for the advancement of the field of study", followed by rarity, degree of preservation and scientific potential:
- The highest category, comprising monuments that are important for the study of the earliest history of the Eastern Alps and the northern Balkans (2.5% of monuments).
- The middle category comprising monuments of importance for the study of the greater part of Slovenia (17.5% of monuments).
- The lowest category comprising monuments of local importance (80% later 60%of monuments) (Mikl Curk 1970).

These had the following meaning in an administrative sense: the first order or category of protection regime meant the preservation of a monument *in situ* unchanged or researched with the possibility of presentation the second order demanded that prior to any intervention research be undertaken, which would decide the eventual fate of the monument the third order merely demanded monitoring of the intervention in space with the purpose of documenting and collecting any finds.

Fig. 11.2: The results of a search for the prehistoric settlement at Vir near Stična in the online GIS Heritage Register (http://rkd.situla.org) (© Ministrstvo za kulturo Republike Slovenije; © Ministrstvo za okolje in prostor Republike Slovenije).

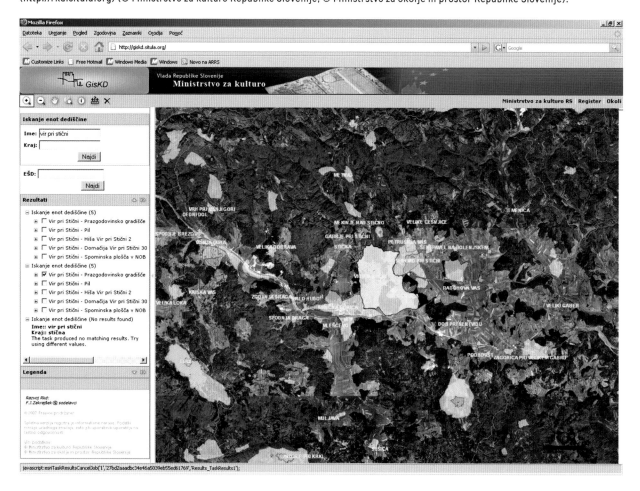

description of cultural heritage unit

1.   IDENTIFICATION

Reference number: -----------------
Name of unit: ----------------------------------
Synonyms for the name:
----

2.   DESCRIPTION

Heritage code: /----/ --------------
Unit type code: /----/ --------------
Unit size code: /----/ --------------

Typological descriptors:

Description:

Dating:
----

3.   LOCATION

Settlement: /----/ --------------

Gauss-Krueger coordinates of centroid
Y: --------   X: ---------   Z: --------- m

Map references:
  1:5000:   /----/ --------------
  1:25000:   /----/ --------------

Description of location:

----

4.   LAND AREA

Approximate land area: ---------   ha

5.   TYPE OF PROTECTION / LEGAL STATUS

 Category of protection: /----/ -------------------

6.   RELATIONSHIP WITH OTHER UNITS

Reference to related unit: ----------------
----

7.   RESPONSIBILITY

Conservation topics:

Regional office responsible for conservation:

/----/ -------------------------------------

8.   REMARKS

Remarks: --------------------------------------

9.   QUALITY OF DATA

Accuracy of the centroid: /----/ -------------
Accuracy of the polygon: /----/ -------------

10.   REGISTRATION
Date: -------------   No. : -------------
Reason: /----/ ---------------------------------

11.   LAST CHANGE
Date: ----------------   No.: -------------
Reason: /----/ -------------------------------

12.   DE-REGISTRATION
Date: ----------------   No.: -------------
Reason: /----/ -------------------------------

13.   NOTES:

Notes:

Fig. 11.3: Form for the description of an immoveable cultural heritage unit.

The monument register for the entire area of Slovenia in the central institution, the Institute for the protection of natural and cultural heritage of the Republic of Slovenia, was never fully realised, the partial registers in the seven independent regional Institutes for the protection of natural and cultural heritage were in reality operationally functional (Mikl Curk 1987). These registers differed amongst themselves in the extent and nature of the recorded data, despite the standardisation proposal (Dular, Tecco Hvala 2002; http://arkas.zrc-sazu.si/).

Changes

An important change in the understanding or definition of archaeological sites occurred in 1981 (UL 1/1981). In addition to the pre-existing category of monuments, the new Natural and Cultural Heritage Act created a new category that of heritage, which was also protected by law in the planning documents on the basis of the expert reports (design) of the specialist organisations (Institutes for the protection of natural and cultural heritage). The idea of the monument was retained for that cultural heritage, which was deigned to have a special cultural scientific historical or aesthetic value. The responsible agency proclaimed them to be a cultural and historical monument with a legal decree. The Decree of proclamation that also detailed the protection regime (restrictions and prohibitions) was passed by the local authority (commune) and by the parliament of the Socialist Republic of Slovenia in the case of monuments of exceptional or great importance for Slovenia as a whole. In both cases this could only be undertaken on the basis of a proposal by the Institute for the protection of natural and cultural heritage, supported by expert reports (design) the preparation of which was founded on a selection of criteria that formed the basis of the evaluation. These criteria were never systematised and formalised, although in practice they formed a relatively homogenous core from which individual conservators drew the basis for their proposals.

Although the Act introduced the categories of cultural heritage and cultural monument in 1981, the obligatory registration of cultural heritage (in addition to cultural monuments) was only defined in 1995 by the Regulation for the managing of central register of cultural and natural heritage (UL 26/1995). The regulation organised the compilation of the central register of cultural and natural heritage, but was never applied to the latter category. It introduced the obligatory citation of the heritage register number and foresaw the information support to the management of the register with a system of electronic forms, which permitted the formation of a single central register in the unified environment of the republic and regional institutes.

The register system was adapted in 2002 with the Regulation on the register of immoveable cultural heritage (UL 26/2002) to the new Cultural Heritage Protection Act (UL 7/1999). The compilation of the register was confined to immovable cultural heritage. In addition to a collection of protection data, the regulation defined a collection of basic data (for cultural monuments) and a collection of documents, but the basic concept of the register, formed on the basis of the regulation in 1995, remained virtually unchanged.

The current system for the protection of immoveable cultural heritage in Slovenia is divided into two basic concepts or categories:

- Cultural heritage.
- Cultural monuments.

The basic category is that of cultural heritage, which receives legal status on inscription in the register of cultural heritage. Heritage may be scheduled as a cultural monument, when it has a special meaning for the state or the local community (commune or region). Heritage receives the status of cultural monument through the Proclamation Act, which is be passed by the government of the Republic of Slovenia, in the case of cultural monuments of national importance, or by the relevant local authority in the case of cultural monuments of local importance. Inscription in the Register of cultural heritage and the passing of the Proclamation Act of scheduling are two different measures for assuring the protection of immovable cultural heritage on two different levels. Inscription in the Register is intended for the protection of the public interest in connection with the protection of heritage. Heritage is identified by inscription in the Register and so is assured compulsory inclusion in the planning process. Scheduling of the cultural heritage defines concrete measures for the protection of a specific unit of cultural heritage (UL 105/2007), which can also include requirements with regard to public access to and management of a monument. Scheduling as a monument potentially permits access to public funds for its protection and revitalisation.

Every unit of heritage is given a unique heritage register number (EŠD) on inscription, which is used in all procedures relating to heritage protection (from recording and documenting to scheduling as a cultural monument). It is also used as a link between modules in the information system, because the register also performs the role of a central database for the information support to the implementation of heritage protection.

Inscription in the register extends to all types of immovable cultural heritage: archaeological, architectural, settlement, memorial and garden-architectural heritage, as well as cultural and historic landscapes. The description of the unit in the register contains the basic facts about the heritage unit in question, which also include details of the spatial location of the unit. The geo-locational data (the central point and the area of the unit) are generally defined on at least a scale of 1:5000.

At the moment there are a total of 25.972 units inscribed in the Register, including a total of 2.687 units of an archaeological character – 1028 monuments and 1659 heritage units (circa 10%).

RKD is in line with the recommendations of Core Data Index (Recommendation 1995), passed by the Council of Europe in 1995 and 1998, from which the core data for documenting architectural and archaeological heritage have been defined.

The initiative for inscription in the register can be suggested to the Ministry of Culture by any legal or private person. The inscription proposal is always prepared at the competent regional office of the Institute for the Protection of Cultural Heritage of Slovenia, in most cases at their own behest. At the moment this preparation and processing of proposals for inscription in the Register is undertaken by 14 archaeologists-conservators within the regional offices of the ZKDS, which is, at least in principle, centralized (cf. Djurić 2007 for the Service organization). The submitter vouches for the veracity of the data. Inscription in the Register is at the discretion of the Minister for Culture. Erasure of entries from the Register or their modification is undertaken in the same manner.

The data in the Register are within the public domain. The public nature of the Register is assured by its publication on the internet (http://rkd.situla.org), the issuing of extracts from the Register and through distribution of data from the register on the basis of special agreements. A specific GIS oriented web service for access to data from the Register is also in preparation.

Evaluation criteria

In the process of creating and establishing a uniform functional data base for the requirements of protection, a hierarchically organised terminology on object types for description of heritage units began to form. This may be in certain cases relatively precise. The terminology has not yet been formally adopted, because it is still in its nascent stage, but its finished segments have been adopted by the internal working groups in INDOK, whilst it is available to the submitters-conservators, for whom its use is mandatory. However this terminology on object types does not reach the level of such tools as, e.g. the Monument Class Description (MCD) of English Heritage, because it was never conceived as a tool in the evaluation process. It is still dependant on the subjective understanding and selected criteria of the individual conservator. In some extreme cases the inscription proposal may be based on the subjective opinion of the archaeologist conservator alone.

The corpus of monuments is evidently biased and extremely modest in extent, not even approximating the hypothesised number of archaeological sites in Slovenia, which most recent assessments suggest exceed 100.000 (Djurić 2007). This is a result of the decentralisation of the service and the absence of a central specialist body that would make it possible to apply unitary standards to the entire country through the homogenisation of inscription proposals on the basis of unified criteria. In the next five years there is an urgent need to standardize and essentially supplement or rather develop the criteria for inscription in the Register, in order to achieve an unitary minimal standard for inscription. It will also be necessary to check the credibility of the existing entries in the Register, especially with regard to the precision of the information pertaining to the content of the registered unit and the suitability of its description. A further reason for the bias in the monument corpus lies in its direct dependence on the political will of the authority, which passes the proclamation act of protection.

Archaeological heritage has a privileged position in relation to other categories of heritage in the field of protection, because *ex lege* no one may destroy or damage it without specialist monitoring. Scheduled monuments are generally not the objects of desire for investors, units of archaeological heritage that are only protected by planning documents are regarded by investor as areas of potential interventions, subject to certain restrictions. This is merely a continuation of the protection regime for the "third class monuments" from the early period of heritage protection in the 1960's, which are still neither intrinsically or spatially defined and so may not even be adequately evaluated. The management of such sites is thus extremely difficult and always at the expense of the site. This may only be remedied by a programme of systematic specialist and custodial evaluation of these heritage units. In other words, the precision of the registered information is of crucial importance for the successful protection of known sites.The sites or registered units present a specific problem and difficulty, because they are not all included in the current spatial planning acts. This means that potential developers do not in principle have direct access to information about the existence of sites in areas under consideration. The only possible access routes for the supply of this information to developers are:

- A proposal by the Ministry of Culture that the spatial planning act in question be amended to include this information,
- Mandatory revision of the area covered by the spatial planning act in the Heritage Register, accessible on http://rkd.situla.org/ or on the interactive map, accessible on http://giskd.situla.org/.

The management of so-far unregistered sites has always been particularly problematic. Proceeding from the Malta Convention and the principles of preventative archaeology, the new Act for the Protection of Cultural Heritage (UL 16/2008) has introduced the institution of the advance assessment of the archaeological potential of all areas that are the subject of developmental interests in planning documents as an obligation of the state.

Integrated conservation

The comprehension of heritage today naturally exceeds the bounds of the consideration of individual objects and artefacts, which are recognised by the component disciplines (archaeology, landscape architecture, architecture, ethnology, history, art history) and their "point-by-point" protection. Integrated conservation deals with large spatial entities and complexes, synergetic values, which exert an influence in the wider area and in various fields.

Some years ago the situation in Slovenia was quite optimistic:

The European Landscape Convention (UL 19/2003) was ratified, creating a unique framework for the formation of spatial policy, which could halt the continuing degradation of spatial identity, on the basis of the European Convention for the Protection of Archaeological Heritage (UL 7/1999a), projects at a national level and also partially at other levels successfully employed methods of integrated protection of archaeological heritage (preventative archaeology methods, reconciling the demands for the protection of archaeological remains with those of the spatial planning, securing finance, inclusion in environmental impact assessment). The passing of the Spatial Planning Act (UL 110/2002) laid the foundations for sustainable spatial development. The Spatial Development Strategy of Slovenia (UL 76/2004) and the Spatial Order of Slovenia (UL 122/2004) were passed as general documents

for the direction of spatial development in the country and as a basis for the reconciliation of sector politics. The local authorities began to prepare a new series of spatial planning documents, which were derived from analyses of spatial development opportunities of individual activities and environmental vulnerability study. These specifically emphasised that private interest must not prejudice the public interest and that spatial management must contribute to the creation of a clearly recognisable spatial order. The Register of Immovable Cultural Heritage was established whose organisation and applicability received their first praise from the ranks of spatial planners themselves. Changes to the Act for the Protection of Cultural Heritage were foretold, which would better define the legal status of heritage, integrated conservation and the possibilities of funding.

Unfortunately things have moved in a different direction. The support for the recognised facts and their importance for integrated conservation did not surpass traditional "point-by-point" protection. The service began to turn in the direction of integrated conservation, but a number of problems remained unsolved.

The separate recognition and evaluation of units by the component disciplines for the same heritage unit or monument. The whole was thus divided into segments, which resulted in the key questions in protection were left open: what was the protected whole, why and how is it protected, what is the relationship between the protected whole and the environment and society? The institutional and constitutional disorder of the field of spatial protection of immovable heritage within the Service leads to unintelligible and inadequate argumentation, consequently leading to the disorganized and unsuccessful functioning of the Service and its inclusion of recognizable values in spatial and other development plans, the inconsistent execution of the consequences of legal status, enforcement on the basis of the registration of heritage (the definition of detailed protection regimes and their inclusion in the spatial planning process, environmental protection – environmental impact assessment, nature conservancy and other developmental plans).

New changes in the planning legislation (UL 33/2007) cut into this sensitive developmental period. These confused not only the administrative authorities, but also in the context of this unregulated situation, in combination with the transition of Slovenian society and intensified support for ownership rights, opened the gates widely to the interests of developers. The interests of development form the point of departure for the preparation of planning acts by local authorities. Demands for the accelerated resolution of ownership and land register affairs form an intrinsic part of this process. The relationship to the inclusion of cultural heritage in planning has thus become increasingly hostile, because the consideration of cultural values are linked exclusively to the units, which have been scheduled as cultural monuments, and not to the entire fund of cultural heritage. There is no guardian for the protection of general architectural and landscape characteristics. Part of the guardianship for these has been undertaken by the protection sphere of activity, which further burdens its work; above all as in the absence of mechanisms and measures the effects are hardly noticeable. The passing of the new Spatial Planning Act (UL 33/2007) has now more than ever before given a platform and support for sector planning and private interest groups in preference to integrated planning and the public interest. This narrows the area of planning simply to the area of settlement and so retreats from the degree of quality in spatial management, which has already been achieved.

Conclusion

In the current situation, consideration of integrated and holistic heritage conservation, as well as the place of archaeological heritage within it, leads to the conclusion that the tendency in Slovenia at the moment is in the opposite direction. It may be concluded that archaeological sites or remains are otherwise suitably protected *ex lege,* but that the poor quality of data and extremely unsuitable number of registered sites in fact leads to the accelerated destruction of archaeological remains. It is thus necessary to seriously consider a unified strategy, similar to the well-known MPP (Monument Protection Program by English Heritage) that would create a research climate for an evaluation and increase in the number of archaeological sites, which would more closely reflect their actual chronological and spatial presence. The new Act for the Protection of Cultural Heritage permits this type of direction and even supports it to the extent that, in the given situation, archaeological sites may even become the foundation and core for the integrated conservation of the landscapes associated with them.

Integrated and holistic heritage conservation may only exclusively be achieved by a suitable change in the existing practice of protection, which is defined at the moment by considerations that are divided between the so-called basic disciplines (archaeology, history of art, architecture, ethnology, landscape architecture, history, etc). It is also defined at the present on a functional level by basic units of organization, municipalities, which were formerly founders of the dispersed Service network. The heritage protection service is now centralized in its entirety and directly dependant on the State (something that is still not fully appreciated in the service), which means that integrated protection can only be realized through a unified specialist approach to a holistic project for individual larger and smaller complexes throughout the entire territory of the state. The modus operandi and internal organization of the ZVKDS will have to adapt to this new system, which is a problem because the continuation of its regional fragmentation is a reflection of its failure to come to terms with the new reality of the collapse of the system of self-government and the urgent need for more effective, much more articulated protection of the public interest in the context of more or less open Neo-liberalism in Slovenia.

phil.mason@zvkds.si

References

ANSI 1975: Arh*eološka najdišča Slovenije (Archaeological Sites of Slovenia),* Ljubljana.

Djurić, B. 2007: Preventive archaeology and archaeological Service in Slovenia, in: Bozóki-Ernyey, K. (ed.): *European Preventive Archaeology. Papers of the EPAC Meeting, Vilnius 2004,* Budapest 2007, 181-6.

Dular, J., Tecco Hvala, S. 2002: *Standardizacija podatkov za nepremično arheološkom dediščino* (V50353-00), Ljubljana, (http://arkas.zrc-sazu.si/).

Klemenc, J., Saria, B. 1936: *Archäologische Karte von Jugoslavien. Blatt Ptuj,* Zagreb.

Mikl Curk, I. 1969: Predlog meril spomeniških redov za arheološke spomenike (Proposition de mesures pour les catégories de monuments archéologiques). *Varstvo spomenikov* 12, 9-11.

Mikl Curk, I. 1970: Nekaj pojmov in smernic iz varstva arheoloških spomenikov (Quelques notions et lignes directrices de la protection des monuments archéologiques). *Varstvo spomenikov* 15, 15-7.

Mikl Curk, I. 1981: Teorija varstva arheoloških spomenikov v naši praksi (Theory of conservation of archaeological monuments in our practice). *Varstvo spomenikov* 23, 81-94.

Mikl Curk, I. 1987: Kako do podatkov za varstvo kulturne dediščine (The manner of obtaining data important for the preservation of cultural patrimony). *Varstvo spomenikov* 29, 21-5.

Pahič, S. 1962: Arheološka topografija Slovenije (Archaeological topography of Slovenia). *Argo* 1/4, 93-120.

Petru, P. 1962: Evidenca najdišč, dragocen vir za reševanje arheološke problematike (Evidence des excavations – source précieuse pour la protection des monuments archéologiques). *Varstvo spomenikov* 8, 59-73.

Petru, P. 1968-9: Izhodišča varovanja nepremičnih arheoloških spomenikov in regionalni plan Slovenije (Points de depart de la conservation de monuments archéologiques immeubles et le plan regional de la Slovénie). *Varstvo spomenikov* 13-14, 9-16.

Radics, P. 1862: *Archaeologische Karte von Krain,* Laibach.

Saria, B. 1939: *Archäologische Karte von Jugoslavien. Blatt Rogatec,* Zagreb.

Recommendation 1995: Recommendation No. R(95)3 of the Commitee of Ministers to Member States on Co-ordinating Documentation Methods and Systems Related to Historic Buildings and Monuments of Architectural Heritage, Council of Europe.

UL 23/1948: Zakon o varstvu kulturnih spomenikov in prirodnih znamenitosti v Ljudski Republiki Sloveniji (Protection of cultural monuments and sites of natural interest in the People's Republic of Slovenia act). *Uradni list LRS (Official Gazette of the PRS)* 23.

UL 22/1958: Zakon o varstvu kulturnih spomenikov in prirodnih znamenitosti v Ljudski Republiki Sloveniji (Protection of cultural monuments and sites of natural interest in the People's Republic of Slovenia act). *Uradni list LRS (Official Gazette of the PRS)* 22.

UL 26/1961: Zakon o varstvu kulturnih spomenikov v LR Sloveniji (Protection of cultural monuments in the People's Republic of Slovenia act). *Uradni list LRS (Official Gazette of the PRS)* 26.

UL 29/1962: Pravilnik registraciji kulturnih spomenikov v LR Sloveniji (Regulation for the registration of cultural monuments in the People's Republic of Slovenia). *Uradni list LRS (Official Gazette of the PRS)* 29.

UL 13/1967: Regionalni prostorski plan SR Slovenije (Regional spatial plan of the Socialist Republic of Slovenia). *Uradni list SRS (Official Gazette of the SRS)* 13.

UL 1/1981: Zakon o naravni in kulturni dediščini (Natural and Cultural Heritage Act). *Uradni list SRS (Official Gazette of the SRS)* 1.

UL 26/1995: Pravilnik o vodenju zbirnega registra kulturne in naravne dediščine (Regulation for the managing of central register of cultural and natural heritage). *Uradni list RS (Official Gazette of the RS)* 26.

UL 7/1999: Zakon o varstvu kulturne dediščine (Cultural Heritage Protection Act). Uradni list RS (Official Gazette of the RS) 7.

UL 7/1999a: Zakon o ratifikaciji Evropske konvencije o varstvu arheološke dediščine (spremenjene) (European Convention on the Protection of the Archaelogical Heritage (Revised). Uradni list RS (Official Gazette of the RS) 7.

UL 25/2002: Pravilnik o vodenju zbirnega registra kulturne in naravne dediščine (Rules on the keeping of the register and joint register of outstanding natural features and cultural monuments). *Uradni list RS (Official Gazette of the RS)* 25.

UL 110/2002: Zakon o urejanju prostora (Spatial Planning Act). *Uradni list RS (Official Gazette of the RS)* 110.

UL 19/2003: Evropska konvencija o krajini (The European Landscape Convention). *Uradni list RS (Official Gazette of the RS)* 19.

UL 76/2004: Strategija prostorskega razvoja Slovenije (The Spatial Development Strategy of Slovenia), *Uradni list RS (Official Gazette of the RS)* 76.

UL 122/2004: Prostorski red Slovenije (Spatial Order of Slovenia), *Uradni list RS (Official Gazette of the RS)* 122, 2004.

UL 33/2007: Zakon o prostorskem načrtovanju (Spatial planning Act). *Uradni list RS (Official Gazette of the RS)* 33.

UL 105/2007: Odločba o odpravi Odloka o spremembah in dopolnitvah Odloka o razglasitvi nepremičnih kulturnih spomenikov na območju Občine Gornja Radgona, Odločba US, Številka: U-I-318/06-13. *Uradni list RS (Official Gazette of the RS)* 105.

UL 16/2008: Zakon o varstvu kulturne dediščine (Cultural Heritage Protection Act). *Uradni list RS (Official Gazette of the RS)* 16.

Vestnik 1962: *Vestnik zavoda za spomeniško varstvo LRS* 1, 18-27.

12 | Protection of archaeological monuments in the Republic of Latvia

Sandra Zirne

An early attempt to record the cultural heritage of Latvia dates to the reign of the Swedish king Gustav II Adolf (1611-1632), when the Swedish antiquarian Martin Asehaneus collected gravestone inscriptions and described church interiors and furnishings in the Vidzeme region. The first half of the 19th century saw the emergence of a more general interest in the cultural heritage of Latvia with the establishment of several societies devoted to the study of ancient monuments and art. State involvement in cultural heritage matters dates to the period of the Republic of Latvia (1918-1940) when, in 1923, a special state institution, the Board of Monuments, was established. Up to the Soviet occupation in 1940, 1,454 monuments had been placed under state protection. After the Second World War, responsibility for different aspects of cultural heritage lay with various constituent bodies of the Council of Ministers and the Ministry of Culture of the Republic of Latvia, as well as institutions under their control.

Cultural heritage is a testimony to mental activities of mankind having two aspects- material and intangible. Cultural heritage is a manifestation of human spirit and scale of values embraced by the meaning of life. Cultural monuments form a constituent part of cultural and historical heritage and are most commonly encountered as cultural and historical landscapes and individual territories, city centres (ancient burial sites, cemeteries, parks, sites of historical events, sites of activity of prominent persons), as well as individual building complexes and separate buildings, pieces of art, equipments and items having historical, scientific, artistic or any other form of cultural value. Today, the protection of cultural monuments in the Republic of Latvia is guaranteed by the State. The system of legislation and normative acts governing the preservation of cultural heritage in the state consists of the Law on Protection of Cultural Monuments, passed in 1992 (amendments 1993, 1995), together with the Statutes of the State Inspectorate for Heritage Protection established by the Regulations of the Cabinet of Ministers of the Republic of Latvia, and the Convention Concerning the protection of World Cultural and National Heritage sites. In addition, another 37 laws and normative acts relate to aspects of cultural heritage protection.

There are 8,517 cultural monuments registered in Latvia and 30% (2,495) of these are archaeological monuments. The list of state protected cultural monuments and amendments to the list is subject to the approval of the Minister for Culture. The list is published in *Latvijas Vestnesis* (the Official Journal of the Republic of Latvia). The list records the name of the cultural monument, its type, heritage value group, location, and date.

Cultural objects of value are also included in the list of state protected cultural monuments. In accordance with the Law on Protection of Cultural Monuments *'cultural objects of value which lay claim to inclusion in the list of State protected cultural monuments shall be subject to State registration irrespective of the fact who owns, possesses or utilises such objects of value. State registration of monuments shall encompass assessment and inspection of monuments, determination of the historical, scientific, artistic, architectonic, archaeological, ethnographic or other cultural value thereof, recording and research thereof, and preparation of registration documents'.*

Public administration of cultural heritage (cultural monuments) preservation and use in the Republic of Latvia is regulated by the Cabinet of Ministers and implemented by the State Inspectorate for Heritage Protection, which was founded in 1989. The State Inspectorate for Heritage Protection is responsible for the inventory. It also prepares draft cultural monuments lists and inscription documents and, as well, ensures that research is carried out on cultural monuments. The research materials are stored in the Monument Documentation centre of the State Inspectorate of Heritage Protection.

The archaeological heritage and the principles for its protection and use are subject to the same legislative norms and laws as other kinds of cultural monuments. The archaeological heritage does not have specific legislation for its protection and use, nor does it have its own heritage institutions. It is considered part of cultural heritage, and on this basis a sub-structure of the State Inspectorate of Heritage Protection, the Department of Archaeology and History, deals with the archaeological heritage.

The protected monuments are divided into two sub-groups: monuments of local importance and those of national importance. The division of archaeological monuments described in the regulations on cultural monuments is based on their chronology and character, scientific value etc. Archaeological monuments of national value include: all archaeological sites (hill-forts (fig. 12.1), settlements, lake dwellings, cemeteries etc.) up to and including the 13th century, all medieval castles (fig. 12.2), fortifications and historical centres of towns up to and including the 17th century; pagan cult sites with features of artificial modification or information about finds or an occupation layer; excavated archaeological monuments of great scientific, culture- historical and educational value; sunken ships and their cargo. Archaeological monuments of local importance include: all cemeteries, settlements and village sites of the 14th to 17th centuries etc. Actually, all preserved, known and identified archaeological sites are included in the list of protected monuments. A monument in some cases consist of two or, more seldom, three archaeological sites forming a united complex, for example, a hill-fort and settlement, settlement and cemetery, a medieval cemetery and church site, so the total number of protected archaeological sites is actually higher (approximately 2600).

The procedure for listing archaeological monuments is centralised. Inclusion of an archaeological monument in the list of State protected cultural monuments is based on a survey to determine its monument group (settlement, medieval castle, hill-fort, ancient burial places), its date if it can be determined, and its state of survival. A final decision rests with the cultural monument registration expert committee of the State Inspectorate for Heritage Protection. Monument surveys gather information about finds, oral tradition etc., and depend very much on the activities of the public and particularly of the local people. This may well explain a great difference in the number of different monument types. The typological group of the hillforts are among those kinds of monuments that includes high number of the sites (there are about 500 hillforts under the state protection); these also are one of the most attractive monuments visible in the landscape of Latvia. Cemeteries make up almost a half of all protected monuments. These figures do not, of course, reflect the real situation in the past. Settlements are rather difficult to recognise on the ground because of their low visibility and scarcity of archaeological finds. More reliable methods of settlement survey are required. The process of mapping archaeological monuments is at an early stage. As yet there is no publicly available digital map of all archaeological monuments in Latvia. Every monument which is

included in the List of state protected cultural monuments has a separate set of documentation (containing maps at a scale 1: 10000, 1: 50000, photographs, plan and descriptions dating from the 19th century onwards).

Protective zones have been established around each monument in line with the law in order to provide for its protection. The size of the protective zone depends on the nature and state of survival of the monument. Where such zones are not defined then a protective zone of 100 metres radius is applied to monuments in towns and cities and one of 500 metres radius in the countryside. All activities within these areas have to be co-ordinated with the State Inspectorate for Heritage Protection. The Inspectorate has the right to stop any economic activities close to cultural monument or in their protective zones in cases where legislation on cultural protection is violated and cultural monuments are endangered. In each district and city of national significance the State Inspectorate for Heritage Protection appoints a state inspector for heritage protection. This person is directly subordinate to the Inspectorate and acts in accordance with the official regulations.

In accordance with the law on Territorial Planning of the Republic of Latvia, the principle of sustainable development is taken into account in territorial planning in order to provide the current and future generations with a high-quality environment, balanced economic development, and ensure rational use of natural, human and material

Fig. 12.1: Hill-fort of Tanīskalns in Rauna, Cēsis district. Living house near the hill-fort was built in the last century.

resources, development and preservation of natural and cultural heritage. Territorial plans for each region must include maps showing all state protected archaeological monuments with their protection zones and these must be taken into account in development proposals. Each spatial plan must be acceptable to the State Inspectorate for Heritage Protection.

In the territorial planning process particular attention must be paid to cultural monuments which are seen as adding value to a location or development. Different bodies dealing with cultural heritage and environmental protection issues co-operate both at regional and governmental level. Cultural heritage preservation requirements are taken into account in Environmental Impact Assessments.

The priority for the next few years is to create a digital record (database and maps) of Latvia's archaeological monuments for public use.

sandra.zirne@inbox.lv

Fig. 12.2: Medieval castle in Rauna is situated about 300 m from hill-fort of Tanīsa kalns.
In perspective both places will be protected as complex of archaeological sites. *Photo: J.Urtans*

13 | Safeguarding Russia's archaeological heritage – the current situation and proposed system changes

Irina Saprykina

History of heritage in Russia

The history of archaeological science in Russia already amounts to over 250 years, yet the history of safeguarding the national archaeological heritage is much briefer. Some supervisory archaeological works were conducted in Czarist Russia, for instance, when the monument of Alexander II was being built in the Moscow Kremlin, and during the construction of the first railways in the middle of the 19th century. However, systematic large scale salvage archaeological works were organized in the 1930 due to the start of industrialization and such major projects as the construction of the Volga-Don and Imeni Moskvy canals, the implementation of the GOELRO (electrification) plan, etc.

During this period, the notion of "salvage archaeology" had not yet been formed, but archaeologists "mobilized" themselves to identify, locate and describe archaeological sites within areas scheduled for major construction work. This formed the basis for the compilation of the first archaeological maps of Central Russia. It should be noted that the very first lists of archaeological sites in Russia (covering primarily the hillforts and kurgan cemeteries) appeared as early as the beginning of the 19th century and were compiled by scientists of the German archaeological school who worked at the Russian Academy of Sciences.

Large scale archaeological excavations on territories scheduled for major construction works began in the 1950s, when the country's economy revived after World War II. During that period, and in accordance with the requirements of planned economy, a Gosplan instruction was issued stating the necessity of salvage archaeological excavations which would be financed out of the construction budget. Archaeological expenses were a separate line in the Gosplan cost estimate. The directive method of construction and the decades of de facto monopoly of the Academy of Sciences over salvage investigations allowed them to conduct major work at the Bratsk and Krasnoyarsk hydroelectric power stations, as well as on other major construction sites, covered by the five-year plans.

During that period, the structure of salvage archaeology had not been finalized yet, but the safeguarding of historical and cultural heritage was taken up by the All-Union Society for Protecting Cultural and Historical Sites (VOOPiK), a public organization. The VOOPiK was not specifically oriented towards safeguarding archaeological heritage as such, yet it organized a movement for regional studies, which permitted the identification of thousands of archaeological sites, thus providing for certification and inventory of those in the 1970s and 80s.

The Current situation

Starting with the late 1990s, which also saw another period of economic growth in the country, preservation of archaeological heritage in Russia comprises many target areas, including: monitoring the current state of archaeological sites, predicting the possible discovery of an archaeological site on the basis of the analysis of various factors, locating archaeological sites and providing for their state registration, elaborating methods for preservation of archaeological sites at the design stage for land use projects, and salvage excavations – as exceptional case. The number of sites discovered increased sharply due to the use of varied methods of location, - interpreting the data from aerial photography and geophysical exploration, predictive superimposition of ancient map and archive data over modern geological structure, determining the probability of discovering sites within a given territory as of the results of correlating geographical landscape and morphological data using GIS technologies (and now Glonass system). The use of the above predictive exploration methods permitted the location of over 200 new archaeological sites, dating from the Mesolithic to the Modern period, in Ingushetia in 2004 alone.

For Russia, the safeguarding of archaeological heritage is especially important, since archaeological materials are frequently the only source for the reconstruction of historical processes, which took place here, up to the 15th century. The evolution of the perception of archaeological sites as part of Russia's cultural and national heritage has come quite a long way. At the present time we are witnessing one of the culmination points of that evolution, which has also been contributed to by the fact that the state is gradually transferring its functions related to safeguarding cultural heritage to local authorities.

At present, the system of safeguarding archaeological heritage (as well as historical and cultural heritage as a whole) is organized in the following way. State authorities in constituent entities of the Russian Federation have the power to establish state agencies (Ministries or Committees) for safeguarding heritage sites. These agencies shall be responsible for the state registration of the sites, provide for their preservation and inspect the condition of the sites, take the required measures for their reconstruction, and elaborate and implement target programs for cultural heritage preservation. These agencies also have the authority to add new data to the archaeological site register in accordance with new information received from archaeologists, that is, to create a database of archaeological sites of regional importance. At present, in accordance with *Law ФЗ-73*, an archaeological site in Russia shall be property of the State and subject to State protection starting from the moment of discovery by a professional archaeologist.

Federal agencies for heritage protection are responsible for safeguarding archaeological sites of Federal importance, the first list whereof was issued by Decree of the RSFSR Council of Ministers in 1960 with an amended version issued in 1995; for maintaining the program of recording known archaeological sites (at present, about 50 000 sites have been recorded in Russia, which is compatible with the recorded cultural heritage of such countries as the Czech Republic or Finland), etc. Thus, the functions of the Federal site protection authorities have been minimized in comparison with those of the local authorities.

Listing archaeological sites

In 2008, the system of safeguarding Russia's archaeological heritage will undergo se*rious reorganization.* In accordance with the latest amendments to the applicable Federal Law, state authorities in constituent entities of the Russian Federation empowered to protect cultural heritage sites of regional importance will have the authority to extend state protection to sites of Federal importance. This calls for a unified state register of cultural heritage sites to be transferred to the jurisdiction of local site preservation authorities, for a list of cultural and historical sites that will not be subject to privatization and for a list of cultural heritage sites to remain under the jurisdiction of Federal authorities.

The creation of the lists in question calls for a definition of the process of submitting the lists of archaeological sites by the constituent entities of the Russian Federation to the Ministry of Culture or the Committee on Property ("Rosimuschestvo"), which should confirm the said lists and return them to the RF constituent entities. Heritage protection agencies in constituent entities of the Russian Federation will also be responsible for submitting information about sites of Federal importance, to which their proposals may be added. The final lists for sites of such status are compiled by Federal heritage protection agencies. The main obstacles here are:

- Lack of a normative and legal base for transferring the cultural heritage sites from federal authority to the constituent entities of the RF.
- Lack of a normative and legal base for distinguishing federal, regional and municipal ownership of cultural heritage sites.
- Lack of inventory lists for the "property", etc.

Even coordination of all the above parameters does not mean that a unified state register will be created. This should differ from the currently available lists, in the fact that every site should have a passport compiled to a given standard. So far, the relevant agencies have not yet developed a standard passport for cultural heritage sites, in accordance with which the sites should be included in the unified state register.

In the field this may create a situation, where newly-discovered sites will only be protected by law after inclusion in the state register and drawing up of the relevant documents, which will certainly take time and may have a negative influence on the functioning of the entire structure of salvage archaeology in Russia. If the above situation is to be expected, then archaeologists have to speed up the processing and submission of the relevant documentation on existing archaeological sites that have not yet been registered for state protection to the heritage protection authorities.

As there is currently no federal documentation standard, archaeologists temporarily use earlier data that was contributed to the "Archaeological map of Russia" project.

The project is over 20 years old, having been launched in the middle of the 1980s. Part of the results has been published under the title quoted above. The project involved the mapping of all known archaeological sites, finding their exact location and positioning, the depth and preservation of the occupation deposits, chronological position, etc. The analysis of this data would allow the future definition of the heritage protection object, one of the main parameters for including the site in the unified state register. The project was initiated and is being carried out by the Institute of Archaeology of the Russian Academy of Sciences; work has currently started on an online version of the Archaeological map of Russia, which would be available to archaeologists for the constant updating of the existing database. The Institute has experience in creating a similar database for recording archaeological excavations.

Description of the sites includes the following data: name of the site, its location including the exact geographical markers and GPS indicators, dating, culture, history of investigations, amount of research, depth of the occupation deposit, analysis of archaeological artefacts, state of preservation, evidence of damage, area of the site and its estimated boundaries, analysis of the landscape, the estimated boundaries of the preservation zone. A separate line should cover the current land use in the territory where the site is located, the cadastral number of the site, the responsibilities of the owner of the land plot, concerning the preservation of the cultural heritage site. Yet this particular information that is especially important for the preservation of the site, can only be obtained in the constituent entities of the Russian Federation. The possibility of obtaining it depends on the good will and understanding of the situation on the part of individual representatives of the executive power.

Compilation of such a map initiates large scale archaeological prospecting, concerning both the control of archive data (some of the sites are known from the beginning of the 17th century), and a target search for new archaeological sites situated in the "blank areas", discovered in the course of mapping. The work records both complete and partial losses of sites, destroyed due to natural and anthropogenic impact. A record is made of damage to the visual perception of the site within the landscape, of the lack of development of protection zones of the site that are situated in construction areas and of other violations of archaeological site protection, data which is submitted to heritage protection agencies in constituent entities of the Russian Federation.

Consequently, it is only elaboration of legal mechanisms for the extremely complex system of archaeological site protection, coordination of separate legal acts and articles of law contained in such fundamental documents as the Land Code, Urban Planning Code, Criminal Code, and closer contact between the controlling and heritage protection agencies that can solve the current problems which Russia encounters for the first time in the course of legal practice and activity directed at safeguarding historical heritage.

dolmen200@mail.ru

14 | How is England's Archaeological Heritage Managed?

Roger Bowdler

Abstract: Responsibility for archaeological resource management in England is divided between national and local bodies. Before discussing their roles, however, we must straightaway acknowledge the vital role of the owners of archaeological sites in safeguarding their asset. Without public support for, and engagement in, the process of protecting archaeology, the system will be bypassed and irreplaceable evidence lost.

Archaeological heritage management is undeniably complex. Beginning with government's role, this article will then consider the legislation behind archaeological conservation and then outline the work of the principal national organisation in this field, English Heritage. Every bit as important, however, is the role of local authorities: this is looked at next. To conclude, a discussion of forthcoming proposals for the reform of the heritage protection system is set out. At time of writing (November 2008), the British Government had yet to announce its intentions in this area.

Government Level

The national government's ministry with responsibility for the nation's heritage, as well as tourism and other roles, is the Department for Culture Media and Sport (DCMS). This is headed by a Secretary of State (currently Andy Burnham MP) with overall responsibility for the Ministry, supported by a more junior minister (currently Barbara Follett MP) with direct responsibility for the heritage. Planning matters (including the management of archaeology within the development process) are the responsibility of another large ministry, the department for Communities and Local Government (CLG).

English Heritage

English Heritage (EH) was established as a non-governmental agency in 1984, when it took on the responsibilities formerly exercised by the Environment Ministry and is the government's expert adviser on historic environment matters. Properly called the Historic Buildings and Monuments Commission, it performs a range of tasks. These include opening 400 properties to the public (mainly ruined castles, monasteries and prehistoric sites); giving grants and advice to private owners; advising local authorities on planning matters; carrying out research and publication; advising government on policy and designation matters; and trying to increase public interest in the historic environment. Its budget in 2007-08 was £178.6M, of which £129.45M was provided by the DCMS, EH's sponsor body. The organisation has a London headquarters and eight other regional offices.

English Heritage advises government on designation matters and on consents for Scheduled Monument Consent,

which is required for most works to Scheduled Ancient Monuments, the formal term for protected archaeological sites of all ages. It also advises on Listed Buildings matters, which is currently a very separate process.

England's regional administration is complex. The country is divided into 376 local authorities. These vary from large cities, such as the City of Birmingham, to smaller urban or rural districts, such as the London Borough of Camden or the New Forest District Council. Although the country is divided into nine regions for administrative purposes, these are very different from the historical provinces, cantons, departments or states encountered elsewhere in Europe and lack the autonomy or resourcing of continental regions.

Legislation

Nationally designated archaeological sites are protected as 'Scheduled Ancient Monuments' under the Ancient Monuments and Archaeological Areas Act of 1979. This is the most recent Act devoted to archaeology: the earliest legislation (apart from 16th century royal proclamations, intended to prevent damage to funerary monuments during the Reformation) dates from 1882, when Sir John Lubbock MP obtained notional protection for a 'schedule' of 69 prehistoric sites. The 1913 Ancient Monuments Act introduced the notion of a preservation order, preventing deliberate destruction. Buildings in religious use and in permanent private residential occupation were excluded from scheduling: a situation which remains to this day. By 1931, 139 Ancient Monuments had been scheduled. A separate system of designating buildings was established in the 1947 Town and Country Planning Act; some sites are both listed and scheduled and a result.

The 1979 Act also introduced the idea of Areas of Archaeological Importance, an area designation which has not been subsequently used at any other places than the earliest group of five historic settlements: Canterbury, Chester, Exeter, Hereford and York. There are currently just over 19,700 Scheduled Monuments, which include around 32,000 individual archaeological items (one scheduled site may comprise a number of separate items such as dispersed hut circles, for instance). The majority of these are found in the south-west of the country, and the great majority of all scheduled monuments are rural in location. The issue of urban archaeology is considered below, after a discussion of the formal designation of archaeological sites.

Designation of Monuments

The range of sites and structures that can be scheduled is very wide. It covers prehistoric sites as well as Cold War sites, industrial complexes, modern military sites, and even a stretch of a 1920s motor racing circuit, at Brooklands in Surrey. Perhaps the youngest items to be scheduled are the Cruise Missile bunkers at the former military airbase of Greenham Common in Berkshire, of 1982-86, (the scene of celebrated womens' anti-nuclear missile demonstrations in the 1980s). English Heritage prepares the recommendations, but it is the Secretary of State who decides. Scheduling is discretionary: the Secretary of State can elect not to schedule a site of clear archaeological interest if he chooses to do so (if its national importance is not clear; if there are outstanding planning permissions which render a designation unviable without considerable compensation; or where the site is more effectively managed through other means such as the planning system). This is a very different state of affairs from the protection system for buildings, where designation is mandatory if the test of special interest is passed. This is but one of the confusions in the present heritage protection system.

Scheduling is very selective, and has aimed to identify the best-preserved or most important examples of various classes of monument. As a result, the proportion of designated sites is quite low: hundreds of thousands of identified sites are not designated, but are instead protected through the planning system (largely in urban areas). The selectivity of this approach justifies the levels of close control that scheduling entails: statutory designation is sparingly applied, in the expectation that close management will preserve the site in as unaltered state as possible. Getting owners on side, and explaining just why scheduling is warranted in the public interest, is of critical importance. Archaeological designation has gone to great pains to develop this outreach aspect of our work,

and some of the lessons it has taught us are now being applied to our approach across the asset range.

The Monuments Protection Programme

A survey in 1984 undertaken by the newly formed English Heritage showed that only 2% of the known archaeological sites, then totalling 635,000, were then scheduled. A carefully planned project, the Monuments Protection Programme, was established in 1986 to address this problem of under-representation (Schofield 2000). It sought to increase this percentage to 10% of known sites within ten years. This was ambitious enough: on top of this target (which had to be revised downwards and given a longer time-scale), it was also decided to improve greatly the quality of designation documentation, to base designations on more thorough academic scrutiny, and carry out full site assessments and mapping. Local authority archaeology services contributed to the Monuments Protection Programme by suggesting potential sites which were then investigated by English Heritage staff and consultants. We will consider the changes to designation documentation below, when we address the issue of documentation.

Certain categories of sites received special attention. This has resulted in some important contributions to understanding, such as the *Atlas of rural settlement in England* (Roberts & Wrathmell 2000). For industrial sites, a new approach was established, in which selection took place through four distinct phases, or *steps*, of assessment. *Step reports* were commissioned on a range of industrial types, and very thorough national appraisal undertaken, resulting in a considerable volume of research. Modern military sites too were given special treatment, with a careful programme of archival research and ensuing publication accompanying the selection of key sites for designation.

In both these latter categories, industrial and military, the issue arose of the inevitable overlap with the very different approach to designating buildings: this will be considered in the second section.

Fig. 14.1: Avebury stone circle at the heart of a prehistoric landscape; one of the largest in Europe and in the guardianship of English Heritage.
Photo: English Heritage

Fig. 14.2: Chester Roman Amphitheatre, an elevated view with excavation. *Photo: English Heritage*

The Monuments Protection Programme made slower progress as it turned to more complex categories of archaeological site, and as overall policy shifted away from site-specific designation towards a more strategic approach, the imperative to complete it became less compelling. The process of designation, of course, can never be 'completed'– new appreciation of known sites (through excavation and research) combined with changing views of 'significance' both in the profession and more generally, means that the concept of a 'once and for all' approach to the identification of sites of archaeological significance is inappropriate, and in an age in which different views about significance have to be reconciled not ignored, this 'once and for all' approach becomes even less appropriate. Numerous sites have been identified as potentially possessing 'national importance' but have yet to be designated. In 2004, ministerial consent was granted to suspend the Programme in order to concentrate on work to inform a new system of heritage protection. At this time too, the archaeologists employed on the Programme were incorporated into multi-disciplinary regional teams in the newly-formed Heritage Protection Department of English Heritage, and ceased to concern themselves solely with archaeological sites. We have therefore been engaged on a much more integrated approach towards the appraisal of the historic environment.

The Consequences of Scheduling

Special permission, called Scheduled Monument Consent, must be obtained if an owner wishes to demolish, destroy, damage, remove, repair, alter, add to, floor or tip material onto a Scheduled Monument. English Heritage advises the Secretary of State on all such applications, and it remains the case that it is still central government which issues this consent. Less than a thousand such consents were granted last year. Even like-for-like repairs, it will be noted, require consent. Some categories of activities are covered by 'class consents' which remove the need for Scheduled Monument Consent application: these include agricultural activity on regularly cultivated land; repairs needed by health and safety reasons; repairs to English Heritage's's own properties; and where a management agreement has been negotiated. All of these class consents are, however, narrowly specified and do not take the place of Scheduled Monument Consent as outlined above. For example, the class consent related to agricultural use one only covers land which is regularly cultivated and has been cultivated in the 10years prior to legislation being applied – even than cultivation is only permissible to a depth of 30cm. Metal-detecting on a scheduled site is not permitted without express consent.

Some grant assistance to owners is available, although applicants are increasingly directed towards the Heritage Lottery Fund for funds as English Heritage strives to maintain its operations with relatively static levels of government funding. Advice on management and conservation is available from Ancient Monuments Inspectors, based in each of the nine English Heritage regional offices. Field Monument Wardens, employed by English Heritage, regularly visit scheduled sites to advise on management and check on condition.

Protecting Archaeology in the Planning Process: PPG 16

How is urban archaeology protected, if much of it is not formally designated? We have seen that a low percentage of archaeological sites enjoy formal protection, and that scheduled monuments are preponderantly located in rural locations. Development pressure is greatest in cities and towns, and this pressure continues to be very intense in many parts of England. This pressure is managed through an important government circular, which constitutes the basis of archaeological development-led management in England: *Planning Policy Guidance: Archaeology and Planning*, or PPG 16, issued in 1990 and still current.

To put it mildly, monumentalising vibrant cities is an unrealistic aspiration. Change is inevitable; modern construction demands deep ground works; finance and time constraints on developers are intense. 'The use of scheduling, which imposes strict controls with the underlying aim of putting physical preservation before adaptation, re-use or change, is therefore not always appropriate in the urban context' (Scofield 2000, 9). This is something of an understatement.

Fig. 14.3: St Augustine's Abbey was founded shortly after AD 597 it is part of the Canterbury World Heritage Site. *Photo: English Heritage*

A few town centres have been extensively scheduled, such as at Cirencester, Gloucestershire (the Roman town of *Corinium Dobunnorum*), but we have an inconsistent tally of larger urban schedulings; London, for instance, only has a very limited number of scheduled sites, covering very specific locations, such as the Guildhall Ampitheatre, a bath house site and the city wall. As mentioned earlier, a select group of historic settlements were named in the 1979 Ancient Monuments Act as *Areas of Archaeological Importance*: namely Canterbury, Chester, Exeter, Hereford and York. This blanket designation was not taken further, however, and no other historic town has joined this initial list. Some local planning authorities have introduced the idea of the Archaeological Priority Area, which places extra conditions on development within the designated area.

Thanks, however, to skilful positioning and an acknowledgement of the issues facing each side of the table, developers and archaeologists working in the planning system have reached a system of mutual understanding. Pre-application assessment of archaeological potential is now standard good practice and in general is the case although the procedures are only based on government guidance (Planning Policy Guidance 16 – PPG16), issued in 1990 by the Department of the Environment, and there is no statutory basis for this; mitigation of the impact on deposits is now an accepted part of planning; proper levels of recording and post-excavation investigation are now widespread. The role of professional groups such as the Association of Local Government Archaeology Officers on the management side and the now renamed Institute for Archaeology (formerly the Institute of Field Archaeologists) across the profession helps to ensure consistency and adherence to appropriate standards.

PPG 16 is undergoing revision, but it is to be hoped that its wise approach to issues of archaeological potential remains in place during the process of updating. Another factor which requires comment is the amount of energy and money which has gone into urban characterisation. English Heritage has, in partnership with local planning authorities, devoted considerable effort towards urban characterisation and the computer-based mapping of archaeological development and potential. Knowing what is of likely significance importance is of crucial importance for owners, developers and managers alike. Designation alone cannot communicate this sensitivity.

What Works Well and What Works Less Well?

The work carried out in the context of PPG16 (mitigating development) has seen a massive increase in the scale of and spending on archaeological field work with important consequences for the structure of professional archaeology in the country. At the same time there has been a very positive impact on the development of shared understanding about, and public interest in the past, raising the profile and providing opportunities for enhancing a sense of place through public engagement with archaeological mitigation schemes (work carried out by the Museum of London Archaeological Service in the capital is particularly noteworthy in this respect). Public engagement is regarded as a very important means of securing better care for archaeological sites: the Council for British Archaeology, the leading amenity group and of high standing, has worked hard in this regard, as has English Heritage.

Fig. 14.4: Kirby Hall, Northamptonshire; is one of England's greatest Elizabethan and 17th Century houses. *Photo: English Heritage*

Unfortunately some aspects of the system work less well. PPG16 is only guidance and is therefore imperfect and there can be failures of the system where a developer is obstructive or unsympathetic. Limited resourcing for local authorities makes the matters of enforcement and compliance very challenging to achieve. It does not offer protection against permitted works for the vast majority of archaeological sites in the rural environment, most of which are not subject to the planning regime which would bring them into the remit of PPG16. There are also some concerns expressed about the quality of some of the work carried out under PPG16 and inadequate procedures for depositing the results of this work in a proper, publicly accessible archive. We need to acknowledge too that our designation basis is inconsistent and incomplete, and that distinctions have developed between archaeology and buildings in terms of their statutory protection and management.

To What Extent are Designated Sites Made Available to the Public?

This question demands consideration on several levels. We shall first consider the matter of public access to designated sites and the associated issue of metal-detecting. Making sites available also includes intellectual access to sites: we will then look at the curation of information, and at how designation is seeking to encourage the wider understanding of significance of archaeological sites in order to build appreciation and care for these places.

Over 19,000 archaeological sites enjoy statutory protection, but only a small minority are open to the public. Scheduling does not bring with it any obligation for the owner to allow public access to the site. Many of the most renowned sites have long been open to the public. English Heritage opens some 400 sites to the public and the great majority of these are of an archaeological character: castles, ruined abbeys and houses. These sites came into the care of central Government, and were transferred into the care of English Heritage on the latter's establishment in 1984. Examples of English Heritage 'guardianship' sites include the Neolithic settlement at Chysauster, St Augustine's Monastery in Canterbury (part of the World Heritage Site, which includes the cathedral too), and the roofless Renaissance house, Kirby Hall, in Northamptonshire. English Heritage takes its duty of educating and attracting the public very seriously: if visitors enjoy their visits, they will develop an interest and build their awareness of the historic environment all around them. These sites are show-cases for demonstrating best approaches to conservation management. English Heritage also

supports Heritage Open days, encouraging access to a wide variety of sites in private ownership and generally raising public awareness of their heritage.

The National Trust, a private charity founded in 1895 with a membership of 3.6 [2.7] million which has become a highly influential body, also manages a considerable number of archaeological sites including the World Heritage Site of Neolithic Avebury. Having acquired very considerable areas of natural beauty, it also manages many monuments in the landscape, both scheduled and unscheduled. As a promoter of best practice, like English Heritage (and its Scottish and Welsh equivalent: Historic Scotland and CADW respectively), the National Trust develops new methods of management, presentation and interpretation.

The great majority of sites lie on private land. Britain's official cartographic arm, the Ordnance Survey, has played a leading role in identifying and recording earthworks. From the 1920s onwards, under the aegis of OGS Crawford, aerial photography greatly expanded the number of identified sites and the Ordnance Survey has continued to update its map coverage. Its fieldwork recording function has subsequently been devolved to the Royal Commission on the Historical Monuments for England (or RCHME), since 1999 a part of English Heritage.

Not all of the archaeological sites marked on maps are designated by any means. Public footpaths enable access to large areas of privately owned land, but there continues to be much sensitivity around the issue of public access. Agricultural land is covered by the 'Country Code', a voluntary set of guidelines for visitors which seeks to minimise damage and disturbance to crops and flocks. The rights of the private owner are affected by scheduling and other heritage designations when it comes to ground disturbance and development, but in terms of public access, designation does not bring a requirement to allow the public to have access. Should public money be spent on the conservation of a site or building, however, issues of public access must be addressed.

Sensitivity over public access has intensified with the rise of metal-detecting. This has become a popular activity and has led to some of the most significant discoveries of artefacts of recent decades. Through considerate negotiation with, and behaviour towards, land-owners, the great majority of metal-detectorists have been able to carry out their investigations without trouble.
The Portable Antiquities Scheme, established in 1997, has built up more positive relationships between metal-detectorists and archaeologists, and through the recording of enormous numbers of objects discovered by metal detectorists made a most significant contribution to our understanding of the past. Sometimes the identification of a site of considerable archaeological potential in terms of recoverable items—an Anglo-Saxon cemetery, for instance- leads to a dilemma for the designator and heritage manager: does highlighting such a site through inclusion on the Sites and Monuments Record, and pinpointing its precise location, increase the vulnerability

Fig. 14.5: Great Western railway works, Swindon. Now also the site of the National Monuments Records. *Photo: English Heritage*

of such sites to damage resulting from illegal activities ('black' archaeology)?

Making sites available to the public does not solely refer to free access to the site in question. Intellectual access too is relevant as well. To begin with, designation was purely and simply an identifier: a site was named, marked on the map, and as duly scheduled. More recently, conservation thinking has laid much greater emphasis on communicating understanding. At the heart of English Heritage's philosophy is the 'cycle of understanding': a cycle of understanding, valuing, caring and enjoying, in which communicating why the historic environment matters is of fundamental importance. From this it follows that designation has an extra responsibility. It cannot simply identify and name: it must explain as well. English Heritage's Heritage Gateway a key example of such accessibility – as is the work done by a variety of organisations to create 'virtual' tours of key sites.

Explanation takes place on numerous levels. Public involvement lies at the heart of the modern archaeological agenda, a development synonymous with the highly effective work of the Council for British Archaeology. Communicating new interpretations and discoveries beyond the profession is regarded as a core responsibility, and the CBA's magazine British Archaeology, edited by committed communicator Mike Pitts, embodies this media-alertness. Alongside media and education issues (the latter a huge topic which cannot be explored here), those of information holding and sharing need to be addressed too. This takes place at national and local government levels.

English Heritage, as the Government's principal adviser on the historic environment, has a lead role in co-ordinating information on archaeological sites, both designated and undesignated. Through its National Monuments Record, based in the historic Great Western Railway works in Swindon, Wiltshire, it makes available site records, aerial photographs, and survey reports, all of which can be accessed via AMIE (this stands for Archives and Monuments Information, England). This is curated nationally, and sits alongside the local repositories of information

which are maintained –or should be maintained- by local planning authorities at local government level.

The critically important local level of information holding is provided by the Historic Environment Records (HERs) formerly known as Sites and Monuments Records. Owing to the complexity of local government organisation in England, these HER's operate at different levels. In some cases (the county of Cornwall, for instance) they cover the larger units of local government and are increasingly integrated with country repositories of historical archives. Separate protection systems for buildings and archaeology encouraged the divergence of systems for holding the relevant information: this challenge has been addressed in the previous section, but it requires re-statement here. The huge increase in archaeological evaluation since the publication of Planning Policy Guidance Note 16, allied to the high levels of urban redevelopment which have taken place in England from this time onwards, has led to a huge volume of material being deposited with SMRs. It is rare in England to find the continental model of local museums playing a leading role in environmental management: there are exceptions, such as the Passmore Edwards Museum in East London, but generally museums concentrate on the curation, presentation and explanation of objects.

English Heritage advises the Secretary of State for Culture Media and Sport on archaeological designations, and prepares the designation documentation for formal approval by the Secretary of State. The nature of the documentation has been undergoing change in recent years. Older designations (of which there are still a very high number) contained very little explanatory material on the sites in question. Their aim was to identify the area being protected; interpretation was minimal, and communication of significance was left to infrequent on-site encounters between Ancient Monument Inspectors and owners. Things have changed considerably in recent years, in terms of our responsibility to communicate significance. Stating something is significant and expecting owners to behave accordingly is seen as high-handed. Restriction on the enjoyment of private property rights needs to be justified by explanation of importance, and the emergence of a higher level of public interest.

Modern designation entries include descriptions of the site in question; an assessment of their claims to national importance; and a contextual section which places the site in terms of its overall class, and explains the development of this category of site. Precise mapping is important, marking the 'constraint area' or the site boundary and small extra margin, within which Scheduled Monument Consent applies and must be sought. These descriptions have become fuller than the scheduling entries of old, with an inevitable impact on rates of productivity. We are aware of the importance of communicating better with owners, however, and are revising our older scheduling entries in order to share an appreciation of the importance and fragility of the scheduled archaeological sites.

Fig. 14.6: RAF Greenham Common, part of the early 1980s cruise missile shelter complex. Similar facilities were also built in Belgium, Germany, the Netherlands and Italy. The site is Scheduled. Photo: English Heritage

A similar process can be observed in the other designation regimes. List descriptions for buildings used to be terse, and merely sought to ensure that the right building was identified. Now that less familiar buildings are being designated, there is a greater need for explanation about the nature of significance. This is undertaken partly to share understanding with the owner, and partly to assist Local Planning Authorities and English Heritage staff in reaching decisions concerning the management of change. If alteration is proposed that does not affect the special interest or character of a listed building, there is a presumption to allow this.

Below-ground archaeology requires an extra consideration: that of archaeological potential. While not all buildings are as understood as is sometimes thought, there is no doubt that an extra level of care is needed in considering potentially damaging works in areas with demonstrable likelihood of yielding archaeological evidence. The places we do not yet understand can have equal importance as those we have long recognised as of national importance.

What is the Greatest Challenge in the next Five Years?

The greatest challenge we face over the next five years is to create an integrated system of heritage protection. The age-old divides between historic buildings and archaeology are no longer helpful in an age which sees the connections, rather than the divisions, between these twin elements of the historic environment, and the public has become confused by the complicated arrangements which have arisen over the course of over 120 years of heritage legislation. Government has clearly expressed its view: a new approach is required to the identification and management of the historic environment. Practitioners and professionals may be adept at navigating their way around the legislation, but for ordinary citizens – the category which includes the largest number by far of owners of designated sites and structures – the system is complex and off-putting. Proposed legislation to put this to rights is currently being developed, and we are awaiting the enactment of the Heritage Protection Bill hopefully during the life-time of the present government. As this is a parliamentary process, led by government, English Heritage awaits the call from the DCMS to take forward these changes.

The overview we have given above will make clear the intricacy of existing arrangements. Summarising such

arrangements is not an easy task: if the reader remains confused by aspects of the situation, this is not to be wondered at.

Let us start to set out the proposed way forward. The Heritage Protection Review was initiated by Government: the Department for Culture Media and Sport published a report named *A Force for our Future* in 2002; this was a response to a major English Heritage publication named *The Power of Place* (2001) which proposed a new emphasis for conservation: the celebration and promotion of the historic environment as a force for social and economic cohesion and advancement. In order to meet this challenge, assessment of the fitness for purpose of inherited approaches was necessary. Did people understand existing systems? Were we doing a good job in terms of promoting interest in the historic environment? Did decision-makers take it into account when planning change? Was a modern approach to heritage management possible with existing tools? In 2003 the Heritage Protection Review got underway properly.

The principal tenets of the Heritage Protection review have been to increase openness; simplify the system; apply flexibility where appropriate; and maintain the rigour of existing approaches. The challenge has been to modernise and simplify, while maintaining levels of protection.

Revising the Designation Basis

A clear challenge is the establishment of an enhanced designation basis for heritage management. To re-write all 400,000 designation entries is unrealistic. They will be transferred over to the proposed Register in their present form, and re-written according to need and to a prioritised programme. Unifying designations enables the connections and reinforcements between sites and buildings and landscapes to be perceived so much better. Historic places are amalgamations of all these elements and need to be treated together. Uniting the relevant designations is thus an important start in bringing about this shift in attitude. As we have seen, the number of designated archaeological sites compared with the total of known archaeological sites is dramatically small: keeping up with new discoveries, and reflecting significance through designation, is one of our greatest challenges.

Access to Information: Historic Environment Records

Much emphasis has been placed above on the role of understanding. Heritage Protection Reform addresses this aspect by setting great store on improving how we curate information. The Historic Environment Records, it is proposed, must develop into integrated, cross-asset tools. Highly significantly, government proposes that all Local Planning Authorities must have access to such services, that they should not be seen as a desirable resource to be consulted if possible, but must be far more integrated into the decision-making process. Historic Environment

Fig. 14.7: RAF Neatishead. An early 1960s Type 84 radar, this is the last surviving large Cold War era radar in the United Kingdom and was used to monitor incursions by Warsaw Pact aircraft and to co-ordinate the response. This site is Scheduled.
Photo: English Heritage

Records has their origin as Archaeological Sites and Monuments Records and have acted as depositories for archaeological records, and since the advent of PPG16 in 1991, for excavation reports. Many Historic Environment Records now include buildings and are becoming wider in their scope (including for example landscape characterisation To become relevant for the spectrum of the whole historic environment, the Historic Environment Records will need to continue this trajectory and to pay even more attention to above-ground structures and landscapes, and present the continuum of human activity to those seeking to understand the places in which they live. Making the maintenance of a Historic Environment Records obligatory is seen by some as one of the major achievements of the Heritage Protection Bill. It will certainly be a considerable challenge to expand them, and to attain the goal of true integration across the board: if a medium-term view is taken for the attainment of this goal, the prospects for delivery are more favourable.

New Designation Approaches

A major conceptual challenge is the alignment of very different approaches to designation. As we have already seen, buildings and archaeological sites have been treated very differently. Through Heritage Protection Reform, two very different approaches are coming together. With buildings, we have pursued a non-discretionary approach which has sought to identify all buildings and structures of special interest for careful treatment in the planning process. Scheduling, as we have also seen, has been highly selective in order to apply a close level of control over the few selected sites deemed most suitable for designation, and has concentrated in recent years on rural sites to the exclusion of urban archaeology. Developing an integrated approach which unites the comprehensive nature of buildings designation with the analytical rigour of scheduling is another major challenge. We also need to develop ways of designating sites of great prehistoric importance which do not have definable structures (a pre-requisite for scheduling): such sites of early human activity as Boxgrove, West Sussex, clearly merit protection and the greatest care in management, but currently fall outside the realm of statutory designation. Rectifying this anomaly is one of the aspirations of the current reform programme.

Coastal and Marine Archaeology

An undeniable challenge which we are beginning to face is posed by marine factors. These can be divided into two broad categories: first, a growing awareness of the marine resource, and a growing stress on its continuity with terrestrial archaeology; and second, the realisation that climate change is likely to impact particularly directly on coastal sites. We still have much to do in terms of terrestrial designation, and we are far from having finished our work on the terra firma. There exists a growing awareness of the importance of the marine archaeological resource, both in terms of submerged landscapes and wrecks, combined with the realisation that economic exploitation of the sea (through deep-sea fishing and aggregates extraction, as well as the increase in wind farms) bed requires a clearer flagging of archaeological sensitivity. This area is a very important challenge for Britain, both as an island nation and as a member of the European Union.

Partnership and Management

As an alternative to regulatory, reactive approaches, greater emphasis is placed on partnership and trust. For many years, management agreements have been brokered as ways of avoiding the needless elements of control through Scheduled Monument Consent: pre-agreed works, with suitable monitoring arrangements, have been put in place where appropriate, and where the owners' interests can be reconciled with the protection of the archaeological resource. This approach is to be rolled out to standing buildings and sites too, in order that heritage management can become less a matter of tight regulation and reactive control, and more a shared approach to positive management: one based on trust, and a shared appreciation of the asset and of the owner's aspirations for their site.

Conclusion

England has, since 1882, evolved a complex system of heritage protection over archaeological matters. Compared with some other countries, it was quite late in establishing a system of state protection for antiquities, and the designation of known sites of archaeological importance is very incomplete. Management of the archaeological resource therefore depends as much on protection through policy, as on protection as a consequence of statutory designation and specific consents. Heritage Protection Reform will bring greater clarity for owners and managers in this regard. It will also end the unhelpful and separatist distinction between archaeological sites, landscapes and buildings. As set out above, management of the archaeological resource is a shared responsibility between national and local government. Development pressure; increasing concerns about marine and coastal archaeology; continuing damage to archaeology through ploughing: these are just some of the challenges which England faces.

We look forward to the next epoch of heritage protection in seeking to address them.

Roger.Bowdler@english-heritage.org.uk

References

Roberts, B. & Wrathmell, S. 2000: An *Atlas of rural settlement in England* (English Heritage 2000).

Schofield J, ed., *MPP 2000. A review of the Monuments Protection Programme, 1986-2000* (English Heritage 2000).

15 | A Centrally Managed GIS System for Protection of Romanian Archaeological Sites and Historic Monuments

Dana Mihai and Mircea Angelescu

Abstract: The Romanian Archaeological Sites and Historic Monuments Inventory Application - eGISpat, a centrally managed GIS system, was designed to provide the functionality to maintain and advance analysis of the geospatial and parametric data, and to produce maps and reports using a nationwide archaeological and historic monuments geodatabase, known as the List of Historic Monuments (LHM). This centrally managed web application was designed and built by ESRI Romania and the National Institute for Historic Monuments of the Ministry of Culture and Religious Affairs. The purpose of eGISpat is to facilitate participation in and support of integrated resource planning by regional branches at the district ('judet') and local government level, and the maintenance of data on the historical record of work on archaeological and historic monuments performed in the districts. eGISpat also covers the historic centre of Bucharest, including archaeological sites (excavated from 1950 -2005) and historic monuments, as well as the digital map, scale 1 2.000, a satellite image and the historical records. All departmental staff are able to work in a web integrated GIS environment and perform business processes for the rapid entry, viewing and dissemination of information. The National Institute for Historic Monuments continues to educate the public and promote preservation for future generations.

Introduction

Archaeology and geography have much in common. Like geographers, archaeologists study places. They collect data in the field and map their findings on many different scales, from a square metre of an archaeological dig to regions covering half a continent. Since the discipline's beginnings in the nineteenth century, when researchers sketched artefacts and landscapes in pencil and watercolour, archaeologists have always been interested in recording and analyzing this information. Over the last decade, GIS and GPS technology has been used to map sites with new precision and to predict where undiscovered sites of archaeological interest might lie.

The challenge

For over four years now, the National Institute for Historic Monuments (INMI) of the Ministry of Culture and Religious Affairs has been in the process of compiling and maintaining a database of 23, 624 archaeological sites known as the official 'List of Historic Monuments' (LHM 2004). In 2005, INMI decided to replace an existing tabular-only system stored in the Microsoft Access application with an advanced server-based application based on GIS technology. The lack of a national information system on the country's cultural heritage was the main argument for implementing a centrally managed GIS system of this kind.

The main purpose of this project is to create a coherent GIS system, in accordance with the current legislation on cultural heritage resources, and a unique network of organizations (NIHM, INMI, Cultural Counties Directorates, and the Ministry of Culture and Religious Affairs' National Institute for Historic Monuments) involved in updating the national heritage resources inventory. This should allow a strategy to be defined and better decision-making support to be offered to the Ministry of Culture and Religious Affairs, as well as allowing easier access to primary information on historic monuments, their unique code, locations, age determination, etc.

Components and capabilities

The eGISpat architecture

The eGISpat is a distributed archaeological GIS system consisting of several components that can be distributed across multiple machines at national level. The key components of the eGISpat application (fig. 15.1) can be summarized as:

- ArcGIS server: hosts and runs server objects. The ArcGIS server consists of a server object manager and one or more server objects containers.
- Web server: hosts the web application and web services that use the objects running on the GIS server.
- Data server: ArcSDE provides a gateway for using, managing and storing a multi-user geodatabase in

Microsoft SQL Server as a database platform, for any client application. Spatial and tabular data are integrated in a common centralized relational database structure normalized through a geodatabase model.

- Web browsers: used to connect to the web application - eGISpat Bucharest running on the web server.
- Desktop applications: ArcGIS Desktop 9.1 and a SOA client application – eGISpat Romania connects via Hypertext Transfer Protocol (HTTP) to ArcGIS web services running on the web server or connects directly to the ArcGIS server over a LAN or WAN.

Definitions and concepts

Before turning to the details, it is useful to review some key terms and concepts that will be used throughout this paper:

- GIS server: The GIS server is responsible for hosting and managing server objects. The GIS server is the set of objects, applications, and services that make it possible to run ArcObjects components on a server. The GIS server consists of a server object manager and one or more server object containers.
- Server object manager (SOM): The SOM is a Windows service that manages the set of server objects that is distributed across one or more container machines. When an application makes a connection to an ArcGIS Server over a LAN, it is making a connection to the SOM.
- Server object container (SOC): A SOC is a process in which one or more server objects runs. SOC processes are started and shut down by the SOM. The SOC processes run on the GIS server's container machines. Each container machine is capable of hosting multiple SOC processes.
- Server object: A server object is a coarse-grained ArcObjects component, i.e. a high-level object that simplifies the programming model for certain operations and hides the fine-grained ArcObjects that do the work. Server objects support coarse-grained interfaces that perform large units of work, such as 'draw a map' or 'geocode a set of addresses'. Server objects also have SOAP interfaces, which makes it possible to expose server objects as web services that can be consumed by clients over the Internet.

- Web server: The web server hosts web applications and web services written using the ArcGIS Server API. These web applications use the ArcGIS Server API to connect to a SOM to make use of server objects and to create ArcObjects for use in their applications.

Geodatabase Model for management of the eGISpat application

The geodatabase model of the official LHM published in 2004 is under development to allow these country-wide archaeological, architectural and historic resources to be managed effectively. The intention is not to store all the information associated with a site, but users will be able to: a) identify the location of historic resources (historic monuments, archaeological sites and ensembles); b) identify internal data files containing site data; and c) link detailed site records and other documents (i.e. photographs, scanned images, documents, text, video etc.) to site locations. Analysis of the structure of the LHM has shown that it includes 23,624 monuments, 18,516 monuments of national and international importance and 5,108 positions representing monuments of local importance. From a typological point of view, the LHM includes 1,762 ensembles and 4,040 architectural and archaeological sites.

The eGISpat application contains information on listed archaeological sites and historic monuments, organized into three large categories, in accordance with the methodology for the inventory of historic monuments: monuments, ensembles and archaeological and architectural sites. In addition, in accordance with Law no. 422/2001, the LHM is divided into four categories: archaeology, architecture, funerary/memorial architecture and public. The geodatabase consists of a set of feature classes, related tables with defined relationships and domains, and also allows business rules, relationships and behaviours to be associated with a combination of spatial and tabular data and administered through the same structure. Figure 15.2 shows the structure of the archaeological sites and historic monuments geodatabase model designed for the eGISpat application.

At this moment, the eGISpat geodatabase model contains the following feature classes:

- Monument: a point feature class representing historic monuments as points.
- Situri: a polygon feature class representing archaeological sites as polygons.
- Ansambluri: a polygon feature class identifying the extent of archaeological ensembles as polygons.
- Localitati: a polygon feature class representing settlements (towns, villages, communes, Bucharest capital)
- Judete: a polygon feature class identifying the extent of administrative boundaries (municipal boundaries)
- Drumuri: a linear feature class representing the road network
- Cai ferate: a linear feature class representing the railroad network
- Rauri: a linear and polygonal feature class representing the hydrographic network
- Dunărea: a polygonal feature class representing the Danube Delta

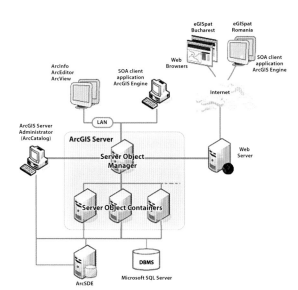

Fig. 15.1: *The eGISpat architecture* – the centrally managed GIS system.

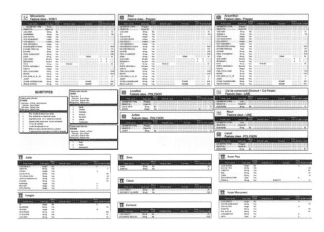

Fig. 15.2: *The eGISpat geodatabase model* – work in progress.

GIS web services implemented on the .NET web server can also be consumed from a Java client. The .NET GIS services (fig. 15.3) were developed using an ASP.NET framework and can be consumed by the client application – eGISpat Romania to:

- Verify the uniqueness of COD2004 (in accordance with Law no. 422/2001).
- Return data and type of all columns from a specified table.
- Read data from one field.
- Delete records using a 'where clause' criterion.
- Return the field type for a specified table.
- Add image files to the geodatabase.
- Create geographical features and their attributes.
- Return an image according to the selection criteria.
- Update attributes of geographical features.
- Perform geodatabase management tasks such as connect and release the connection.

This function can also manage and authorize the user/role and tasks, so that Read, Insert, Update and Delete operations can be performed only after an authentication process.

Associated tables contain most of the attribute information or identify links to site records and documents. The tables contain information about the administrative unit ('judeţ'), geographical region, historic monument identifier, staff name, listed or unlisted status, etc. Domains facilitate the standardization of site information. The domains are based on definitions and terminology used in the LHM 2004 in accordance with Romanian Law no. 422/2001 and include site condition, geographical zone and jurisdiction.

eGISpat GIS web services

The web services described in this paper are SOAP based. SOAP is the messaging framework that defines a suite of XML elements to communicate to arbitrary systems. Web services are discovered using Universal Description, Discovery, and Integration (UDDI), a metadata structure that categorizes web services. Once discovered, the Web Services Description Language (WSDL) is read to understand how to call and invoke services. The WSDL is simply a standards-based XML file readable across platforms. Users are not allowed to connect directly to the server. Their access is restricted through a web service catalog, a web service that only exposes the subset of server objects that the administrator chooses to expose. On the web server, the web service catalog is used also for publishing server objects as web services over HTTP. These

eGISpat Romania – Web service client application capabilities

The eGISpat web services are a set of related application functions (API) that can be programmed against over the Internet. These application web services are implemented using the native ASP.NET web service framework and are called by the .NET client application – eGISpat Romania.

Users with access to the web service catalog can:

- Display the map of the Romanian Archaeological Resources with multiple layers such as roads, streams, historic monuments, etc.
- Save a map document as a raster file (JPEG, BMP, TIFF, WMF etc.).
- Pan and zoom in, zoom out throughout the map.
- Zoom to the full extent of the data.
- Identify features on a map by pointing at them.
- Search and find features on the map.
- Display labels with text from field values.
- Draw graphics features such as points, lines and polygons.
- Add descriptive text.
- Select features by pointing at them.
- Find and select features with a SQL (Structured Query Language) expression.
- Transform the coordinate system of map data.
- Perform geometric operations on shapes to create buffers.
- Submit advanced spatial and attribute queries.
- Select features and generate reports related to one or more historic monuments, archaeological sites or ensembles.
- Add and delete image files and geographical features in the geodatabase.
- Perform geodatabase management tasks.
- Validate values entered during the create and update process.

Fig. 15.3: *eGISpat Romania – GIS web services.*

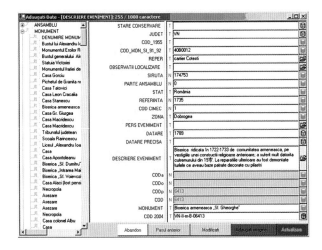

- Create and update geographical features and their attributes (fig. 15.4).

Bucharest Historic Centre web application

History
The historic centre of the city of Bucharest was awarded legally protected status in 2001 in view of its city planning and architectural values. The historic centre area contains archaeological monuments and sites dating back to the Medieval period, including the Medieval ensemble 'Curtea Veche' (representing The Old Royal Court), and churches and inns built before 1800. Most listed monuments date from the second half of the 19th century. They have been joined by some of the most original monuments from the inter-war period. We should note that many of the historic monuments were built on or include parts of the cellars of older structures (dating from the 17th – 18th century).

The buildings in the historic centre can be grouped into the following functional areas: commercial area (Lip-scani Street and Calea Mosilor Street), *functional area* (Calea Victoriei) and residential area (Stelea Spatarul Street and Radu Calomfirescu Street). The archaeological monuments located in these areas represent a large variety of architectural programmes. The royal residence area 'Curtea Veche' represents the main axis of the Medieval town, around which other parts of the town developed: the marketplace, several churches (Stavropoleos, Sf. Gheorghe Nou, Sf. Gheorghe Vechi, Coltea, Doamnei), inns that have been in use for centuries (Hanul lui Manuc, Hanul cu Tei, Hanul Polonezilor, Hanul Patria), houses with shops on the ground floor and lodgings above (Lipscani

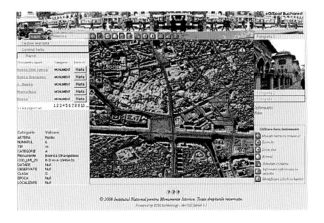

Fig. 15.4: *eGISpat Romania* – the ability to create and update geographical features and their attributes.

Street, Calea Mosilor Street, Selari Street and Smardan Street), dwellings (the 'round-windowed house' at 15 Radu Calomfirescu Street), public and cultural institutions built in the late 19th and early 20th century, hospitals (Coltea, the Romanian Postal Services (PTTR) hospital), commercial arcades (the Macca-Villacrosse arcade and the French passage), and hotels (Fieschi Hotel).

Bucharest's built heritage has been preserved despite severe damage (a great fire in 1847, several earthquakes) and large-scale city planning and architectural programmes. Curtea Veche represents the Medieval construction system dating back to the 15th – 16th century and decorative elements from the Brancovenian period, and includes other monuments typical of the same period, as well as the churches of Coltea, Razvan and Stravopoleos, which are true architectural pearls.

Historic Centre web GIS application – eGISpat Bucharest
INMI is currently involved in developing a GIS project for the historic centre of Bucharest that will provide a tool to help planners and preservationists assess historical and cultural resources in Bucharest. The pilot project is based on the suitability of GIS technology for spatial data analysis and is designed to allow better monitoring of the national LHM.

The technical team and ESRI Romania decided to build a web GIS application – eGISpat Bucharest (fig. 15.5) using ArcGIS Server technology and incorporating the historic resources geodatabase, a digital map scale 1:2 000, IKONOS satellite imagery courtesy of GeoEye, representative setting, registration files, plan photographs, building footprints, streets, sidewalks, rivers, etc.

eGISpat Bucharest capabilities
The web application – eGISpat Bucharest allows the user to perform the following functions via a LAN or Internet connection:
- Display the map of the Historic centre of Bucharest with multiple layers such as roads, streams, historic monuments, archaeological sites, etc.
- Pan and zoom in, zoom out throughout the map.
- Zoom to the full extent of the data.
- Move back or forward one display.
- Identify features on a map by pointing at them.
- Search and find features on the map.
- Interactively toggle layers on and off.
- Display labels with text from field values.
- Draw images from satellite imagery.
- Draw graphic features such as points, lines, circles and polygons.
- Insert descriptive text.
- Select features inside boxes, areas, polygons and circles.
- Select features within a specified distance of other features.
- Find and select features with a SQL (Structured Query Language) expression.

Fig. 15.5: Web GIS application of the Historical Centre.

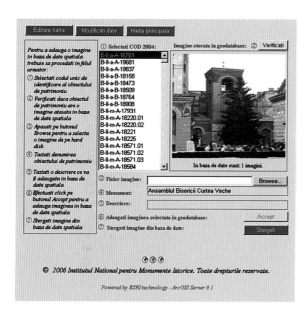

- Find locations on a map from a defined address or intersection.
- Transform the coordinate system of map data.
- Perform geometric operations on shapes to create buffers.
- Submit advanced spatial and attribute queries.
- Manipulate the shape or rotation of a map.
- Select features and generate reports related to one or more historic monuments and archaeological sites.
- Print maps on A4 paper.
- Add and delete image files in the geodatabase (fig. 15.6).
- Perform geodatabase management tasks.
- Create and update geographical features and their attributes (fig. 15.7).

Conclusions

This project represents the first phase, involving the creation of a centrally managed GIS system for Romania's archaeological and historical resources. For the second phase, INMI will be applying for additional funding to field check the existing geodatabase information and to scan additional surveys. The final phase will involve adding archaeological sites using Trimble GeoExplorer GeoXT, GeoXH, Recon GPS Card and the ArcPad application to complete the project. For INMI eGISpat is the first step in the creation and implementation of an enterprise

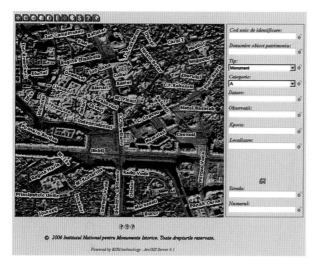

Fig. 15.6: *eGISpat* Bucharest – the ability to add and delete image files in a geodatabase.

GIS system that will be applied to the national historic resources inventory. A national cultural heritage network is urgently needed. Using a geodatabase model will allow better management of the National Archaeological Directory and the List of Historic Monuments.

The major benefits of the eGISpat application are:
Significant operational and risk/cost reductions as compared to common practical experience where each user tends to have a 'private' database that is not centralized or shared by other users within the organization.

A centralized archaeological geodatabase allows users to modify the geodatabase schema, or to integrate new information into the application according to their needs. All their changes are simply documented in the UML diagram and the geodatabase is updated. Advanced ArcGIS users are able to directly access the eGISpat geodatabase for advanced spatial analysis and mapping. All non-GIS specialists are easily able to access spatial data using the eGISpat interface. All departmental staff are able to work in a centrally managed GIS environment and perform business processes for rapid multi-user editing, viewing and dissemination of cultural heritage resources. Advanced GIS web services are delivered to several organizations (INMI, Cultural Counties Directorates, and the Ministry of Culture and Religious Affairs' Institute for Historic Monuments). eGISpat is a performance tool to help decision-makers at national level efficiently manage cultural heritage resources. Implementing a centralized management system using state-of-the-art GIS technology will also allow us to support the geospatial specifications and standards required by the European Union. The eGISpat Geodatabase Model offers better decision-making support for administration, rehabilitation and preservation, and also for the promotion of our national cultural heritage resources. This enterprise GIS project will also enable the implementation of sectoral policies and strategies in accordance with our specific requirements.

As such, eGISpat is a useful tool for research and planning purposes on a variety of scales. The eGISpat Geodatabase Model can provide practical benefits, including more efficient planning, and incorporation of cultural resources into local and country-wide planning processes at an early stage. The ultimate goal is to reduce disturbance of cultural resources and increase our knowledge of the past.

danelise@hotmail.com

Fig. 15.7: *eGISpat* Bucharest – the ability to create geographical features and their attributes.

References

Arroyo-Bishop, D. & Lantada Zarzosa, M.T. 1992: The ArcheoDATA System: A Method for Structuring a European Archaeological Information System (AIS). In Larsen, C. (ed.) Sit*es and Monuments: National Archaeological Records, C*openhagen: The National Museum of Denmark, pp. 133-156.

Davidson, T.E. 1986: Computer-Correcting Historical Maps for Archaeological Use. *Historical Archaeology* 20 (2): 27-37.

ESRI Press (2005), ArcGIS 9: *ArcGIS Server Administrator and Developer Guide.*

European Convention for the protection of archaeological heritage, La Valetta, ratified by Romania through the Law no. 150/1997.

European Convention for the protection of archaeological heritage, 1985, Granada.

European landscape Convention, 2000, Florence NSW Heritage Office, Policy, Standards and Guidelines. http://www.heritage.nsw.gov.au/06_subnav_02.htm.

RO-Legislation: Law no. 421 of 2001 establishing the requirements and regulations governing historic monuments and cultural resources. Standards and Guidelines for Consultant Archaeologists (Archaeological Fieldwork). www.culture.gov.on.ca/english/culdiv/heritage/acsp_bulletin-july2004-e.doc.

Society of Museum Archaeologists, MDA, Standards in Action: Working with Archaeology http://www.mda.org.uk/standarc.htm.

The National Park Service, Office of the Secretary of the Interior, Protection Of Archaeological Resources. http://www.cr.nps.gov/local-law/43cfr7.htm Ontario Archaeological Society, 2004, Archaeology Customer Service Project: Status Report - http://www.ontarioarchaeology.on.ca/oas/Pages/Moc_status_report.htm.

16 | Places – Landscapes. Listings – Assessments. Some ideas about the numerical evaluation of archaeological landscapes

Christian Mayer

Abstract: This paper approaches landscape as a concept that goes beyond lists of objects that can be found in a defined area of the earth's surface. Using a list to reconstruct a landscape is shown as adding something that by its nature is not included in a list of such objects but is essential to the concept of landscape. Therefore, using a list to discuss a landscape or to assess a single site within a landscape means implicitly adding something that does not have the same sensual qualities as the entries in a list. Consequently, for an individual to speak about a landscape is to create a landscape. And, of course, each creates his or her own landscape. To make explicit the implicit element of the concept of landscape, a quantitative approach is introduced in this paper and applied to the data of the Austrian National archaeological survey.

Some methodical considerations

In preparing for this paper I identified a parallel between working with an archaeological landscape and assessing sites. This parallel lies in the fact that in both working with landscape and assessing an archaeological situation one refers to something that does not exist in the same sense as data do. This fact becomes obvious when one tries to define landscape. Obviously, landscape at its most basic refers to a section of the earth's surface. But surely this is a reduction because while landscape comprises something that relates to the surface of the earth, it is not explicable by geodesy. The very special character of this something becomes clear when a landscape has to be transformed into data. Of course, the first step is to provide a list of objects found in the area of study but, of course, this list does not suffice as a picture of the landscape of the area. To complete the picture, one has to add something that lacks the sensual qualities of objects. That is why landscape, paradoxically, is not visible.

Archaeological databases do not comprise this mysterious something but adding personal experience and common sense to data creates a landscape. Since personal experience is by definition individual and there is still no agreement as to what common sense is, there is a vast number of different landscapes. So talking about places as well as assessing an archaeological situation by referring to a list of sites means to create a landscape implicitly. Can we move on from creating landscapes implicitly? Is it important to create landscapes explicitly? These questions must be answered since landscape is not fiction. But one wonders whether the process is scientific. Certainly, different landscapes created implicitly and referring to the same piece of ground do have something in common beyond geodesy. Although this brings us back to the problem of listings mentioned already, suppose for illustrative purposes a landscape can be resolved into numerable elements. By combining some or all of these elements and assigning different weights to them we can create what appear to be different landscapes (fig. 16.1).

1.00	0.00	0.00
0.00	0.00	0.00
0.02	0.00	0.00

0.00	2.70	0.00
0.00	0.00	0.00
0.00	0.70	0.00

0.00	0.00	0.00
0.00	0.00	1.07
0.00	0.00	0.98

Fig. 16.1: Aspects of a landscape.

As the number of elements and their possible weights can vary, one should think of different numbers, combinations and weights of elements as aspects of the same landscape. All of these aspects provide a certain insight into landscape and are informative. Therefore the problem in dealing with landscape is not finding the true landscape but finding out how a certain aspect of a landscape was created. My view is that it is necessary to show what elements and what weights are used to describe landscapes explicitly.

A database: Austria's National Archaeological Survey

To illustrate the problems and demonstrate an approach to solving them, I shall use data from Austria's National Archaeological Survey. The focus will be on the quality of knowledge of Austria's archaeological landscape. This is informed by the historical and legal situation in general and the situation in regard to the protection of historical monuments especially.

The authority in charge of archaeological monuments in Austria is the Bundesdenkmalamt, an institution founded in 1918 and given legal powers in 1923. Of course, both the institution as well as the legislation have forerunners (Frodl 1988; Brückler 1991; Niegl, 1976; Niegl 1980) but the law of 1923, amended and rewritten to some extent, is still in force. This law contains two important articles concerning the reporting of finds and sites and the publication of these reports. Reporting of sites to the Bundesdenkmalamt is obligatory. This obligation extends not only to reports on sites but since 1999 includes the obligation to deliver detailed information about excavations as well. In turn the Bundesdenkmalamt is obliged to give information about these reports to the public. This is done via the series 'Fundberichte aus Österreich', where these reports are listed. Enhanced by drawings of finds and short scientific papers 45 volumes have been published since 1921. Additionally, in recent years detailed accounts of sites have been published in two series of monographs.

Originally, no inventory of archaeological sites was carried out, and it was only in the 1960s that site reports were compiled. Each site was treated as a topographical unit. Data were stored as paper files. Since 1993 these data have been completely reworked and stored in a conventional database (Mayer 1996; Mayer 2002). At the moment about 85 % of Austria's territory has been included in the National Archaeological Survey. This database has now been transformed into a GIS. At least six archaeologists work constantly on data input.

The data model underlying the database can store all information about sites regardless how much is actually known, an important feature since some of the older reports contain limited information but, nevertheless, are important sources of information about Austria's past. The database is to some extent public which means that full information about single sites are given to owners, archaeologists and private persons well known for their interest in archaeology. Mass data is passed on only in special cases. Reduced information, that is a simplified dating and classification of sites, is given to other authorities, to land developers and planners. Usually this is done by an official statement by the Bundesdenkmalamt which contains a list of sites, measures to be taken and a comment on the archaeological situation of the region in question.

The Bundesdenkmalamt does not publish maps that can be used by planners as the number of unknown sites in Austria has to be considered as higher than the number of known ones. Users of such maps tend to understand these maps as fixed and do not take precautions to prevent the destruction of unknown archaeological sites. Sites not under legal protection do not have an explicit legal status, which means they could be ignored by planners, other authorities or during construction but there is an article in Austrian law that allows the Bundesdenkmalamt to stop any work on a site, and to give it legal status. This article persuades many planners to cooperate with the Bundesdenkmalamt to protect archaeological sites.

Some history of the Cultural Resource Management in Austria

So as to provide a better understanding of the situation, a short outline of the history of heritage protection in Austria is set out here. In 1850, the Commission on the Protection of Historical monuments was installed (Frodl 1988). This council of 'beati viri' with high aims, some staff and even money but – as there was no law on monument protection yet - without executive power relied on volunteers, called Correspondents or Conservators, who reported to the Commission and recommended measures and funding. The Commission included some scientists that played important roles in the development of heritage protection policies, among them Alois Riegl. Around 1911 the Commission was transformed into an institution which consisted not only of volunteers but of a number of public servants, too. Among these were the 'Landeskonservatoren', officials that were responsible for certain parts of the county.

The end of the Austro-Hungarian Monarchy and the new Constitution brought about changes that were to be of crucial importance in the following years (Frodl- Kraft 1997). The constitution of the Republic of Austria of 1920 differentiates between legal matters of federal and of central interest and regulation. Matters of heritage protection were considered part of the latter, being imposed on all nine federal states equally. In 1923, a law on the Protection of Monuments, based on the views of Alois Riegl, was passed, thus providing a legal basis for operation. The organizational structure imposed in 1911 lived on in the activities of Correspondents. These had permission to act as representatives of the Bundesdenkmalamt in making inquiries and small excavations for periods of two, later four years respectively. In fact, most of the reports and most of the finds were made by these Correspondents. Since the state had and has no legal claim on archaeological finds, most of them donated or sold finds to local museums or to national institutions such as universities or the museum of Natural History in Vienna. Some of these correspondents founded their own private collections which often formed the core of local museums. Usually those conducting excavations had little or no archaeological training. In fact, excavation as the key method for the retrieval of very complex information about the past and not simply as an extraction method for precious goods was accepted only fairly late in Austria. In regard to excavation the practice has been to store the documentation of the excavation with the finds. Since

1999, there is a legal obligation to provide a copy of the documentation to the Bundesdenkmalamt.

Political and economic circumstances in the 1920s and 1930s had a severe impact on archaeology in the Republic of Austria. Bundesdenkmalamt staff numbered only 18 employees in 1934 (Frodl-Kraft 1997, 465). Among these, only G. Kyrle was a trained prehistoric archaeologist and when he left the organisation in 1925, there was no archaeologist on the staff. In 1934, when the government was overthrown and replaced by a proto-fascist corporative system, the Bundesdenkmalamt was dissolved and became a department of the ministry of Education ("Zentralstelle für Denkmalschutz"). Decentralising tendencies resulted in the establishment of an institution subordinated to the nine federal states and the central ministry at the same time, thus submitting monument protection and science to the arbitrariness of bureaucracy and political orders.

After 1938, when Austria became part of the Deutsches Reich, the former Austrian legislation on protection remained in force. In 1940 the Zentralstelle was replaced by an 'Institut für Denkmalpflege' that had no executive power (Brückler 1990). Executive power was transferred to the seven newly formed local authorities ('Gaue'). The intention was that the new institute would serve as a scientific agency but in fact the new administrative bodies acted like the old ones; official contacts were not welcome.

The Institut für Denkmalpflege had two departments, one for Art History and the other for Prehistory, the latter being led by K. Willvonseder. For obviously ideological reasons, this department was better equipped with staff and money than its forerunners and even had its own laboratories. Of course, World War II had a huge impact on archaeology in Austria. The construction of roads and military facilities led to some large-scale excavations. On the other hand, male archaeologists were called up to military service some never returning from war. Finally, the new department lost its head in 1942 when K. Willvonseder decided to enter the personal staff of the head of the SS, Himmler.

Originally, each of the newly formed local administrations was supposed to have its own archaeologist but this did not happen. Only in Carinthia was an archaeologist employed; in Vienna and Lower Austria the duties were executed by the Institute. So the situation remained as it had been before. If there was any activity it was carried out by the Institute or by volunteers.

After 1945 the Republic of Austria was re-established and the Bundesdenkmalamt was re-instituted by combining the former Gaukonservatorate and the Institut für Denkmalpflege into one body. Again it became the authority on the protection of monuments, now enhanced by a department for archaeology, in German called the 'Abteilung für Bodendenkmale'. As before, based on the constitution of 1920 and the law of 1923, monument protection matters were being administered and executed by the central government. In other respects the old ways of doing things survived; archaeology still relied on volunteers to report on sites and do some rescue excavations.

After the war, the governments of the federal states took over the running of some local museums; this was a major change from the pre-war situation. These museums were originally founded and run by historical societies in the first half of the 19th century. Always connected to the local governments as a result of public servants being active in these societies, the connection became closer when the economic situation worsened and the museums became more and more dependent on public money. After World War II these Museums, called 'Landesmuseums' were administered by the federal states or their personnel were officials of the administration of the federal states. Now, one can observe the opposite development in the move to privatise cultural institutions. These museums did have lists of sites as part of inventory of their archaeological collection but only a few of the museums attempted to provide a complete list of sites in their respective federal state. Only the list for Vienna is computerized and accessible through the internet. Today, some of the federal administrations use these lists as their main, even exclusive, source of information on archaeological sites and their own archaeologist as experts in planning processes, thus maintaining a pre-war tradition that viewed a central administration as incapable of having local knowledge.

Because of this situation it is not even possible to know the number of archaeologists who work in the field of monument protection. At present the Bundesdenkmalamt employs 11 archaeologists. Four have their offices in the capitals of some federal states, the other five in the headquarters in Vienna. This small group are responsible not only for the listing of sites but also the legal side of the protection of monuments, as well as editing the annual reports and managing about 90 % of a year's excavations. Infact, the staff of the Bundesdenkmalamt does all the legal and the organisatorial part of the excavations. Since there are only very few research excavations in Austria, this brings a lot of work for the Bundesdenkmalamt. Certainly, we employ lots of people – not necessarily archaeologist - that work at these excavations, but since the museums have neither founding nor staff, no the storage facilities of finds and no infrastructure for archaeology, all these aspects has to be provided by the Bundesdenkmalamt. In addition to the 11 archaeologists employed by the Bundesdenkmalamt, there are about 65 archaeologists in Austria employed by universities, museums and other public institutions, and possibly another 60 work in contract archaeology. The number of archaeologists in the state is fairly modest for a population of 7.8 millions.

The Austrian archaeological landscape – well known?

To return to the issue of archaeological landscapes, it is clear from the foregoing that for an objective discussion of Austria's archaeological landscape, terms and arguments used must have a methodological foundation. This, in particular, applies to the term 'well known'. Finding out what is meant by well or poorly known may lead to an endless discussion in the first place. In fact, the discussion is needless. Looking at the records in a database, we see that not all record fields can be filled-in for each site because the information available for each site will vary. Intuitively, we feel that we know some sites better than others. However we need to turn intuition into an operable tool. Technically, turning objects into database

empirical relative   *projected onto*   symbolical relative

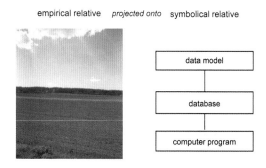

```
        data model
            |
         database
            |
      computer program
```

Fig. 16.2: Empirical and symbolical.

records is a projection of an empiric relative onto a symbolic relative (fig. 16.2). The symbolic relative is called a data model and defines which information and by which logical structure data are stored. Based on a data model, one can design a representation of the data as a database and write a computer program.

A data model not only prescribes what information is to be collected by splitting objects of interest into attributes but regulates the terms used to describe the entries as well. These terms are related to each other and a valid data model has to reproduce the relationships between the terms used as well. Therefore, a proper data model will hold much of the information that may be required about a site, but in a form that is not easy to deal with. The task is to choose a form that is more suitable.

In fact, speaking of a site as being well or poorly known is a problem of quantification or, in other words, a problem of measuring on a scale. Scales play a key role in quantification since their properties determine the statistical means that we can employ to describe our archaeological landscape and assess an archaeological situation. So let's have a closer look. The notion of knowing more or less about something implies the existence of a larger/smaller relation. Suppose we want to qualify the notion of knowing the localisation of a site well or poorly. Certainly we know the localisation of a site best if we know the actual extent of a site. This would cover the ground parcels, the cadastral unit, the municipality, the county, the province, the country – or we simply do not know anything about the location of the site. Obviously, the larger/smaller relation between the terms constitutes an ordinal scale. Although using an ordinal scale is already a sort of quantification, this type of scale is not satisfying from a practical point of view, since the statistical methods applicable are not as powerful as statistical methods for scales of more complex properties. To construct such a scale for the exactness of location,

there is something else to consider. One may feel that the ranks of the ordinal scale proposed are somewhat coarse. But one can add some more values like juridical district or group of parcels named by a traditional name. In fact one could find many more stages to describe the exactness of location. Of course, not all of these stages are reasonable in application but nevertheless it is obvious that the ranks already mentioned are just blocked values. This means that the properties of the scale used to measure the exactness of location allows key statistics of a distribution like mean and standard deviation to be computed.

The data model of the Austrian National Archaeological Survey has four components that are measurable on scale like the one described (fig. 16.3). To characterize a site by the sum of the scores of these scales, an additional relation has to be realized. This relation is the independence of the four variables measured. Independence is achieved if the actual value of any particular property is not determined by the value of another one. For example, in Austria it is common to think of the Hallstatt Culture as being synonymous with the Early Iron Age and Reinecke's phases Ha C and D. Of course, this not true since the Hallstatt Culture does not occur throughout the whole of Austria nor is the duration of the Hallstatt Culture restricted to Ha C and D. In fact, the concept of dating relies on a time scale that is independent of events. For the data model used in Austria this independence is given for all four components and can be proved by statistical means. Therefore it is possible to sum the values of each variable to characterize each site by a single value. Formally speaking, an empiric relative is projected onto a numeric relative or the degree of knowledge of a site is measured on an absolute scale.

Before some results of actual computations will be presented one further point should be made that is important in working with such scales. Basic to the application of any scale is the pre-condition that is must be clear what the scale applied actually measures. The scale used for dating does not measure how old a site is or whether a date in a report is true or not; but it gives information on how detailed the knowledge of the chronology of a site is. Therefore the four scales are called the degree of knowledge in respect to location, dating, cultural affiliation and class of site. The sum of these four is called the degree of knowledge of a site.

Some Maps

As an example, data from a number of areas of Austria will be discussed, namely the federal states of Salzburg, Upper and Lower Austria, Burgenland and Carinthia. In the maps about 15,000 places are shown (fig. 16.4). Data is given for three periods. The actual numbers used to score the measures are arbitrary. For the following computations the scores sum to a maximum value of 12. It is not difficult to see in fig. 16.5 that the distributions of scores for each period are quite different. There are scarcely any sites that reached a value of 12 since only very few sites in Austria are completely known. The proportion of sites scored with a value of 11 is remarkably high for Germanic sites. This is

empirical relative   *projected onto*   numerical relative

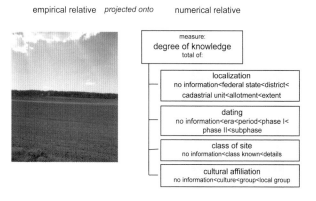

```
            measure:
      degree of knowledge
            total of:

    localization
    no information<federal state<district<
    cadastrial unit<allotment<extent

    dating
    no information<era<period<phase I<
    phase II<subphase

    class of site
    no information<class known<details

    cultural affiliation
    no information<culture<group<local group
```

Fig. 16.3: Measuring the degree of knowledge of a site.

due to the fact that these sites are especially interesting to private collectors and also because they are of particular interests to one scientist in the archaeology department of the Bundesdenkmalamt. The Neolithic period has an especially high proportion of scores of 5 and 10. The explanation for the lower score is that while about a quarter of all Neolithic sites have a relatively precise location their dating is very inexact. The high proportion of sites scoring 10 results from the high number of sites that can be dated to the early and middle Neolithic. Although these statistics are informative, they do not provide a satisfying description of a landscape as the spatial component is lacking.

For the first map (fig. 16.6), an index of the median score of the knowledge of sites and the area of cadastral unit has been computed and transformed into a map using Krigeing. The regional differences are obvious. Certainly, we would be glad if we could interpret this map as the hot spots of the historic settlement of Austria. But of course, this would be too simple an interpretation since the values we are using to produce this map measure the degree of knowledge of sites and not the their true spatial distribution. Additionally, the map contains only places

where archaeological finds were actually made. Further, the more fieldwork carried out in a region the greater the overall quality of scientific knowledge about it. Therefore the map is a measure of the activity of archaeologists. In fact, it is easy to recognize the effects of the activities of institutions and even of single persons. In the northwest, at the Austrian-German border the activities of a private collector over a 15-year period are indicated on the map by yellow shading. Moving east, the work in the Roman city of Wels/Ovilava and Linz by the Landesmuseum of Upper Austria and the city museum of Linz are reflected on the map. The impact of the long-lasting excavations at the Roman city of Lauriacum is reflected in our knowledge of the region. North of St.Pölten along the lower River Traisen Valley and further east a region rich in archaeological activity and home to a number of local museums is indicated by the yellow shading. Data on the archaeology of that part of Lower Austria north of the River Danube we owe, in the main, to the activities of local museums which, except for the museum in Poysdorf, were all founded at the end of the 19th or at the beginning of the 20th century. The yellow to orange coloured areas at the border of Austria with Slovakia are due to the archaeological work carried out to facilitate the construction of a dam alongside the River March in the 1920s and 1930s. The activities of a number of museums in the area to the south of Vienna, all founded in the second half of the 19th century, are reflected on the map. The Burgenland achieves prominence on the map owing to the activities of a private collector until 1938 and the Burgenländisches Landesmuseum after 1938. In the southernmost part of the Burgenland near the small village of Heiligenkreuz, archaeological survey in advance of the construction of a motorway undertaken by the Bundesdenkmalamt, results in a yellow spot in an otherwise blank region. Finally the yellow spot in Tyrol is due to the long-lasting excavation

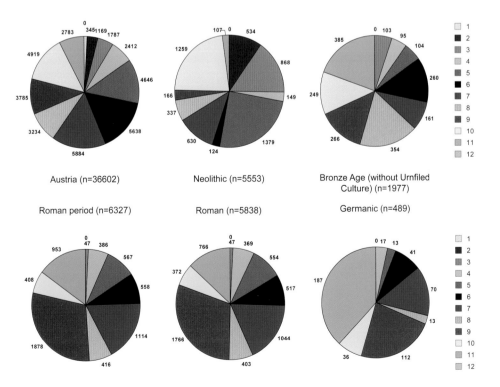

Austria (n=36602)

Neolithic (n=5553)

Bronze Age (without Urnfiled Culture) (n=1977)

Roman period (n=6327)

Roman (n=5838)

Germanic (n=489)

Fig. 16.5: Distributions of scores.

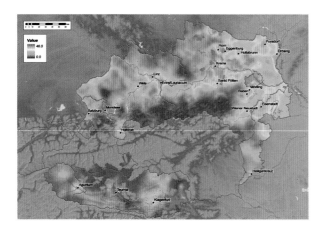

in the Roman city of Aguntum. The contribution of the Landesmuseum of Carinthia, located in Klagenfurt, is also reflected in yellow on the map.

The degree of knowledge of Neolithic sites is plotted on the next map (fig. 16.7). The picture is again uneven

Fig. 16.6: Degree (all periods), value: median degree of knowledge / area of cadastral unit.

with a strikingly high concentration of better known sites in north-eastern Austria. As before, it is easy to recognize the specifics of Austrian prehistoric archaeology. The activities of a private collector at the Austrian–German border are reflected on the map. North of Hallstatt, the settlements of the Late Neolithic Mondsee Culture along the sea banks are indicated by yellow shading. The general picture is dominated by the north eastern Part of Lower Austria and to a minor extent by the Burgenland. In fact, most of the sites date, as already mentioned, from the Early and Middle Neolithic and belong to cultures easily recognized by their ceramics. When a coefficient of the median of the degree of knowledge to distance to the nearest Neolithic site is computed and mapped, the picture changes dramatically (fig. 16.8). Now, only a few spots reach higher values appear, demonstrating how strongly knowledge of the Neolithic period depends on

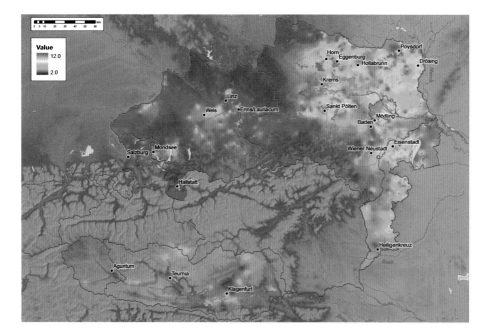

Fig. 16.7: Neolithic; value: degree of knowledge.

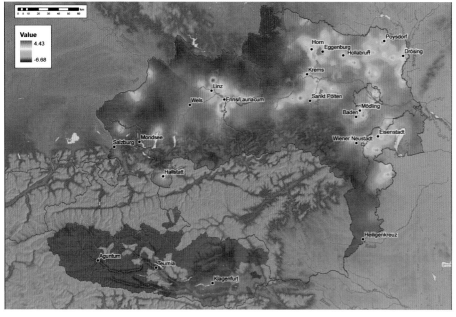

Fig. 16.8: Neolithic; value: median knowledge / area estimated by distance to nearest neighbour (logarithmic).

very few sites. One detail should be mentioned; south of Lauriacum some orange spots denote Neolithic sites that came to light during motorway construction. These sites changed the picture of the archaeological landscape there completely.

As for the Neolithic, the picture of the Early and Middle Bronze Age is dominated by sites in the North East of Austria (fig. 16.9). The level of Bronze Age activity in other parts of Austria is simply unknown. In fig. 16.10 the coefficient of degree of knowledge and distance to the nearest neighbour is plotted. Again the map illustrates how strongly knowledge of the Early and Middle Bronze Age depends on very few sites. This map is especially strongly determined by the activities of a single person. North of St. Pölten the late J.-W. Neugebauer, member of the Bundesdenkmalamt, worked for over 20 years, excavating, along with much else, about 6,000 graves from the Early Bronze Age.

Fig. 16.11 displays the scores of the sites of the Roman period. The map is dominated by the Germanic sites in the

north eastern part of Lower Austria. Unlike the maps for other periods, some other regions of Austria are shaded yellow like the Southern Burgenland. The explanation for this is the reports in the 1920s and 1930s by a Correspondent of the Bundesdenkmalamt, who was also the head of the local police, of a mass of grave mould dating from the Early Roman Period.

The mass of Germanic sites with high scores north of Vienna is striking but deceptive, as these sites are of special interest to a number of collectors that liaise with the Bundesdenkmalamt, where one staff member takes a particular interest in this period. In fig. 16.12 the coefficient of degree of knowledge and distance to the nearest neighbour is plotted. This makes clear that in reality Germanic settlement sites are poorly known. I refrain from comment on Roman settlement and invite the reader to test her or his knowledge on the Roman limes in Austria. Also visible are Roman period activities in Aguntum in Tyrol and the results of research done on Roman roads around Hallstatt.

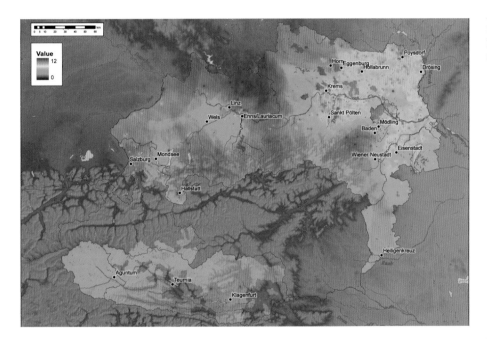

Fig. 16.9: Early and Middle Bronze Age; value: degree of knowledge.

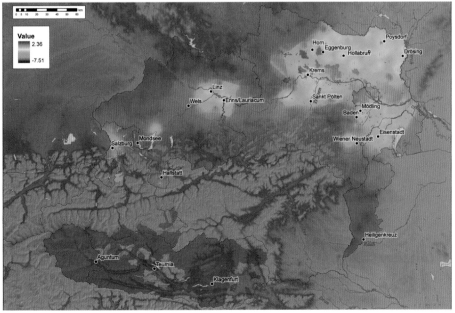

Fig. 16.10: Early and Middle Bronze Age; value: median knowledge / area estimated by distance to nearest neighbour (logarithmic).

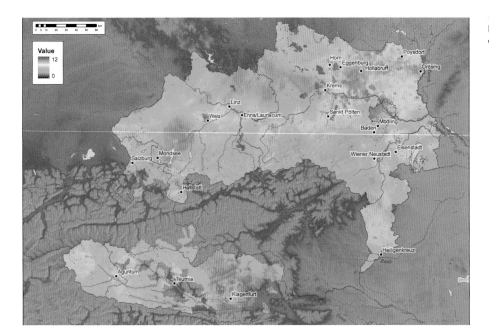

Fig. 16.11: Roman Period: value: degree of knowledge.

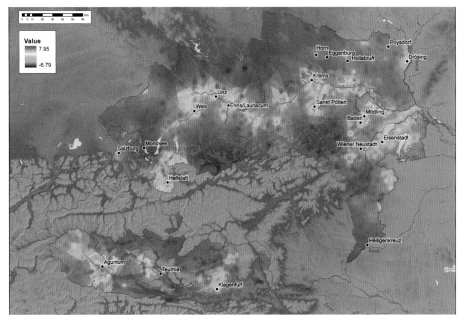

Fig. 16.12: Roman Period: value: median knowledge / area estimated by distance to nearest neighbour (logarithmic).

Some methodological aspects - revisted

But are maps an explicit creation of an archaeological landscape? Definitely not, since points on a sheet of paper are just another representation of a list. So what was added to produce the maps presented in this paper? Firstly, I used a data model that projects data into a form suitable for statistical computations. Secondly, to actually produce the maps a statistical concept called spatial processes was used. This comprises a method that estimates one of the parameters of a spatial process. This method is the quite well known Krigeing (Cressie 1993). By compiling the maps, we created the archaeological landscape and it is only by going through the whole procedure of creating the maps that we can fully assess and interpret them.

But is it necessary to make such efforts? The answer to this is definitely yes. From a scientific perspective, generalising about Austrian cultural phenomena on the basis of the available information is not valid. The Austrian archaeological landscape is mainly a landscape of Austrian archaeologists. Certainly, presenting a list of sites alone as a picture of the Austrian archaeological landscape would not suffice. What is more, using maps like the ones presented in this paper without a methodical analysis of the degree to which sites are 'well known' or 'badly known' would not be persuasive in a discussion with planners or government agencies, bodies that base their own decisions on rigorous scientific techniques, comparable to the ones presented in this paper. Appeals to 'personal experience' or 'common sense' will not suffice in this context.

chrmayer@chello.at

References:

Brückler, Th. 1990: Die "Verländerung", die
     österreichische Denkmalpflege in der NS- Zeit
     und die Gründung des Instituts für Denkmalpflege
     1940. Österreichische Zeitschrift für Kunst und
     Denkmalpflege 44, 184-94.
Brückler, Th. 1991: Vom Konsilium zum Imperium.
     Die Vorgeschichte der österreichischen
     Denkmalschutzgesetzgebung. Österreichische
     Zeitschrift für Kunst und Denkmalpflege 45, 160-
     173.
Cressie, N.A.C. 1993: Statistics for spacial data, New
     York.
Frodl, W.1988: Idee und Verwirklichung. Das Werden der
     staatlichen Denkmalpflege in Österreich, Wien.
Frodl-Kraft, E.: 1997, Gefährdetes Erbe. Österreichs
     Denkmalschutz und Denkmalpflege im Prisma der
     Zeitgeschichte. Wien.
Mayer, Ch. 1996: Fundstellenbezogene Daten
     in der Abteilung für Bodendenkmale des
     Bundesdenkmalamtes. Fundberichte aus
     Österreich 35, 321-66.
Mayer, Ch. 2002: Some aspects of SMR management in
     Austria. In: Garcia Sanjuan, L. & Wheatly, D.W.
     (ed.): Mapping the future of the past, Sevilla, 37-45.
Niegl, M.A., 1976: Die Entwicklung der generellen
     gesetzlichen Normen betreffend das Fundwesen
     und die archäologische Forschung in Österreich,
     Römisches Österreich 4, 189-202.
Niegl, M.A., 1980: Die archäologische Erforschung der
     Römerzeit in Österreich, Österreichische Akademie
     der Wissenschaften, Philosophisch-historische
     Klasse Denkschriften 141.

17 | Protecting archaeological sites in a larger context – a Finnish challenge

Marianne Schauman-Lönnqvist

Background

As a former part of the Swedish realm, Finland has a long tradition in the inventorying of ancient monuments. By the royal decree issued on 28 November 1666, the Crown declared all ancient monuments and sites in Sweden protected and ordered an inventory of them. This work was carried out by the clergy, who sent in antiquarian-topographical descriptions of their parishes to the newly established Central Office of National Antiquities in Stockholm. These so-called "clerical reports" were also delivered from Finland (Edgren 1995, 50).

The efforts to obtain an inventory of the ancient monuments to be protected in Finland in the 17th century were with some exceptions not continued until the latter half of the 19th century, when archaeology in Finland, now under Russian rule, gained a position as an academic discipline. The Finnish Antiquarian Society was founded in 1870 and the State Archaeological Commission, the predecessor of the National Board of Antiquities was established in 1884. One year earlier an imperial decree on the protection of ancient monuments was issued and a more systematic survey of ancient monuments then started. Surveys that covered defined spatial areas as counties or parishes and surveys that focused on a specific theme were carried

out. The inventory of the hillforts in South-west Finland by Hjalmar Appelgren that resulted in his thesis (Appelgren 1891) deserves to be mentioned as an example of the latter type of survey.

The decree of 1883 protected the archaeological heritage automatically, but the threats were not of major concern for the archaeologists. The ancient monuments in rural Finland were thought mostly to be considerably well preserved, as the country was so sparsely populated and land use so insignificant. The visible monuments, such as Bronze Age burial cairns, were situated on hilltops outside the inhabited village areas and thus as a general rule did not obstruct farming activities and so were more or less undamaged. The early inventories mainly registered visible monuments, even if the majority of the finds collected were of Stone Age date and were derived from subsoil deposits. Many of the Stone Age implements were found during ploughing. Finds of Iron Age date were recovered in connection with building and other activities in the village plots. These find sites were noted, but no efforts were made to deduce the size of the possible sub-soil site. The main objective of the inventories was to find new monuments and sites for research. Even if the archaeologists took an interest in and carried out excavation on subsoil

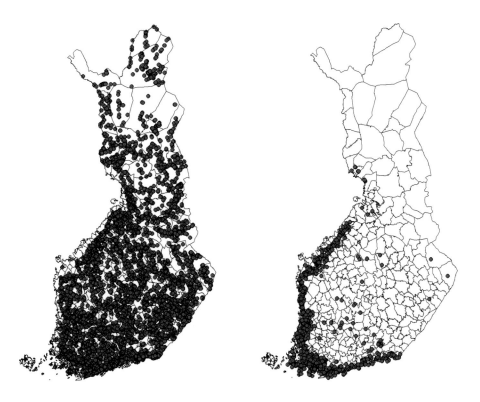

Fig. 17.1 (left): The distribution of Stone Age dwelling sites. National Board of Antiquities.

Fig. 17.2 (right): The distribution of Bronze Age burial cairns. National Board of Antiquities.

Fig. 17.3: The Stone Age dwelling site Hundbacken in Pedersöre.
Shallow floor depressions reveal the subsoil site in the forest.
Photo: Mirja Miettinen, National Board of Antiquities

sites, they were rarely totally excavated and their extent remained largely unknown. The same policy continued more or less until the end of the Second World War.

The post-war rebuilding entailed land use on a new scale. Even agriculture endangered archaeological heritage to an extent unknown earlier, as among other things new ploughing equipment reached the subsoil level containing the Stone Age dwelling sites. A planning and development act was passed in 1959 and the State Archaeological Commission found itself in a new role delivering opinions on plan proposals. However, planning at that time was mainly focused on densely inhabited areas (Littow 2006, 23). The rural agricultural areas remained unrestricted by the new planning legislation. Developments that endangered ancient monuments in these areas in this period were hydroelectric plants and road construction. Heritage management was included in the related planning processes and carried out rescue excavations when needed.

The Antiquities Act
The current Antiquities Act was passed in 1963. The act extends automatic protection to all ancient monuments and sites and prohibits their excavation, burial and disturbance without permission granted by the National Board of Antiquities. The Antiquities Act lists the types of ancient monuments, which are immoveable monuments, including both subsoil and underwater monuments, e.g. earth and stone mounds, cairns, stone circles and other stone settings, pre-Christian graves, cemeteries, stones with inscriptions, rock art, traces of grinding or hammering, mines and hunting pits, sacrificial springs, trees and

stones, immoveable natural objects associated with old traditions, tales or significant historic events. There is no specific age given to the monuments to be protected, only that they ought to be abandoned. Shipwrecks of over hundred years in age are also defined as immoveable ancient monuments. It is for the National Board of Antiquities to determine, which ones are monuments to be protected. It is stated in the proposal for the Act that if anyone is uncertain as to whether an object is an ancient monument or not the National Board of Antiquities should be consulted. The Antiquities Act further states that in planning, those responsible for the plans shall establish, whether the plan will concern ancient monuments. This gave the National Board of Antiquities some authority to intervene in the planning process.

The survey work intensified in the 1960s. New information on monuments and their location in the landscape helped in the discovery of more complex sites and even new categories of monuments.

The present heritage management organisation in Finland
The National Board of Antiquities attached to the Ministry of Culture is the central authority responsible for heritage protection in general. The Department of Archaeology of the National Board of Antiquities is in charge of the management of archaeological heritage. One of its main assignments is to supervise land use from the aspect of heritage. The Board is also the body that issues excavation licences. The Board keeps the national register of archaeological sites. The work is carried out in the central office in Helsinki and in two regional offices, Vaasa and Hämeenlinna. The Board has also delegated this authority to eight provincial museums; Jyväskylä, Kajaani, Lahti, Rovaniemi, Savonlinna, Turku, Tampere and Vaasa.

The register of archaeological sites
The situation today relies to a great degree on earlier developments. The current data base inventory was built up in the 1990s on the basis of the earlier surveys, supplemented with recent survey material. Approximately 200 - 300 new sites are registered every year. For the moment the data base includes circa 22,000 protected monuments. The National Board of Antiquities lists ancient monuments in two categories, those that must never be touched and those that can be, so to speak, eliminated by excavation. The first category consists of monuments of outstanding value, but also of types that for some reason have become rare in particular regions, but may be common elsewhere.

The inventory comprises different categories of information. The basic information is the type of monument, the name of the site and municipality, the location and the coordinates and a brief verbal description of the monument.

Fig. 17.4: Bronze Age burial cairns at the World Heritage site
Sammallahdenmäki in Raumaa.
Photo: Leena Koivisto, National board of Antiquities

There is a link to the topographic map site of the National Land Survey of Finland and the site is displayed on the map. When the boundaries of the site are determined they show on another map. Some of the registered data, such as the identity of the land owner, is accessible only for the officers of the National Board of Antiquities. The inventory is also accessible on the web for browsing.

The objective has been to carry out a basic survey of the entire country, but the resources have been insufficient to realise this in the short term. This work is still on-going. The Finnish experience indicates that a survey is out of date in 20 – 30 years. Refined survey and field walking methods with aid of GPS and GIS combined with new research results concerning the archaeological heritage forces the authorities to renew the surveys once in a generation. Finland is a large country and as the available resources for survey activity are limited, surveying will, as has been mentioned above, always be a constantly ongoing process. Basic surveys with municipalities as defined units are realized by the National Board of Antiquities budget funding. The provincial museums also carry out surveys in their regions. However, these surveys are insufficient. If planning concerns an area, where the archaeological inventory is outdated or the data insufficient, the planner is required to fund an archaeological survey together with other necessary investigations, as is stated by the current Land Use and Building Act of 2000. Very varied areas are surveyed as a result of the different survey approaches. The National Board has published a survey manual in order to obtain similar information irrespective of the surveying party (Maaranen & Kirkinen 2000). As the National Board of Antiquities is the authority that defines the ancient monuments, only an officer of the National Board of Antiquities can make the approbation and register the monument in the inventory. The register procedure is followed by the sending of a notification to the landowner.

The inventory data used in the heritage management

The register is the basic tool for the protection of the ancient monuments. It is used by the officers in the National Board of Antiquities and the provincial museums in their daily work.

The inventory data are however used by various other authorities as well as by private land owners and companies. The universities also have limited access for research purposes. The inventory comprises different categories of information and only basic information, such as the type of monument, the name of the site and municipality, the location and the coordinates and a brief verbal description of the monument are delivered to these users.

Even if the inventory is the basic tool for the protection of the ancient monuments, there are some difficulties in using it due to lack of essential information. When a new site is found, it is not always possible to determine the extent of the site, especially if it is a buried site. The surveyor can deduce the extent to some degree by the surface finds in the ploughed fields. The only means in forested areas is to dig test pits in critical areas, based on an analysis of the topographical situation, but these only give an approximate result. A completely reliable assessment would require the excavation of trial trenches. The site is registered in the inventory with the remark that the full extent is unknown. Forest companies use data from the register, when operating with computer-equipped log harvesters. When the data is insufficient, the forest worker has difficulty in avoiding damage to the sites, at least at the perimeter. Warnings are given not to go too close to the site in some cases, especially when harrowing deforested areas before replanting.

The imprecise nature of the data also complicates the planning situation. When the exact boundaries of the ancient monument are unknown, a trial excavation is needed to establish the size of the protected monument before the protected area of the monument in question can be entered into the plan. Even if the register lacks some information, the protection work can not be carried out without the aid of it.

Fig. 17.5: A Bronze Age burial cairn at Kylmäkorvenkallio, Rauma.
Photo: Leena Koivisto, National Board of Antiquities

Fig. 17.6: The Iron Age cemetery Mäksmäki in Masku.
Photo: Teija Tiitinen, National Board of Antiquities

How to protect the archaeological heritage when all ancient monuments are automatically protected?

The long tradition of protecting all ancient monuments gives a promise of great security for the archaeological heritage. Difficulties arise when it comes to the protection not only of single monuments, but also of larger areas, where the monuments can be understood in their original context. The Antiquities Act states that ancient monuments include an area of land necessary for the preservation of the remains in question and for providing sufficient space around them in the view of their nature and significance. The provincial environmental centres can, on application by the land owner or the National Board of Antiquities, confirm the boundaries of the ancient monument and the necessary protective area needed for its preservation. The centre can also issue special regulations concerning the land use of the protective area, thereby ensuring the value of the monument. Unless the boundaries of the monument concerned are laid down by the regional environmental centre, the protective area is only two metres wide from the visible perimeter of the monument.

A protective area of two metres around the monument is far too narrow and the question of protective areas has always been a great concern for the National Board of Antiquities. All sites and monuments are equally protected according to the Antiquities Act, but they are divided in two groups in the inventory: those of outstanding value that should be preserved undamaged for coming generations under any circumstances and monuments that can be excavated, when land use demands it.

For a long time the strategy of the Board to ensure the protection of the most outstanding monuments and their surroundings was to have the boundaries of these monuments and their protective areas laid down by the regional environmental centre. This work has been extremely resource consuming as the land owners, almost without exception, appeal to the administrative court against the decision made by the regional centre. The boundaries of 30 ancient monuments and their protective areas have been defined so far.

The article in the Antiquities Act concerning the protective areas has been tested many times in court. The administrative court has generally taken a very restrictive attitude towards the extent of the protective areas. An exceptional Viking Age monument complex, comprising a hillfort, a cemetery, a settlement site in the intervening area between the latter two sites and the environs of the entire complex, was threatened by a planned motor way. According to the initial plan, an exit was projected on the settlement site, between the hillfort and cemetery. The National Board of Antiquities requested the determination of the boundaries of the monument and its protective area by the regional environmental centre. The landowners, who expected an increase in the value of their assets due to the coming motorway, opposed the submission during the negotiations carried out between them and

Fig. 17.7: The Iron Age cemetery Mäksmäki in Masku in winter time.
Photo: Teija Tiitinen, National Board of Antiquities.

the regional environmental centre. However, the centre determined the boundaries of the monument complex, but defined a less extensive protective area, than that which had initially proposed by the National Board of Antiquities. The land owners appealed against the protective area to the administrative court, as they found the regulations unfavourable. They claimed that new development was restricted and only current agricultural land use was allowed. The court decided in favour of the land owners and rejected the protective area with the argument that it was too large. The National Board of Antiquities appealed this decision to the Supreme Administrative Court, which retained the decision of the boundaries of the ancient monument complex, but rejected the boundaries for the protective area, on the grounds that the protective area was larger than was necessary to ensure the safety of the monument. The Supreme Administrative Court stated also that cultural landscape "per se" cannot be protected by the Antiquities Act. This statement has been taken as a precedent for similar cases.

Consequently the National Board of Antiquities has given up the strategy of continuing the practice of having the boundaries of the most important ancient monuments and their protective areas defined by the regional environmental centres.

Ancient monuments and planning

As the Antiquities Act does not provide the necessary tools for protecting ancient monuments in a larger landscape context, other means to obtain these objectives must be found. The evident instrument for this matter has always been the planning process. However, the National Board of Antiquities has not always been successful with in the protection of large area complexes, even if is an important participant in the planning process.

In 1983, the National Board of Antiquities, in cooperation with the Ministry of Internal Affairs, the ministry then responsible for the environment, published an inventory of the most important archaeological areas that required

protection (Valtakunnallisesti merkittävät esihistorialliset suojelukokonaisuudet 1983). This inventory covered far too large areas to be taken seriously into consideration by planners and decision makers and it has also in other ways become outdated some time ago. The inventory cannot be used as a tool in planning and a new edition should to be published.

With no specific guidelines to rely on, the National Board of Antiquities has fought for the protection of archaeological reserves, case by case, with varying results. At the end of the 1980s, the motorway from Helsinki to Tampere was projected close to an important archaeological site, a hillfort and a cultural landscape of extraordinary value. There were no formal reasons for altering the plans, but strong opposition from archaeologists, as well as the public, forced the motorway construction authorities to do so. The case shows that plans can be altered without resort to judicial action, but it requires a lot of resources.

The new land use and building act was passed in 2000. It states that when a plan is drawn up, approved or ratified, the provisions of the Antiquities Act should be observed. There are three levels of planning. The province or county plan, the zone plan and the detail plan. The provincial plan is summary and produced by the provincial authorities and ratified by the Ministry of Environment. The zone and detail plans are internal municipal decisions. The detail plans are mostly plans for urban areas, but there are also other examples, such as shore line plans, which are drawn up in rural areas with the purpose of controlling holiday home development. The National Board of Antiquities aims to have all ancient monuments entered on plans at all levels. The scale on the provincial plans does not always allow this and they are listed instead in an appendix. They are drawn up with the greatest possible accuracy on the other plans. Reserves for the outstanding archaeological area complexes are drawn up on the province plans.

Fig. 17.8: A Troy Town, probably constructed in the 18th century, on an island in the archipelago of the Gulf of Bothnia.
Photo: Kaisa Lehtonen, National Board of Antiquities

The National Board of Antiquities maintains a dialogue with the planning party in its efforts to restrict the exploitation of heritage. The Board aims to minimize the rescue excavations to be carried out, even if a possibility of allowing development after due excavations does exist. The succeeding generations of archaeologists will always have better facilities to extract knowledge from the monuments and if exploitation can be avoided, it is seen as a benefit. All other threats to the archaeological heritage should be taken into account, even if some of them are almost unavoidable. Acid rain, caused by air pollution, adds to the acidity of the already acid soils. This results in the accelerated corrosion of fragile metal artefacts. Hydroelectric dams create basins, which cause the erosion of riverside and waterfront sites (Schauman-Lönnqvist 2007, 54). Whenever the possibility of preserving heritage exists it must be taken. All effort is made in the planning process to restrict development activities to areas without any ancient monuments. The National Board of Antiquities makes suggestions for reserves in the plans to ensure the preservation of the surroundings of the most important monuments. The planners have recently adopted this way of thinking and are willing to make such reserves. However, when economic values are endangered by the heritage on a larger scale, the political decision makers do not always agree on such an approach to protection and are not willing to decide in favour of reserves.

The National Board of Antiquities can in some cases raise some funds to buy some land to ensure the preservation of archaeological heritage. Land ownership is however not a primary function for the Board. In order to achieve a broader understanding of the protection of ancient monuments in their surroundings, where they can be understood as part of a larger context, emphasis in heritage management ought to be laid on education on all levels.

Marianne.Schauman-Lonnqvist@nba.fi

References

Appelgren (-Kivalo), Hj. 1891: S*uomen muinaislinnat. Tutkimus vertailevan muinaistieteen alalla.* S*uomen Muinaismuistoyhdistyksen Aikakauskirja* 12. Helsinki.

Edgren, T. 1995: Några synpunkter på rannsakningarnas Finlandsdel. *Rannsakningar efter antikviteter – ett symposium om 1600-talets Sverige. Kungl. Vitterhets Historie och Antikvitets Akademien. Konferenser 30:50-61.* Stockholm.

Littow, P. 2006: Kaavoitus ennen maankäyttö- ja rakennuslakia. *Maankäyttö 4/2006*; Helsinki, 22-24.

Maaranen, P. & Kirkinen, T. (eds.) 2000: *Arkeologinen inventointi. Opas inventoinnin suunnitteluun ja toteuttamiseen.* Helsinki.

Schauman-Lönnqvist, M. 2007: Rescue Archaeology in Finland – Goals and Practices. In Katalin Bozóki-Erney ed. *European Preventive Archaeology. Papers of the EPAC Meeting, Vilnius 2004.* Budapest, 51-56.

Valtakunnallisesti merkittävät esihistorialliset suojelukokonaisuudet: 1983. Sisäasiainministeriö. Kaavoitus- ja rakennusosasto. Tiedotuksia 3/1983. Helsinki.

18 | A new inventory for the Lower German Limes (Rhine-Limes) 2005 – 2007

Jürgen Kunow

Abstract: In 1987, Hadrian's Wall was granted World Cultural Heritage status, to be followed in 2005 by the Upper German-Raetian-Limes. Since then, the UNESCO has decided to place the entire length of the European Limes on the World Heritage list of protected monuments. The Lower German Limes is a part of this European monument. A nomination for World Heritage status necessitates the production of a completely new inventory of the monument. This is a prerequisite for a successful application. The Archaeological Monuments Services of three states (Rhineland-Palatinate, North Rhine-Westphalia, The Netherlands) must work together to develop a uniform scheme for cataloguing the monument. The scheme adopted for the North Rhine-Westphalian section of the Limes, which is some 225 km in length, is explained in some detail. This is of general interest, but is of particular interest for custodians of other sections of the Limes in river landscapes, e. g. the Danube.

The most fundamental task in the preservation of archaeological monuments is generally considered to be the making of inventories. Thus, by means of three main activities - namely determination (in the sense of recognition), description and evaluation of the existing archaeological material – the basis is laid for the heritage management of upstanding and sub-surface monuments. It may, at first, appear surprising that we should begin again to record the existence of archaeological material for the Lower German Limes, in whose legionary fortresses and auxiliary forts the first extensive and exemplary excavations were carried out more than a hundred years ago, and which have been the subject of so much scholarship. That this is necessary becomes evident when hard questions, relevant to the practical preservation of the Lower German Limes, are asked, such as:

What percentage of the approximately 27 hectares of the large legionary fortress *Bonna* in the urban area of today's Bonn has not been built upon, and/or destroyed, and therefore would be accessible for any future research? Or, which precise sections of the Limes-road are actually known? Or, where exactly did the Limes run in Lower Germany, i.e. where was the river bed of the Rhine in Roman times?

At present nobody can answer these elementary questions with certainty. Surveys and synopses that would collate separately recorded data material according to specific questions are missing!

In order to understand our work on a new inventory of the Lower German Limes, it is, firstly, necessary to visualize two sets of circumstances. One relates to the research work done hitherto on the Limes and the archaeological institutions which carried it out and are still responsible for them today. The other concerns the invitation by UNESCO to register the Roman Limes on the World

Heritage List as a single linear monument, traversing many modern states, and as a testimony to a common historical past.

I will begin with a few words – which at this point is all that is possible anyway – about the history of research on the topic. Scientific research on the two large German sections of the Limes, the Upper German-Raetian Limes and our section, the Lower German Limes, both began in the first half of the 19th century, as a result of the work of interested lay people, antiquarian and historical societies, as well as former military personnel. The year 1892 became the key year for the Upper German-Raetian Limes, with the founding of the Reichs-Limeskommission under Theodor Mommsen. During the next four decades or so, this border section was systematically researched and in 1937 the last of 56 publications on the topic appeared. Thereby a complete inventory was created of the 550 km long Limes section, with its approximately 900 watch towers and 120 large and smaller military forts, from which both heritage management and research still benefit today (Planck 2002). Research on the Lower German Limes pursued a completely different course. Here the emphasis was on extensive excavations which were carried out at individual prominent locations, such as the legionary camps *Novaesium* (Neuss) by C. Coenen in the years between 1887 and 1900, or *Vetera I* (Xanten) by H. Lehner and F. Oelmann from 1905 to 1934. In the case of auxiliary forts the excavations of A.E. van Giffen come to mind. Between 1941 and 1953 he was able to almost completely examine the fort of a cohort in Valkenburg in the Netherlands (Bogaers & Rüger 1974, 40-43; Bechert & Willems 1995, 95-97). Impressive as these investigations are, they remained examinations of individual locations. How these sites related to each other was not looked at nor was any recognition given to their role as part of the Roman Limes. After the Second World War, Harald von Petrikovits coined the term 'Lower German Limes' and postulated that the individual camps were interconnected and part of a linear border (Petrikovits 1959). His insight was finally accepted by the scientific community in the 1970s (Bogaers & Rüger 1974; Gechter 1979; Bechert & Willems 1995). This accords with the ancient name for this border area, *limes ad Germaniam inferiorem*.

The necessity for a first comprehensive inventory of the Lower German Limes can be very concisely justified – which brings us to the second point. This is a prerequisite, along with the so-called management plan, for a successful application for registration on the list of world heritage sites. After Hadrian's Wall (in 1987) and the Upper German-Raetian Limes (in 2005) became part of the World Heritage List (Planck 2002; Breeze & Thiel 2005; Thiel 2008) UNESCO requested the bordering states to treat the Roman Limes as a common monument worth protecting. The Lower German Limes now appears to be a 'missing link' between two already registered Limes sections; a situation that cannot be rationally explained to the public or politicians.

Within the framework of the project 'Bestandserhebung Niedergermanischer Limes (NGL)', designed to run for some five years (2005 to 2010), the focus is now

concentrated on comprehensively dealing with four areas of responsibility (Kunow 2007):

- to record and document the condition of above-ground and sub-surface remains of the Lower German Limes, including all facilities which are proven to have been used or operated by the Roman Army;
- to formulate and consolidate a programme for the protection and maintenance of this linear monument in the context of ongoing urban and regional development along the Rhine;
- to increase public awareness of the related individual monuments and museums under one common 'brand name';
- to develop new interdisciplinary research questions about the Roman Limes, including the former 'Vorfeld' and the 'Hinterland'.

To return to the Lower German Limes, the project had to be planned so that not only the part in North Rhine-Westphalia would be taken into consideration but also that part of the Limes in other areas. As is known, the Lower German Limes began in the south in *Rigomagus* (today: Remagen, Rhineland-Palatinate), ran along the Rhine through what is today the Federal State of North Rhine-Westphalia and reached the North Sea, *Mare Germanicum*, at *Lugdunum*

Fig. 18.1: Course of the Lower German Limes between Remagen (Rhineland-Palatinate, Germany) and Katwijk (Netherlands) with demarcation of the various archaeological departments' responsibility (cf. Kunow 2007, 28 fig. 13 with additions).

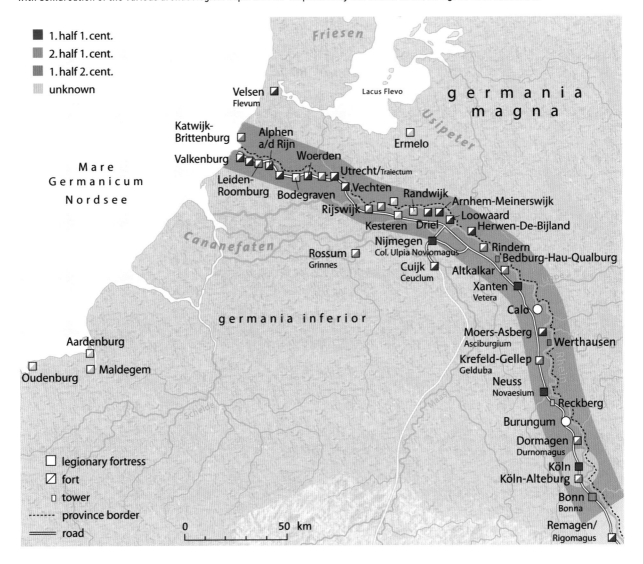

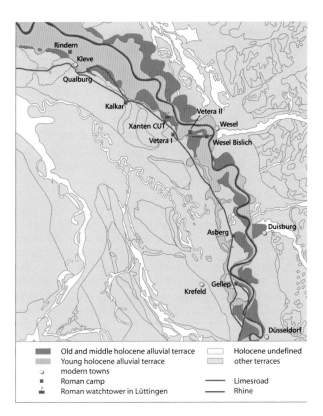

Fig. 18.2: Map of the pre-Roman (= old and middle Holocene) flood-plain terraces, as well as Roman and post-Roman (= young Holocene) terraces on the German Lower Rhine between Düsseldorf and Rindern (cf. Gerlach 2007, 101 fig. 94).

Neuss, Duisburg, Krefeld or Nijmegen, which have to be integrated in this large-scale inventory.

Looking at the European Limes of the Roman Empire as a whole, the longest sections of the imperial border ran along rivers, namely the Rhine and (especially) the Danube. Land boundaries created with earthen or stone walls and ditches, like Hadrian's Wall, or rather the Scottish Antonine Wall, and the Upper German-Raetian Limes, were only constructed where no such natural frontiers were available. Therefore a so-called 'Wet Limes' or River-Limes was actually the norm. However, this involves exceptional features. On the one hand, border security with man-made buildings (wooden palisades, earthen mounds, stone walls, ditches, etc.) was unnecessary here, and on the other hand – and this is considerably more important for heritage management – river landscapes are especially dynamic areas, from a physical-geographic (permanently shifting rivers) as well as from a cultural-geographic perspective (settlement areas intensively used by people). We have to devote our attention to both these aspects.

(today: Katwijk, Netherlands) (fig. 18.1). The total length of the Lower German Limes can only be approximately given as about 380 km, as the course of the Roman Rhine – at least as far as our Federal State of North Rhine-Westphalia is concerned, with about half of the river's length (approx. 225 km) – is still not precisely known. There are five state archaeological services involved – namely those of the German Federal States of the Rhineland-Palatinate, North Rhine-Westphalia (Landschaftsverbände of Rheinland, Westfalen-Lippe and the City of Cologne) and of the Netherlands (Rijksdienst voor het Oudheidkundig Bodemonderzoek; more recently: Rijksdienst voor Archeologie, Cultuurlandschap en Monumenten, Amersfoort) – and diverse town archaeological units such as those of

For the Rhineland – in the Netherlands they know considerably more about it – one initial fundamental question was to clarify the course of the Rhine in Roman times. Here we started a common research programme with the Geological Service of the Federal State of North Rhine-Westphalia, in order to bring together the existing geological, archaeo-botanical and archaeological data from various archives (Gerlach 2007). The aim was to date the post-Ice Age, i.e. Holocene sedimentation of the Rhenish alluvial plains. Fig. 18.2 shows a simplified result. The illustration of the younger post-Ice Age flood-plain terraces (from the birth of Christ until present) indicates those areas where we can presume that the Rhine flowed during Roman times. In some regions, for example around Xanten, we even know of several courses which the Roman Rhine took and here we can not only define areas, but also linear courses. The changes in a river-course are made particularly evident by the situation at Xanten. In Roman times the town of *Colonia Ulpia Traiana* (CUT) was connected to the Rhine by a harbour and could be reached by ship. Today the Rhine flows at a distance of about 2 km from it.

But not only the physical-geographic, but also the cultural-geographic aspects are decisive for a river landscape. Roman forts and settlements near the river often became the starting point for the foundation of civilian towns, which were then able to develop into modern cities (with reference to the Rhine: Nijmegen, Cologne, Bonn, Mainz, Strasbourg; in the case of the Danube: Regensburg, Vienna, Budapest). Therefore today the Roman remains lie in inner city areas and are more or less completely built over, which makes particular demands on

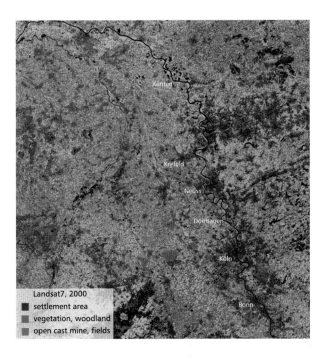

Fig. 18.3: Present urban density along the Rhine as seen on satellite imagery. Here Roman camps and settlements functioned as the nucleus of modern towns (cf. Kunow 2007, 29 fig. 14).

the protection of the sub-surface cultural heritage. The Lower Rhine, above all in its southern section, is now an enclosed and intensively occupied area of modern settlement with a population of almost 10 million inhabitants (fig. 18.3). The Roman camp of antiquity, *Durnomagus*, now also lies in the middle of a modern town, whose name, Dormagen, still serves as a reminder of its Roman foundation. Dormagen serves as a good example of how work on compiling an inventory of archaeological remains can be carried out within the problematic area of an inner city. The Roman auxiliary camp, *Durnomagus*, was established for a cavalry unit, a so-called *ala*, which was stationed here in the 1st and 2nd centuries. In the 1960s and 1970s, in particular, following comprehensive rescue excavations, the 3.25 hectare camp was extensively built over. *Durnomagus* belongs to the best known alae-forts on the Limes, with 1.18 hectares examined, which corresponds to 36.1% of the total area of the camp. In the framework of compiling an inventory the first objective was to assess all excavated areas containing features relating to the

Roman camp (Becker 2007b) and to integrate them into an overall plan (fig. 18.4). The further, decisive question was to determine how much undisturbed area remains for heritage protection and research, for it was evident that the rescue excavations alone had caused losses to an extent of more than one third of the camp area. There were further disturbances due to house construction, laying pipes, etc., which had been carried out without any archaeological control, and whose exact location and depth could only be ascertained by referring to planning department files and related documents. In addition, modern cellars were surveyed when no architectural plans were available, in order to record the extent of the disturbance. All the destroyed areas were entered into an 'Automatische Liegenschaftskarte', the digital mapping scheme used by the official land registry in Germany for every kind of town planning. It is accurate to a scale of centimetres. Moreover, the "Automatisierte Liegenschaftskarte" is linked to a data-base that brings together information about the area from all town planning as well

Fig. 18.4: Plan of the cavalry fort at Dormagen including excavation areas and Roman building structures (cf. Becker 2007, 110 fig. 103 with additions).

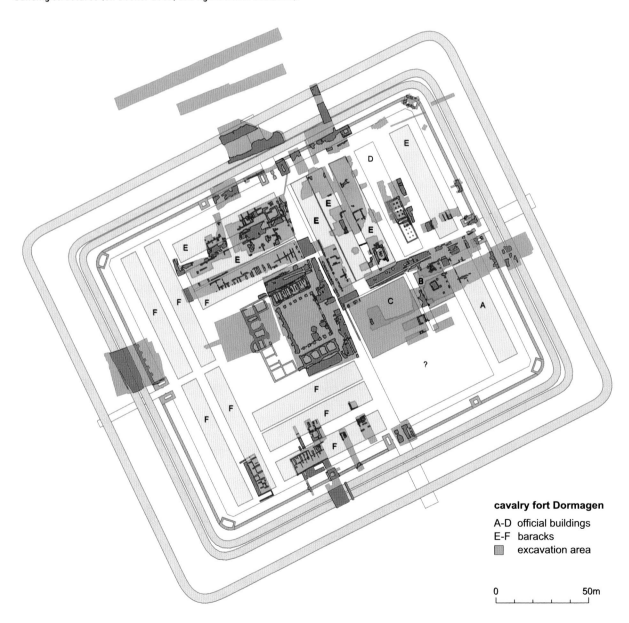

cavalry fort Dormagen

A-D official buildings
E-F baracks
◼ excavation area

0   50m

as archaeological documentation. At a glance, information on precise plots of land related to excavation areas can now be recognized, including excavation plans (fig. 18.5 above), as well as loss-zones as a result of building (with different categories depending on the extent of destruction) and those protected areas which are still intact (fig. 18.5 below). It is thus possible to establish the basis for town and regional planning which protects our heritage. In the case of Dormagen, to our surprise it turned out that, despite extensive modern building and its location in the inner city, about half the area of the former Roman camp had not been destroyed. Before beginning work on compiling an inventory, we had assumed that the loss rate would be 80% or more!

Based on this example, inventories of all of the military installations along the Lower German Limes will be made in the coming years and documented cartographically, according to data in the 'Automatisierte Liegenschaftskarte'. Work on the legionary camp *Bonna* (Bonn), which is about ten times larger than that at Dormagen, and poses very similar problems today with its inner city location, has advanced very well. Military installations along the Limes include the so-called point and area elements, such as camps, watchtowers, etc. and the production centres set up by the military, such as potteries and brick- and tile-works. Furthermore, the so-called linear elements of the Limes road must also be added to the inventory (Becker 2007a) and – as described above – the

Fig. 18.5: Comparison of excavation results (above) and present preservation of features (below) in the southeastern corner of the Roman cavalry fort in Dormagen (cf. Kunow 2007, 29 fig. 15 with additions).

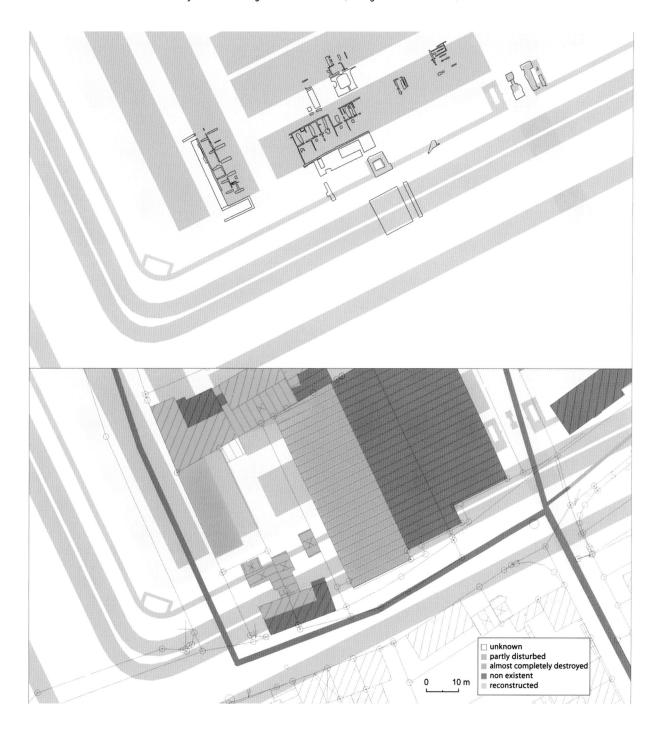

unknown
partly disturbed
almost completely destroyed
non existent
reconstructed

0   10 m

Roman Rhine. However, our interest goes beyond the mere course of the Rhine. The military operated supply installations to secure raw materials, both in the hinterland and at the front line of the Limes, such as quarries (e.g. for trachyte in the Siebengebirge near Königswinter, or for limestone at Iversheim) and mines for extracting ores (iron ore, lead, copper in the Eifel and in Bergisch Land). Numerous areas of quarrying and mining can be chronologically assigned to Roman times and functionally to the military as their operator. Such indispensable infrastructural elements, without which military logistics would have been impossible, will also be included in the inventory of the Lower German Limes.

The inventory of the Lower German Limes, which will be developed over the coming years, is going to form the basis – as I described it at the beginning – for all further applications which should follow. Among these the protection and management concepts for the Lower German Limes are paramount, although better access to Roman monuments for the public and for tourism also feature. At present no precise date can be given as to when North Rhine-Westphalia will be able to submit its section of the Roman Limes (hopefully as a bi-national application, together with the Netherlands) for inclusion in the World Heritage List of UNESCO in Paris. Nonetheless, I am certain that the Lower German Limes will one day be part of the UNESCO Heritage Site called the 'Roman Limes'.

Other European states are now working on similar data bases for other sections of the European Limes and it is to be hoped that in future this will be followed by the Limes in Asia and North Africa (Breeze, Jilek & Thiel 2005; Klee 2006; Thiel 2008). Then we will have an absolutely unique protected world heritage site, with a total length of 5,500 km which connects a multitude of states in Europe, Asia and Africa – hopefully in the mutual interests of our peaceful future.

Juergen.Kunow@lvr.de

References

Bechert, T. & Willems, W.J.H. (ed.) 1995: Die *römische Reichsgrenze von der Mosel bis zur Nordseeküste*, Stuttgart.

Becker, Th. 2007a: Untersuchungen am Straßensystem entlang der römischen Rheingrenze. *Archäologie im Rheinland* 2006, 105-07.

Becker, Th. 2007b: Neue Erkenntnisse zum römischen Auxiliarkastell Dormagen. *Archäologie im Rheinland* 2006, 110-12.

Bogaers, J.E. & Rüger, C.B. (ed.) 1974: *Der niedergermanische Limes. Materialien zu seiner Geschichte*, Köln.

Breeze, D. & Thiel, A. 2005: *The challenge of presentation. Visible and invisible parts of the Frontiers of the Roman Empire World Heritage Site in the United Kingdom and Germany*, Amsterdam.

Breeze, D., Jilek, S. & Thiel, A. 2005: *Frontiers of the Roman Empire – Grenzen des Römischen Reiches – Frontières de l'Empire Romain*, Edinburgh-Esslingen-Wien.

Gechter, M. 1979: Die Anfänge des Niedergermanischen Limes. *Bonner Jahrbücher* 179, 1979, 1-129.

Gerlach, R. 2007: Wo war der Rhein zur Römerzeit? Ein Beitrag zum Rhein-Limes-Projekt. *Archäologie im Rheinland* 2006, 100-02.

Hanel, N. 1995: Vetera I. Die Funde aus den römischen Lagern auf dem Fürstenberg zu Xanten. *Rheinische Ausgrabungen* 35, Köln (2 vol.).

Klee, M. 2006: *Grenzen des Imperiums. Leben am römischen Limes*, Stuttgart.

Kunow, J. 2007: Der Niedergermanische Limes in Nordrhein-Westfalen. *Archäologie im Rheinland* 2006, 27-30.

Petrikovits, H. v. 1959: Der niedergermanische Limes, in: *Limes-Studien. Vorträge des 3. Intern. Limes-Kongresses in Rheinfelden/Basel* 1957 (= Schriften des Institutes für Ur- und Frühgeschichte der Schweiz 14) 88-95.

Planck, D. 2002: Das Limesprojekt – Schutz, Erforschung und Präsentation am Beispiel von Deutschlands größtem Bodendenkmal. *Berichte der Römisch-Germanischen Kommission* 83, 2002, 191-206.

Thiel, A. 2008 (ed.): *Der Limes als UNESCO-Weltkulturerbe*. Beiträge zum Welterbe Limes 1, Stuttgart.

19 | The PALAFITTES database – An archaeological site inventory crossing state borders

Albert Hafner

The idea of preparing a UNESCO world heritage candidature for the Neolithic and Bronze Age lake-dwellings of Switzerland first emerged in 2004, when pile-dwelling research was celebrating its 150th anniversary. In that same year the idea was transformed into action when all States Party to the World Heritage Convention were asked to draw up a tentative list of sites with world heritage potential.

In Switzerland an expert group checked all 35 candidates for the tentative list and chose five projects. The aim was to submit only projects with a real chance of success. All candidatures should comply with the Global Strategy for a Balanced, Representative and Credible World Heritage List, launched in 1994 by the World Heritage Committee. The overall aim of the Global Strategy is to ensure that the List reflects the world's cultural and natural diversity of outstanding universal value. In December 2004, the Swiss government added the pile-dwellings project to the Swiss tentative list (http://whc.unesco.org/fr/listesindicatives/2038). In January 2008 the government of France agreed to include the French sites on its own tentative list.

Inclusion in the tentative list was the first step towards the international candidature process which has been undertaken in close collaboration with the Swiss Federal Office of Culture (part of the Swiss Ministry of Culture), and the national focal points of the participating countries (Austria, Germany, France, Italy and Slovenia). The candidature dossier will be examined by ICOMOS and UNESCO in 2010-2012.

Though the Archaeological Service of the Canton of Berne first took the initiative in 2004, since June 2008 the organisational lead is in the hands of "PALAFITTES", a Swiss organisation based in Hauterive (Canton of Neuchâtel). The aim of the organisation is to support the world heritage candidature of "Pile-dwellings in lakes and bogs around the Alps". It works closely with archaeological heritage managers in the cantons of Aargau, Berne, Fribourg, Geneva, Luzern, Neuchâtel, Nidwalden, Obwalden, Schaffhausen, Schwyz, Solothurn, St. Gallen, Thurgau, Vaud, Zug and Zurich. The candidature is supported by Swiss Archaeology, Basle, the Swiss association of Cantonal Archaeologists (Verband schweizerischer Kantonsarchäologinnnen und Kantonsarchäologen) and the Swiss UNESCO Commission. International partners include the cultural heritage institutions (Landesämter für Denkmalpflege) in Baden-Württemberg and Bavaria, Germany, the Italian Ministero per i Beni e le Attivita Culturali in Rome, the Austrian Ministry of Culture, the French Ministère de la Culture in Paris and the Slovenian Ministry of Culture in Ljubljana.

By the end of 2006 the cantonal institutions for archaeological heritage management in Switzerland had produced the first complete database of all known pile-dwelling sites in lakes and bogs between Lake Geneva and Lake Constance. Data from Baden-Württemberg have now also been integrated, and France, Austria, Italy and Slovenia are currently preparing their databases. The database currently consists of 446 recorded sites in Switzerland and 121 in Baden-Württemberg. The last inventory of pile-dwelling sites in Switzerland dates back to 1930. The outstanding feature of this new database lies in the fact that it is the first common inventory to cross cantonal and national borders.

The inventory of the pile-dwellings is designed mainly to comply with the guidelines for the preparation of serial nominations to the World Heritage List. To keep it as simple as possible the database covers only basic information. Archaeological heritage management institutions may however add more information about a site at any time, according to individual need. The aim of the inventory for the UNESCO pile-dwelling world heritage project is to summarize the most important information on one sheet of A4 paper. There are at the very least good practical reasons for this limitation, as it makes it simple to produce and reproduce physical copies.

The inventory also includes a map on a scale of 1:10 000 defining the core area and buffer zone of each site.

Fig. 19.1: Example of a map from the PALAFITTES database. The site on the adjacent sheet is marked in darker green.

Several adjacent sites may of course exist within one buffer zone. The core area described in the adjacent sheet of the database is coloured in darker green than the neighbouring sites. With its combination of listing information and site mapping, the inventory for the UNESCO pile-dwelling world heritage project is a valuable tool.

The following information is listed in the database:
- Title of the inventory.
- Number of the object.
- State Party.
- Regional administration unit (canton, Bundesland, region).
- Name of the object (community and place name).
- Coordinates (national system).
- Global coordinates according to World Geodetic System 1984 (WGS84).
- Altitude of the site relative to sea level.
- Responsible institution and logo of the institution.
- Inventory code of the responsible institution.
- Size of the site (core zone).
- Size of the buffer zone.
- Site category (landscape and environment, preservation and potential, risk potential).
- Dating of the site.
- Summarized description of the site.
- Bibliography.

The database in the MS ACCESS format has been completed with related files (graphic data from the maps, logos and addresses of institutions). Graphic data exist as printable high-resolution files or as screen-optimized versions. The bibliography of the database has been generated from a MS EndNote database.

More information about the database and the mapping of the sites can be obtained from the Archaeological Service of the Canton of Berne or from PALAFITTES.

albert.hafner@ erz.be.ch,
christian.harb@palafittes.ch
www.palafittes.ch

Pfahlbauten - Prähistorische Feuchtbodensiedlungen des Alpenraumes

Objektnummer		Staat **Schweiz**		Kanton **BE**

Objektname	**Sutz-Lattrigen - Hauptstation**

Weltkoordinaten		Landeskoordinaten	Achse N-S	**582 370** m
			Achse E-W	**216 240** m
			Meereshöhe	**428** müM

Zuständige Institution
Archäologischer Dienst des Kantons Bern
Brünnenstrasse 66

CH - 3018 Bümpliz

Inventarnummer	Grösse der Fundstelle	Grösse der Pufferzone	Fundstellen-Kategorien	1. Landschaft und Umgebung	A
326.170	**3.2** ha	**19.8** ha		2. Erhaltung und Potential	A
				3. Gefährdung	C

Datierung	✔ Neolithisch	Jahre v.Chr.	☐ 5000 - 4000	✔ 3500 - 3000	☐ 2500 - 2000	☐ 1500 - 1000
	☐ Bronzezeitlich		✔ 4000 - 3500	☐ 3000 - 2500	☐ 2000 - 1500	☐ 1000 - 500

Die Hauptstation umfasst mindestens acht Siedlungsphasen: 3825-22 v.Chr., 3638-37 v.Chr., 3596-66 v.Chr., 3412 v.Chr., 3202-3121 v.Chr., 3094-89 v.Chr. 3043-3036 v.Chr. und 3015-13 v.Chr. (vorläufige Daten, n = etwa 8000-10000 Dendroproben).

Kurzbeschreibung der Fundstelle

Der Uferabschnitt der Gemeinde Sutz-Lattrigen befindet sich am Südufer des Bielersees. Die sogenannte Hauptstation mit den Teilen "Innen" und "Aussen" wurde 1854 erstmals in der Literatur genannt. Die Fundstelle wird in allen wichtigen Publikationen des 19. Jahrhunderts erwähnt, obwohl nie umfangreiche Ausgrabungen stattgefunden haben.

Die Fundstelle befindet sich in einer westexponierten langgezogenen Bucht mit einer breiten Flachwasserzone. Nur ein ganz kleiner Teil des Siedlungsareals befindet sich unter Land. Seit den Rettungsgrabungen 1988-2004 (Umfang etwa 19.000 qm) und den Schutzmassnahmen (Umfang etwa 6000 qm) sind die gefährdeten Zonen entweder archäologisch dokumentiert oder durch Geotextil und Kiesschüttungen vor der Erosion geschützt.

Die Rettungsgrabungen 1988-2004 sind Teil des Gesamtprojekts "Seeufersiedlungen Lattrigenbucht", das als eines der grössten Unternehmen im Bereich der Unterwasserarchäologie der Binnengewässer gelten kann. Dabei wurden nicht nur zehntausende von Funden sondern auch mehr als 13.000 Hölzer geborgen. Die wissenschaftliche Bearbeitung der Befunde verspricht zahlreiche grossflächige Dorfgrundrisse und detaillierte Einblicke in die Siedlungsentwicklung von etwa acht bis zehn prähistorischen Dörfern geben. Das jung- und spätneolithische Fundmaterial stellt eine hervorragende Ergänzung zu den Fundkomplexen von Twann dar, die als Referenzkomplexe für die Schweiz gelten. Das Fundmaterial ist abgesehen von Vorbernoch unpubliziert.

Bibliographie (Auswahl der wichtigsten Literatur)
Winiger 1989, 72-85; Hafner 2005, 41-48.

Fig. 19.2: Example of a print-out from the PALAFITTES database. The most important information about each pile-dwelling site is summarized on one sheet of A4 paper. The basic version of the database was designed as a tool for the geographical identification of property. The database can be expanded according to individual needs, but the basic version is the same in all participating countries (Switzerland, Austria, Germany, France, Italy and Slovenia).

20 | Listing and protection of archaeological sites in Europe – summary

Leonard de Wit and Leon Ziengs

Introduction

The 9th Heritage Management Symposium was held in Târgovişte, Romania, from 6 to 8 May 2008. The subject of the meeting was 'Listing archaeological sites, protecting the archaeological landscape'. After the meeting, all participating countries were sent a questionnaire containing approximately 20 questions about the process of listing and the protection of archaeological sites.

The responses were compared to identify similarities and differences in the way the countries concerned manage their heritage. Some responses were more or less identical: one could say that all countries list and protect their archaeological heritage in roughly the same way. But there are of course differences, too. The main similarities and differences in terms of listing, legal issues and heritage management are set out below. This is not an exhaustive analysis considering the circumstances in each country in detail, but merely an impression based on the answers received. We should point out that the responses suggested that certain terms used in cultural heritage management are not used in the same way in all countries. The definition of terms such as 'monument' and 'registration' can vary from country to country. There may therefore be a certain amount of 'noise' in the responses and the analysis. Every attempt has, however, been made to give as clear and representative a picture as possible.

Listing

Similarities

All countries indicated that they have a system for listing archaeological sites and historical landscapes on the basis of inventories. Such lists are a requirement under the law in all countries except Finland and France. The aim is generally to identify sites and landscapes so that they are visible or protected during the planning process. In some countries, however, lists are kept mainly for other purposes. In France, for example, registration takes the form of a document management system that is above all a research tool, while in Scotland the registration process also serves the interests of education and tourism. Responsibility for updating the lists is centralised in almost all cases. One exception is Poland, where 16 regional inspectors have this responsibility.

No single country responded to the question of whether there is a direct link between site protection and the protection of historical landscapes with an unequivocal 'yes'. Historical landscapes as such are not listed in most countries. However, it would seem that the historical value of the surrounding landscape is often used as a supporting argument for listing archaeological sites. Most countries indicated that the protection of historical landscapes does not necessarily cover the areas where the most important archaeological sites are situated. Countries tend to collect data on sites for selection in more or less the same way. Not surprisingly, they all use common methods like field visits, surveys and archive and desk studies. Most countries reject predictive modelling as a possible basis for registration. Only proven values are considered. The German state of Bavaria is a notable exception, however. There, licenses are subject to a legal requirement to intervene at sites 'where archaeological monuments are suggested or predictable'.

Differences

The information countries give about their method of listing is much less uniform. Is it based on objective criteria and parameters, or on expert judgment? In some countries, registration depends on expert opinion, while in others objective criteria are the crucial factor; sometimes it is based on both. Most countries say they take an interdisciplinary approach, or aspire to do so.

The responses to the question of whether listing is supported by scientific research are notable for their variation. Most countries state that the data on which listing is based are generally derived from scientific research. However, several countries also said that this was not the case, or not entirely: there is either no obligation to base registration on research, it does not happen systematically, or no scientific research is conducted at all.

Legal issues

Similarities

Uniformity on legal issues was found particularly in the response to the question of whether protection implies preservation in the long term or whether the demand for space tends to lead to preventive excavation. Although the majority of countries aim for long-term preservation, most answers suggested a certain degree of conflict between preservation in the long term and regional development or economic interests. France and the Swiss canton of Bern both indicated that protection sometimes has to make way for 'appropriate change' such as house and road building. In such cases, rescue excavations are performed.

Differences

There are major differences between the countries when it comes to the legal implications of listing sites and monuments, in particular. As indicated above, Finland has no legislation on this issue and so there can be no legal implications associated with listing. In France, listing has no enforceable legal implications for third parties, and rights of ownership remain unaffected. In Bern, local authorities are obliged to report planned projects in protected areas to the archaeological service, which produces a report that affects the decision on whether to grant a permit. In the Czech Republic, listing places restrictions on farmers in connection with protection, and can lead to permit applications being rejected. Property developers must not damage protected monuments. The same applies in Slovenia. In Scotland, heritage sites may be negatively affected only for 'developments of national importance'. In Poland the heritage service gets a say in the sale and division of protected sites. In Bavaria and the Netherlands the owner of a protected site is obliged to apply for a permit to make any changes to it once it has been listed. In England, agreement must be reached with the archaeological service before any work can be carried out on listed sites, subject to a fine for non-compliance. Switzerland, pointing at an important indirect implication of listing, indicated that listing makes it easier to qualify for a grant.

There are differences between European countries in terms of the compensation available to the owners of listed sites, too. In most countries, owners are eligible for only a negligible amount, if at all. In Bavaria, the Czech Republic, Poland and Slovenia, they are eligible for compensation, though the conditions differ considerably. In Poland, owners must demonstrate actual loss to qualify for compensation, while in Slovenia there must be deterioration in the conditions for economic exploitation of a cultural monument, and no prospect of replacement with another activity. In the Netherlands, on the other hand, owners qualify for compensation when their application has been *rejected*.

The funding of measures to preserve sites also varies. A few examples: in Sweden the conservation of sites is financed with state money. in the canton of Bern, the owner has a responsibility to maintain the site, albeit in collaboration with the authorities. Grants are also available for the purpose. In Bavaria, the polluter pays principle is applied. In France, ownership of sites is gradually transferred from the state to the local authorities, though the state does continue to provide financial support. In Slovenia the owner qualifies for assistance from the public purse after a public tendering procedure. There seems to be no clear policy in England and Latvia.

Heritage management

Similarities

The responses to the questions on heritage management are notable for their similarities. Only Switzerland and Slovenia replied that the national system offers only administrative protection; Sweden indicated that physical protection is possible but very seldom used in order to keep the sites accessible to all. All other countries claim they do take physical measures. Examples given mainly include measures such as placing marker buoys and signs on shipping routes above archaeological findspots, building supporting walls and covering sites. Many countries have no programme for monitoring the quality of sites, though all countries do inspect their monuments and historic buildings, albeit not always on a regular basis. Disturbance of sites is dealt with in most countries by the administrative courts, which can impose fines. A large proportion of the countries (France, England, Finland, Latvia, Poland and the Netherlands) also theoretically have the option of taking action under criminal law.

With the exception of the Czech Republic, Sweden and Finland, all the countries have a similar policy on permitted developments at listed sites. In most countries, listed sites are not fully protected. Protection might, for example, mean that developers must take account of listed sites, or are obliged to involve the archaeological service in developing their plans. Preventive archaeology is common at these sites. Bavaria, on the other hand, permits anything 'as long as the site is preserved'. In most places sites are freely accessible to the public. Only in England and Poland is this less so, the reason given being that many sites in these countries are on private land. All countries say they are engaged in public education on the heritage. It is not, however, clear whether countries have a central policy. All countries also record knowledge and information on the sites. Interestingly, in almost all countries this information is available to the public online.

l.de.wit@cultureelerfgoed.nl

Fig. 20.1: The Netherlands, Renkum - Oosterbeek. The oldest existing church in the Netherlands from the 10th century is also one of the most important memorials of the Battle of Arnhem (1944) (P.A.C. Schut).

Annex: questionnaire including received answers

Questionnaire

This questionnaire contains questions on the process of listing or protecting archaeological sites.

I. Listing

> *Does your country have a system (statutory or otherwise) for listing archaeological sites and historical landscapes? How would you describe the purpose of this process?*

Bern (Canton):

The canton of Bern, like all other cantons in Switzerland, must list its archaeological sites (Bern: AI). The inventory of the sites is included in the cantonal legislation (Bern: DPG, Art. 23).

Bavaria:

Yes; Denkmalschutzgesetz of 1973 (only constructions and archaeological sites, not concerning historical landscapes) www.blfd.bayern.de

Czech Republic:

Archaeological sites may be listed as "cultural monuments" and the process of listing is stated by the Act on Cultural Monuments (No. 20/1987). The purpose of this process is to set up a special regime of management of things and areas declared as "cultural monuments". There are also records on other archaeological sites which are not declared as "cultural monuments". These records have some significance for the protection of archaeological heritage, too.

England:

Yes. There is a statutory process for designating buildings (known as listing), archaeological sites (known as scheduling) and parks and gardens (known as registering). There is also a non-statutory list of battlefields. There are currently over half a million nationally designated historic assets in England.

The whole of the historic environment is important and Government planning guidance such as Planning Policy Guidance 15 and16 ensure that the historic environment is considered as part of the planning process, however, designation flags some historic buildings, monuments, landscapes and areas as of special importance nationally or even internationally and worthy of particular attention. Following the White Paper 'Heritage Protection for the 21st Century', the system is undergoing reform which will make it more unified, make designation decisions easier to understand, improve access to records, speed up decisions and put the historic environment at the heart of an effective planning system.

Finland:

The archeological sites in Finland are automatically protected, and an inventory of them is kept. The historical landscapes of national importance are listed. The emphasis lays on the historical monuments and the built heritage, the archaeological monuments are not specifically taken into consideration albeit they are often situated in these landscapes. A list of archaeological area complexes of national importance carried out in 1983 is out of date and has to be renewed. The purpose of these lists has been to help area planners to take larger entities into consideration and not only focus on single sites or monuments.

France:

France has a GIS/DBMS application bringing together all the data from the "archaeological map". It is both a document management system and a research tool, and it includes archaeological data from all over France. It is not a protection system in itself, but it goes well beyond being just a list of monuments with archaeological and historical value. Above all, it is a warning system for the land developers and political decision-makers who can access it. The tool is continuously developing, as it includes all new data arising from either research work (studies and analyses, prospecting, scheduled digs etc.) or from digs and diagnostics in the context of preventive archaeology (archaeological investigation prior to development work).

Fig. 20.2: The Netherlands, Renkum - Duno. The half-circular Huneschans (10th century) is situated 40 metres above the Rhine using the natural steep slope of a moraine height at the open side (P.A.C. Schut).

Latvia:
Protection of cultural monuments in the Republic of Latvia is guaranteed by State.

The main documents are a Law "On Protection of Cultural Monuments" adopted by The Supreme Council of the Republic of Latvia in 1992. Chapter Three of this Law is "State Registration of Cultural Monuments", Section 12 of this Chapter is "Organisation of State Registration of Cultural monuments":"Cultural objects of value which lay claim to inclusion in the list of State protected cultural monuments shall be subject to State registration irrespective of the fact who owns, possesses or utilizes such objects of value. State registration of monuments shall encompass assessment and inspection of monuments, determination of the historical, scientific, artistic, architectonic, archaeological, ethnographic or other cultural value thereof, recording and research thereof, and preparation of registration documents." The List of State protected Cultural monuments and amendments thereto shall be approved by the Minister for Culture.There are 8'517 cultural monuments registered in Latvia (see table 20.1)

Poland:
Yes, it does. The purpose is many-sided: mainly for routine activities of the Archaeological Heritage Service (it serves as a base for preparing archaeological opinions on the local plans and proposals of localization of planned developments), but also it is often used for research and for preparation of archaeological information for general public.

Scotland:
Strategically, inventories of all known sites are compiled at two levels:
- At national level, the responsibility lies with the Royal Commission on the Ancient and Historic Monuments of Scotland (a state-funded body which is largely free to operate independently, within the resources allocated to it). It is long-established practice that reports on new discoveries and of work on known sites are sent to the Commission, which makes this information publicly available, electronically through its on-line database and physically to researches and others who visit its offices in Edinburgh.
- At county ("Council Area") level, planning authorities have a responsibility under planning rules to have access to expert advice and a record (Sites and Monuments Record, or SMR) of all known sites. This information is primarily for use in the territorial planning and development control system, but may be used for education, tourism, etc. Increasingly, county authorities are combining SMRs with other historic environment records (for example records of listed historic buildings) to create Historic Environment Records or HERs.

County and national records work in co-operation, although this is not always perfect. County records often hold information about the management, and sometimes tourism potential, of sites which is not held in the national record. The national record tends to concentrate slightly more on academic and factual aspects. Note that being in one of these inventories does not bring automatic legal protection to sites, although planning law requires all known sites to be considered during development, according to their significance.

To be given formal legal protection, sites must be "scheduled" by the government agency responsible or regulatory authority, Historic Scotland (HS). This agency is a part of the national civil service, but has relative freedom over its operational activities. Scheduled monuments have strong restrictions over what may be done to them: any action likely to "alter, damage or destroy" a monument – even if intended to help conserve it – requires written consent from the Scottish Government. In practice, HS deals consent applications. Note that consent for works affecting scheduled monuments is required in all circumstances, and is not restricted to projects governed by the planning system – for example it is required in circumstances where permitted development rights exist, such as forestry work, extension of public utilities or small-scale building work on farms.

Fig. 20.3: The Netherlands, Groesbeek - Watermeerwijk. Artifical lake, the source of the Roman aqueduct of Nijmegen (Cultural Heritage Agency, Amersfoort).

At present about 8000 scheduled monuments exist in Scotland, from a population of approximately 100 000 known sites at which remains are believed to survive.

Slovenia:
YES. It is intended for the statutory protection of archaeological heritage alone in the planning process and for all categories of monuments.

Sweden:
All known archaeological sites and monuments are recorded in a geographical database (see question 1 under II *Legal issues* and question 9 under III *Questions related to heritage management*).

There are different kinds of lists for the historical landscape: National heritage areas – landscapes that are pointed out as important in a national perspective. Protected areas (such as national parks) – mainly protection of natural landscapes, which often includes historical landscapes.

Switzerland (Confederation):
The Confederation has three official inventories under the law for cultural and natural heritage and one under the law of the protection of cultural property in time of war:
- Inventory of settlements worthy of protection (ISOS).
- Inventory of historical roads and fairways (IVS).
- Inventory of landscapes and natural sites of national importance (BLN).
- Inventory of archaeological sites and historical monuments to be protected in case of war (KGI).

The Netherlands:
Yes, archaeological monuments can be designated protected national monuments under the Monuments and Historic Buildings Act 1988. The purpose of this is to guarantee their long-term preservation *in situ*. An archaeological monuments map also shows all known sites of archaeological importance, and is used by provincial and local authorities in their planning procedures.
There is no provision for the designation of historic landscapes.

Who is responsible for the process of listing (centralised and/or decentralised)?

Bern (Canton):
In Bern, as in other cantons, the cantonal archaeological institution (responsible for all archaeological interventions) is responsible for the process of listing (Bern: DPV, Art.18).

Bavaria:
Bayerische Landesamt für Denkmalpflege (BlfD), centralised.

Czech Republic:
It is a centralised process; the decision on listing a site is done either by the Government of the CR (higher status of monuments) or the Ministry of Culture of the CR (lower status). The National Heritage Institute (NHI) in Prague is responsible for recording listed sites in the Central Register of Cultural Monuments. The records (databases) of other archaeological sites are carried out both in the NHI and in the Institutes of Archaeology of the Academy of Sciences of the CR (IA ASCR) in Prague and Brno.

England:
Each national designation regime is different. At present the Secretary of State for Culture, Media and Sport is responsible for designating buildings, wrecks and ancient monuments. Parks, gardens and battlefields are designated by English Heritage. World Heritage Sites are inscribed by UNESCO. Since 1st April 2005, English Heritage became responsible for the administration of the listing system. Under proposed legislation, DCMS will devolve responsibility for national designation on land in England to English Heritage.

Finland:
The National Board of Antiquities keeps the inventory of the archaeological sites. The National Board of Antiquities together with the Ministry of Environment has listed the historical landscape areas of national importance. The old list of archaeological area complexes of national importance of 1983 was the result of cooperation between

Fig. 20.4: The Netherlands Winsum - Harssensbosch. Two successive former *borg* sites (houses of Groningen nobleman) and a road from the 14ᵗʰ and 16ᵗʰ century are still visible in the polder landscape north of Groningen (Paul Paris, Amstelveen).

the National Board and the predecessor to the Ministry of environment.

France:
The state is responsible for the archaeological map. The data is supplied by the local departments in each region, and is held centrally by the IT department of the Ministry of Culture.

Latvia:
The process of listing is centralised.
Public administration of cultural monuments in the Republic of Latvia is regulated by the Cabinet of Ministers and implemented by the State Inspection for Heritage Protection, which is responsible for identification, examination and registration of cultural monuments.

Poland:
It is decentralised to the level of Regional (Voivodeship) Inspector of Historical Monuments (including archaeology) and its Office (16 in the country, each having some local Branches).

Scotland:
Inventories are maintained under the direct supervision of trained professional archaeologists, who are employed by national or county authorities. It is these professional curators who have responsibility of the quality and accuracy of records.

Although there is no legal requirement to do so, it has for many years been standard operating practice that all who are engaged in archaeology in Scotland send reports to the Royal Commission, and deposit their original documentary and photographic records with the Commission at the end of projects. This applies to everyone, whether they are working in development-led archaeology, the academic sector or as unpaid vocational enthusiasts. Where projects affect protected sites (scheduled ancient monuments, see below) or are governed by planning conditions, it is usually required by the regulatory authority (national or county) that records are deposited within a specific period of time after the fieldwork is completed.

The list of scheduled monuments is based upon material contained in national and county inventories, and is created by professionally trained archaeologists employed by HS. Scheduled sites are not nationalised, i.e. taken into state ownership - they remain the property of the landowner, who must observe restrictions on his activities which arise from scheduling.

Slovenia:
The Institute for the Protection of Cultural Heritage (or rather its conservators) is responsible for proposal preparation (decentralised), the administrative decree is issued at a ministerial level (centralised).

Sweden:
Centralised.

Switzerland (Confederation):
ISOS: Office for the Inventory of settlements worthy of protection mandated by the Federal Office of Culture (BAK).

IVS: Special office in the Federal Office for Roads (ASTRA) mandated at first by the Federal Office of Culture and actually in the Federal Office for Roads (ASTRA).BLN: Federal Office for environment (BAFU).KGI: Federal Office for the protection of the population (BABS).

The Netherlands:
The Minister of Education, Culture and Science is responsible for designating national monuments. Practical responsibility for this task is delegated to the Cultural Heritage Agency, which is also responsible for updating the archaeological monuments map. Local authorities are increasingly producing detailed maps showing sites of local or regional importance.

Fig. 20.5: Germany, Nettersheim. Roman sanctuary to the Mother Goddesses "Görresburg" (Rheinisches Amt für Bodendenkmalpflege, Bonn).

Please describe the method used for listing. Is it based on objective criteria and parameters or on expert judgement? What criteria exist for assessment and selection and what procedures can be used in practice? Is an interdisciplinary approach taken?

Bern (Canton):

In Bern: Archives, scientific knowledge of the site, surveying (expert judgement) are the main criteria for the definition of an archaeological site. The size of the site is defined after survey. In practice, if a site is not well known the protected area around it will be accordingly larger.

Landscape knowledge and secondary interdisciplinary criteria like geology and soil science are also used to define the probability of existence of a site.

Bavaria:

Objective criteria as listed in extensive guidelines; regular and systematic listing through BLfD, but also after proposal by persons "affected"; interdisciplinary approach between archaeology and building department.

Czech Republic:

Listing of sites is mostly based upon an expert judgement and on an administrative decision.

England:

Current designation regimes use a range of different criteria to identify what is suitable for protection. Buildings are listed on the basis of 'special architectural or historic interest', monuments and wrecks are selected on the basis of 'national importance', and parks and gardens when they are of 'special historic interest'. The final decision is a result of expert judgement of evidence against these criteria, and more detailed non-statutory selection criteria, and then, where appropriate, a recommendation to the Secretary of State. Published criteria are now available, and procedures now include consultation with the owner. We strive to work in a more interdisciplinary way but existing legislation prevents full integration at present.

Finland:

The listing of historical landscapes is based on expert judgment. The approach is to a high extent strictly historical but landscape architectural aspects are perceived. In the plans to renew the list of archaeological area complexes of national importance estimation criteria will be developed and an interdisciplinary approach be used. Geographic, geological and historic factors will be taken into account.

France:

Archaeologists from the regional archaeology departments in the DRACs (Directions Régionales des Affaires Culturelles, or regional cultural affairs departments) sift through the literature and reports on studies and digs, checking the information (site visits, expert analyses etc.) and incorporating it into the database. The data is geo-referenced and structured according to the standards of the database. Everything is checked scientifically by government archaeologists as it is entered. No selection of sites takes place at this stage; choices are made later on the basis of analysis carried out when responding to enquiries. The expertise of the state archaeologists working in the regions is fundamental, and it is they who, based on archaeological data, suggest methods for protecting both archaeological sites and historic landscapes.

Latvia:

Mainly, objective criteria are used to characterise the archaeological monuments (sites): group of monument (settlement, medieval castle, hillfort, ancient burial places), dating of monument (if it's possible), surviving of monument.

Fig. 20.6: Germany, Mechernich – Vussem. Aquaduct of the roman water-conduit form Cologne (Rheinisches Amt für Bodendenkmalpflege, Bonn).

Register contains data on state protected culture monuments – monument name, type, value, location and marker dedication or erection date. Information about monument owners will be added soon, with limited public access.See above, also conclusion of Cultural monument registration expert committee of State Inspection for Heritage Protection.

Poland:

Listing of sites is a long-term all-Polish project called "Polish Archaeological Survey" (Polish abbreviation: AZP), carried our since 1978 according to precise rules (see: http://www.ooda.pl/badania_azp_eng.htm The basic standard does not include interdisciplinary measures; however in many cases the extended standard, including chosen non-destroying methods, is applied.

Scotland:

The national and county inventories usually include all material submitted, with information about the source. Except in cases of the most obvious error or over-enthusiasm, inventories are inclusive rather than critically selective at point of registering data.

The question of the significance/importance of sites in inventories is usually addressed "in theory" only during scheduling (see below). The question is addressed "in practice" during the consideration of development proposal.

To be eligible for scheduling, a site must contain (or be believed to contain) physical remains of national importance. The law does not define "national importance", but formal criteria for selection have been developed by HS, and these have recently been refreshed following public consultation. Essentially they are similar to those used in many other countries, considering factors such as rarity, completeness, representativeness, potential, etc.

During the consideration of whether or not to allow development, all known sites are assessed according to their significance and the likely impact of the development upon them. Usually, scheduled monuments are automatically protected and excluded from development (unless

considerations of national importance apply). For all other sites, the developer (or archaeologists working for him) will normally put forward an assessment of these matters, which the regulator (usually the county planning authority) may challenge.

Slovenia:

Listing is based on expert judgement. Criteria are based on proved evidence (from destructive and non-destructive interventions) of existence for sites, or probability (toponyms, single finds, etc.) for areas. An interdisciplinary approach is used, particularly with regard to architectural and settlement heritage.

Sweden:

The method used for listing is based on expert judgement. In section 1 in the Heritage Conservation Act there is a list of those ancient monuments and sites that are protected and expert judgements are based on this list. The National Heritage Board also has guidelines how this list shall be used in practice.

An interdisciplinary approach is sometimes taken especially if the site or landscape is of interest both for its archaeological and natural qualities.

Switzerland (Confederation):

ISOS: The Federal Commission for the Protection of Nature and Cultural Aspects advises in the making of the list by the Office for the Inventory of settlements worthy of protection mandated by the Federal office of Culture (BAK).

IVS: The Federal Commission for the Protection of Nature and Cultural Aspects advises in the making of the list by the Federal Instances (ASTRA).BLN: The Federal Commission for the Protection of Nature and Cultural Aspects advises in the making of the list by the Federal Instances (BAFU).KGI: A group of experts accompanied the making of the list, which was based on more or less objective data defined by the archaeological services, the offices for the protection of monuments and the museums together, under the authority of the Federal Office for the protection of the Population (BABS).

Fig. 20.7: Germany, Bopfingen – Ipf. Truncated-conical butte with its oval plateau und graded fortifications (Late Bronze Age – Roman Times) on the flat slope to the east (Photo O. Braasch, Landesamt für Denkmalpflege Esslingen).

The Netherlands:
If sites are found by chance or during mapping, they are evaluated as a matter of course on the basis of their physical quality (preservation and intactness) and scientific criteria (rarity, information value, scientific value, group value and representativeness). A score is given, which determines whether a site is selected for the archaeological monuments map. If a site scores highly enough to be added to the list of legally protected monuments – the aim of which is to produce a representative list of monuments – and it represents a major addition to our knowledge of the history of the Netherlands, it will be eligible for statutory protection. In evaluating sites, the landscape setting is now increasingly taken into account, drawing on the knowledge of other experts (historical geographers, botanists, archaeozoologists etc.) where possible.

| *Is there a direct link between site protection and the protection of historical landscapes?*

Bern (Canton):
In Bern: Traditionally, the landscape had little importance in the making of the inventory. Actually, it is taken more in account, especially in regions which are not so well known. The accent is put on the development of a representative inventory for the whole canton.

Bavaria:
No

Czech Republic:
Exceptionally. An example could be the battlefield around Slavkov, Moravia ("The battle of three emperors", 1805).

England:
We do not designate historical landscapes as such, though World Heritage Sites and Conservation areas often contain a number of individual designations. Designed historic landscapes are also eligible for protection if they are on the Register of Parks and Gardens: cemeteries, formal landscapes and public parks can thus be protected. Some historic working landscapes like medieval settlement sites have been selected for scheduling. Often, however, natural designations such as Areas of Outstanding Natural Beauty and National Parks, incorporate historic landscapes.

Finland:
There is no direct link. As mentioned earlier the sites are automatically protected. The historical landscapes are protected by planning.

France:
The link between the archaeological data and the protective measures can be established by the GIS. This linkage is not dynamic, but the work should find a place in the "architecture and heritage atlas" expected in September 2008.

Latvia:
In some cases archaeological monuments are a separate part (monument) of the historical landscape.

Fig. 20.8: Germany. Limes Road of the ' Obergermanischer Limes' between Murrhardt and Welzheim. (Photo O. Braasch, Landesamt für Denkmalpflege Esslingen).

Poland:
The latter is sometimes applied as the extension of the former one, usually in form of A Landscape Park – zone chosen for its natural and historical values (including archaeology), with eliminated possibilities of any further industrial & urban development as well as with limited agricultural activities.

Scotland:
This data is obtained by consideration of documentary records (including aerial photographs), by site survey and inspection and in some cases by exploratory excavation or geophysical survey.

Slovenia:
There is no direct link between site protection and the protection of historic landscapes.

Sweden:
No.

Switzerland (Confederation):
In the cases of the national inventories (ISOS, IVS, BLN but also KGI) the landscape is very much taken into account.

The Netherlands:
No, there is no direct link. However, landscape values can be used as additional arguments for site protection. Where a high density of archaeological remains is found in a limited area, the entire area will be protected, thus encompassing part of the landscape.

Does the protection of historical landscapes cover the areas where the most important archaeological sites are situated?

Bern (Canton):
In Bern, only three sites have a superior protection, and all three are landscapes.

Bavaria:
-

Czech Republic:
Exceptionally. For example, the Early Medieval hill-fort of Pohansko (Břeclav) is part of the World Heritage Site Lednice-Valtice Cultural Landscape (cultural landscape of the 17th-20th cent.).

England:
There are no dedicated historical landscape designations, though as set out above, areas of historical landscape often fall within areas of natural designation. The most important archaeological sites are protected, but some categories of site, especially those without structures or without evidence of human works, evade eligibility at present.

Finland:
Not always.

France:
The national archaeological map is used to prepare the porter à connaissance (literally "bringing to the knowledge"), a preliminary planning document which is one of the first channels of heritage protection information

Fig. 20.9: Poland, Giecz, district of Środa Wielkopolska. One of the important centres of Early Polish state: a hill-fort (9th-11th century) with relics of stone architecture (palatium with chapel, ca 980).

for political decision-makers. Based on the selected and organized data, protection mechanisms such as zones de protection du patrimoine architectural, urbain et paysager (ZPPAUP, architectural, urban and landscape heritage protection zones), secteurs sauvegardés (protected districts) or the protection due to Monuments historiques or listed buildings (listing, registration on the Inventaire Supplémentaire or supplementary inventory) or to natural and historical sites may be proposed. There is no direct link between the archaeological map, with its major monuments, and these types of protection, which depend on variable local conditions and regional strategies.

Latvia:
Not only.

Poland:
Abundance of archaeological objects is one of the factors to choose such an area.

Scotland:
Potential or predicted values can be taken into account, but the case must be carefully made: if there is a major impact on a development, then strong arguments are required. Developers may be required to investigate archaeological potential and provide unbiased evidence if they claim a site which is assessed as high potential has no/little archaeological value.

Slovenia:
Historical landscapes only exist as a general category of 19th and 20th century landscapes in the Slovene system. They do not incorporate archaeological sites, which are separately protected ex lege.

Sweden:
Sometimes.

Switzerland (Confederation):
In the case of KGI, IVS and ISOS, the historical landscape protection covers the most important archaeological sites. BLN covers mostly natural landscapes and sites.

The Netherlands:
There may be a coincidental link.

❙ *Is listing supported by scientific research?*

Bern (Canton):
In Bern, the listing is based on scientific research as well as on practical prospecting and archive work.

Bavaria:
Yes.

Czech Republic:
Yes, mostly.

England:
Scientific research is often carried out in the area of conservation, materials and archaeological and buildings survey, however, this is not a specific factor in the designation decision – though rarity and fragility are considerations.

Finland:
No.

Fig. 20.10: Poland, Moraczewo, district of Gniezno. Typical local hill-fort in Greater Poland, with twin rampart (tribal and early state period, 8th-11th cent.).

France:
The researchers are involved in both putting together the data (diagnostics, digs, literature reviews, prospecting, analysis etc.) and in using it, e.g. for documentaryresearch or spatial analysis. Under certain conditions, they can also export data from the national database into their own databases, contributing to a better knowledge of the territory, a renewal of the approaches to historical landscapesand the definition of an archaeological intervention strategy determined by regional government departments.

Latvia:
Sometimes, but it's not a system.

Poland:
On the basic level – by its most simple forms, i.e.: archive query + fieldwalking + analysis of the materials found. Before more important decisions (on scheduling the site, etc.), detailed surface reconnaissance, air photos and/or test trenches are often applied.

Scotland:
Such information is made available to the regulatory authorities, and can be used. However, if a site discovered by the developer's team, before or during work, is then legally scheduled, so that the development is halted or adversely affected, the developer is entitled to seek financial compensation or judicial review. Therefore, such "hostile schedulings" are very, very rare. If important new sites are discovered in this way, it is usual to negotiate for preservation and, if this fails, to allow for full excavation and recording (at the developer's expense).

Slovenia:
Listing is supported by scientific research to a certain extent, but it is not mandatory.

Sweden:
Yes.

Switzerland (Confederation):
On a federal level, the listings are completed. They were made by specialists. The continuation, usually done by researchers is supported by a professional commission.

The Netherlands:
The data on which the process of listing is based are obtained by means of scientifically accepted methods. The Cultural Heritage Agency has also conducted a programme designed to produce a representative list of protected archaeological monuments. The study highlighted gaps in the list, indicating where priorities should lie.

How are the data needed for assessment and selection obtained?

Bern (Canton):
For the cantonal inventory, data is provided by the archaeological service itself or through other cantonal instances (Cantonal office for the protection of nature, etc.)

Bavaria:
?

Czech Republic:
Archaeological survey, archival background research, etc.

England:
A mixture of consultation, field visits and/survey, archival and desk-based research.

Finland:
The inventories are studied, surveys and studies in the terrain are carried out.

France:
All the archaeological information available is recorded in the national database, including incomplete or unverified information, which is identified with a specific status. This makes it possible to express a doubt as to the location, nature, dating or quality of an item in the database.

Fig. 20.11: Romania, Sarmizegetusa Regia. Dacian Fortress.

Latvia:
Mainly, based on survey of place. (Photo, physical parameters, historical sources, information about dating, artefacts, previous collections in museums, maps).

Poland:
By use of the methods mentioned above.

Scotland:
I do not understand how this is different from the question regarding predicted values.

Slovenia:
There is an increasing emphasis on the use of data acquired through non-destructive methods, in combination with desk top analysis. There are also cases of intuitive assessment.

Sweden:
Field surveys.

Switzerland (Confederation):
For the federal inventories, data is obtained through the cantonal instances.

The Netherlands:
The data that allow a site to be evaluated are initially gathered on the basis of a desk study. If necessary, this is followed up by a preservation assessment, which will involve the use of boreholes or test trenches, depending on the particular question being addressed.

> *Are only proven values considered, or are predicted values also taken into account (role of predictive modelling)?*

Bern (Canton):
In the canton of Bern, as well as in most Swiss cantons, predictive modelling is now slowly being taken into account, especially for special geographical zones (High Mountain regions – Lakesides). Listing is used as an instrument for preventive archaeology.

Bavaria:
For archaeology: according to the Denkmalschutzgesetz art. 7.1 permission to alter or excavate has to be obtained also for sites where archaeological monuments are suggested or predictable by the circumstances.

Czech Republic:
A prediction is mostly considered not to be enough to declare an area as "cultural monument".

England:
Designation is based on proven values, though there is scope to consider the potential of known sites when a designation decision is made.

Finland:
Only proven values are considered.

France:
The archaeological map includes a wide variety of archaeological data, including environmental data arising from diagnostics or analyses, which can enable government archaeologists to suggest reconstructions of how historical landscapes have evolved. This kind of information, generated through collaborative work with other researchers, can in some cases be similar to predictive data. As a result, it can be recorded on the archaeological map as specific zones (sensitive zones, vulnerable zones, zones under threat etc.). This never rules out preventive archaeology operations, but does serve as a guide for regional strategy in terms of protection and study.

Latvia:
Only proven values.

Poland:
So far, predictive modeling is neither popularized in Poland, nor has it any legal meaning as an argument for the protection.

Scotland:
There are agreed criteria for assessing importance, including for scheduling. But these require expert judgment to

Fig. 20.12: Romania, Biertan. Fortified Evangelic Church.

apply in each individual case. The size or depth or number of items within any area is never used as a criterion in its own right, but only combined with consideration of the significance of these factors. Therefore one could characterize the Scottish situation as an expert-led system operating to publicly-agreed rules.

Slovenia:
Predictive modelling has proved to be unreliable and unsuitable, because the results obtained so far are too general, or can not be used for sites of poorly known or unknown periods.

Sweden:
In the case of a larger development project the County Administration Boards can decide that a special survey (both a desk-based assessment and a field survey and limited test excavations) should be conducted. The purpose of the special survey is to find ancient sites which are unknown and not listed.

Switzerland (Confederation):
Federal inventories: Only proven values are considered.

The Netherlands:
A predicted archaeological value is not considered an adequate basis for a protection decision.

> *To what extent is the process of listing strategically driven? Is there a focus on sites and landscapes that are under threat, or on the opportunities for sustainable preservation?*

Bern (Canton):
The global archaeological strategy in Switzerland takes listing into account. Bern has a five year strategy allowing the development of a representative list including predictive models aiming for a sustainable preservation which should also allow a better management of threats.

Bavaria:
The evaluation of the existing list (120.000 "buildings", 950 ensembles, 55.000 archaeological monuments) is strategically driven with a focus on areas that are under particular pressure or with a certain political background; sustainable preservation: occasional.

Czech Republic:
We cannot talk of any clear strategy in the CR. Sites are listed mostly because of the existence of features of evident archaeological value. Sometimes the degree of threat may be considered, too. In some cases, the historical significance (known from written sources) and the symbolic value of the site are stressed (e.g. the Levý Hradec hill-fort or the Prague Castle, both known as the earliest centers of the Czech Early Medieval state).

England:
The process of designation is at present largely reactive in nature and we try to give attention to all sites currently under demonstrable threat. Much of our current work is driven by spot-listing in relation to public proposals or development threat. Under Heritage Protection Reform, we hope to move towards a more pro-active designation approach, which, through expert consideration of threat and public consultation of interest, will be able to strategically identify certain categories of designation as a priority. We wish to work on thematic, strategic levels, but also to continue to be responsive to threat.

Finland:
-

France:
The current application (Patriarche, still under development) contains a module for creating zones in which it is presumed that archaeological diagnostics should be imposed. The establishment of these zones, for which regional government is responsible, is based on both the data in the national database and on the uncertainty of what is known. In these zones, developers know that their projects will be subjected case by case to examination by government archaeologists. These regional choices contribute to defining the planning of scientific activities based on assessments presented to the scientific supervisory bodies overseeing French archaeology, the CIRA

Fig. 20.13: Hungary, Aquincum. Part of the Civilian town (Hungarian Archaeology at the turn of the Millenium 2003, p. 228).

(inter-regional commission for archaeological research) and the CNRA (national council of archaeological research). These strategies have a considerable impact on land management from the viewpoint of sustainable development, such as Monument Historique protection creating easements, the constitution of archaeological reserves by local authorities or conservation through research: preventive archaeological digs following diagnostics. The archaeological map is also used as a primary source of information in putting together government bodies' responses to development and land use plans (plans locaux d'urbanisme (local development plans) or schémas de cohérence territoriale (territorial cohesion schemes)) in what is known as the porter à connaissance planning documents which local authorities are responsible for implementing.

Latvia:
Both- focus on sites and landscapes under threat and on opportunities for sustainable preservation.

Poland:
Usually it is a "practical" compromise of both factors.

Scotland:
In Scotland our protection programme operates strategically, with the objective of reviewing the state of knowledge and providing necessary protection across the whole country. The time-span (30 years) for complete review of the whole country means that we operate area-by-area. The operational order in which areas are reviewed may take account of generic threats – for example we may choose to look at areas where large-scale forestry is planned, or where some new category of development is likely, such as wind farms – but it may also be decided simply because we believe certain areas are "under-scheduled" base don our knowledge of what sites exist there.

Scheduling is intended to support long-term protection and preservation, and is not undertaken as a tactical measure to force developers to excavate more fully than they might if sites were not scheduled. The planning and development control system can normally achieve such tactical goals without the need for scheduling. Therefore the intention is to reserve scheduling as an "accolade" for the most important sites, to achieve preservation, and not as a short-term "tripwire" to trigger investigation if a development is proposed.

Slovenia:
The listing process is mainly dictated by the planning acts of individual local authorities, which essentially means that listing focuses on sites under threat.

Sweden:
Some National heritage areas have been created because of a clear threat.

Switzerland (Confederation):
Federal inventories: The focus is to have a list of sites of national importance, which have to be better protected than others. This means that the role of the lists is more one of sustainable preservation.

The Netherlands:
Protection policy focuses mainly on sustainable preservation. It is used on an ad hoc basis to rescue sites under threat, as a form of correction to the policy of safeguarding archaeological findspots as much as possible via planning.

II. Legal issues

Please describe briefly the legislation pertaining to the listing of archaeological sites and monuments.

Bern (Canton):
Each canton has its own legislation.
For the canton of Bern: Law and decree for the protection of cultural heritage (DPG and DPV).

Bavaria:
Denkmalschutzgesetz of Bavaria of 1973, Art. 1, 1.4, 2, 12.1

Fig. 20.14: Hungary, Visegvár. The Middle Age royal citadel (Hungarian Archaeology at the turn of the Millenium 2003, p. 347).

Czech Republic:
The Act on Cultural Monuments 20/1987 and its updates considers four types of monuments: cultural monuments (individual important items or archaeological features - sites); national cultural monuments (individual most important items or sites); monument zones (larger areas of historic landscape) and monument reservations (most important larger areas). All types may have protective zones around them.

England:
Archaeological sites and monuments are scheduled under the 1979 Ancient Monuments and Archaeological Areas Act. Marine wreck sites are covered separately by the 1973 Protection of Wrecks Act. The legislation dates back to 1882 but has been extensively developed since then. Sites of special archaeological interest can range from caves to aircraft crash sites. Historic, architectural, traditional, artistic or archaeological interest comprises the test for scheduling: there has to be enough interest in the opinion of the Secretary of State (the Minister) for scheduling to be warranted. There is a presumption that scheduled sites will be preserved in situ. All works to them require consent, with certain exceptions.

Finland:
There is no legislation pertaining to the listing of archaeological sites and monuments.

France:
The national archaeological map, as defined by the Code du Patrimoine or Heritage Code (L 522-5), is the database of georeferenced archaeological information covering the whole country. It is constructed in collaboration with public archaeology research establishments and local authorities, which may have their own archaeology departments. Parliamentary debates in 2001 and 2003 clarified the nature and objectives of the national archaeological map, clearly identifying its incompleteness and evolving nature and the need to incorporate it into consideration of land development. It acts as a single inventory managed by the state based on a continuously-fed database bringing together all the available valid archaeological data. It has two roles: a scientific tool for heritage knowledge and a warning system for everyone involved in land development. A decree in application of the Code du Patrimoine (L 552-6) provides for extracts from the national archaeological map to be communicated to, among others, the authorities responsible for authorizing construction.

Latvia:
Law "On Protection of Cultural Monuments", the List of State protected Cultural monuments.
Inspection works according to the Cultural Monuments Protection Law of the Republic of Latvia, Convention Concerning the Protection of the World Cultural and Natural Heritage and 37 other different laws and regulations concerning cultural heritage, By-laws of the State Inspection for Heritage Protection, as well as regulations issued by the Ministry of Culture and State Inspection for Heritage Protection.

Poland:
See: http://www.ooda.pl/akty_eng.htm
and: http://www.ooda.pl/podstawy_prawne_eng.htm

Scotland:
- The whole country is assessed over a time period which is not too long (depends on resources, etc)

Fig. 20.15: Slovenia, Gorice pri Famljah. V Snožetih prehistoric barrows (Arhiv Odd. Za arheologijo, Filozofske fakultete, Univerze v Ljubljani, D. Grosman).

- Areas are selected for the annual assessment and selection programme according to knowledge of what is there – new discoveries, current programmes of academic research and generic (but not specific) threats.
- Guidelines for selecting sites for legal protection are publicly agreed.
- Experts are trained to apply the guidelines fairly to specific cases, and there is good quality control built in, with senior staff checking the work.
- The work of assessment is done openly, and the local public are consulted, involved, given an opportunity to comment and informed of outcomes.
- Landowners receive written notification of site visits and the fastest possible news of decisions reached (whether to schedule or not), with a chance to ask for explanations or changes. (Human Rights).
- Confidential personal information must be protected. (Data protection).
- The list of scheduled sites is maintained in an up-to-date and accessible format, with all necessary information such as the exact location, geographical extent, map, description, reasons for scheduling. The best technology should be used (e.g. Internet, GIS) provided this does not act as an obstacle by restricting access to those with highly specialised equipment or skills.

Slovenia:
The protection of cultural heritage in Slovenia is regulated by the Cultural Heritage Protection Act (2008, formerly 1999).

Archaeological cultural heritage is protected by law on the basis of its inscription in the heritage register or on the basis of the granting of the status of monument.

Immovable cultural heritage (including archaeological sites) acquires its legal status of heritage on the basis of its entry in the heritage register. Registered archaeological heritage is protected directly by the law.

Individual items of heritage may be granted the status of a cultural monument if they:
- represent a substantial achievement of human creativity or contribute to cultural diversity,
- are important part of the space or heritage of Slovenia,
- serve as source for understanding historical processes or phenomena and their connection to present culture and environment.

In case of exceptional importance on national level they may be granted the status of monuments of national importance; they may be granted the status of monuments of local importance in the case of special importance on a regional or local level.

An initiative for proclamation may be submitted by the public institution responsible for heritage protection, and by any private or legal person. The official proposal for proclamation shall be prepared by the public institution responsible for heritage protection. Owners of the monument shall be informed about the proclamation procedure. An act on the proclamation of a monument of national importance shall be adopted by the Government of the Republic of Slovenia; an act on the proclamation of a monument of local importance shall be adopted by the responsible body of the region or municipality.
A proclamation act shall comprise
- the identification of the monument,
- the values on which the proclamation is based,

Fig. 20.16: Slovenia, Kazlje. Vahta prehistoric hillfort (Arhiv Odd. Za arheologijo, Filozofske fakultete, Univerze v Ljubljani, D. Grosman).

- the regime of protection of the monument.
- the buffer zone and the regime of protection in the buffer zone if
- necessary,
- the provision of public access to heritage,
- demands on management and the possible obligation of the adoption of the management plan,
- register of the movable objects, which are part of the immovable monument.

On the basis of the proclamation act a note designating a single monument or archaeological site shall be entered in the register.

Sweden:

The Heritage Conservation Act gives a general protection to sites and monuments which means that all permanent ancient remains defined by the law, whether they are known or not, are protected. Sites and monuments are defined as traces of human activity in past ages, having resulted from use in previous times and having been permanently abandoned. This definition also includes natural formations associated with ancient customs, legends or noteworthy historic events, as well as traces of ancient popular cults. Examples of sites and monuments are graves, cemeteries, settlements, rock art, boundary markings, harbour facilities, different kinds of ruins and cultivated land.

Switzerland (Confederation):

National law for the protection of natural and cultural heritage (NHG) and the national law for the protection of cultural heritage in time of war (KGS-Gesetz).

The Netherlands:

The Monuments and Historic Buildings Act 1988 lays down national regulations concerning the protection of monuments and sites. It provides for 'protectedmonuments' to be listed in a national register. The register includes both historicbuildings and archaeological sites.

What are the legal implications of the listing of sites and monuments?

Bern (Canton):

The implications differ from canton to canton since they are dependent on the cantonal laws.

In Bern, the local authorities must announce projects in protected zones (listed) directly to the archaeological service, which makes a report on the measures to be taken. These are then included in the construction permit. The owner must take in account those measures.

Bavaria:

Demand for preservation (owner's responsibility), permissions are necessary for the alterations and destruction.

Czech Republic:

The development projects must pay attention to the status of cultural monuments, there are restrictions for the agricultural managements, building permission may be refused, etc.

England:

Effective designation forms the basis for decisions about the way we manage change to sites and monuments flagged as of national importance. It aims to strike a balance between protecting what is important and enabling appropriate change. Scheduled Monument Consent is required for works to scheduled sites, listed building consent for buildings and licenses for activities on Historic Wreck Sites. There are penalties for non-compliance with conditions. English Heritage is automatically consulted on all proposals affecting scheduled monuments.

Finland:

No implications.

France:

The national archaeological map is not directly enforceable in relation to third parties. It does not create easements that would affect the exercise of propertyrights.

Fig. 20.17: Spain, Las Médulas,(León province). In Roman times the most important gold mine. Las Médulas Cultural Landscape is listed by the UNESCO as one of the World Heritage Sites.

Latvia:
See above.

Poland:
The Heritage Service must be consulted for all development works; in case of property of state and local authorities also selling and division of the plot of ground must be accepted by them.

Scotland:
For scheduled sites, only developments of national importance will be allowed if this leads to destruction or serious damage. For other sites, the significance of the site will be balanced against the significance of the development. In all cases, preservation in situ will be the first objective and mitigation only a second-best option.

Compensation is only available if scheduling takes place after planning permission has been obtained and the refusal of scheduled monument consent leads to the development becoming impossible or much more expensive. Compensation is never available if sites were known about and/or already scheduled before the application was made for planning permission or scheduled monument consent.

Scheduled sites are inspected by field staff employed by HS (target: once very 5 years, more frequently for sites known to be at risk). Written reports, sketch plans and digital images are submitted after each visit and added to a database. There are (limited) financial resources available from HS to assist owners to maintain sites in good condition, and funding opportunities may also be available through agri-environment schemes. Maintenance of sites is not compulsory for owners, so grants or agreements are used. The state can (through HS) undertake work itself in cases of extreme need, but this is rare - working with landowners is the norm.

Slovenia:
It is mandatory to take cultural monuments and registered archaeological sites into account in planning documents.

Sweden:
It is prohibited, without permission to disturb, remove, excavate, cover over, by building development, planting or in any other way, to alter or damage ancient sites and monuments.

Switzerland (Confederation):
The federal lists are used as instruments for the federal and cantonal instances.

If a site or object is on a national list, it is easier to receive federal grants for its excavation, restoration, etc., although this is not the sole factor to receive grants. The direct management of the listed national sites is carried out by the cantons.

The Netherlands:
Anyone who wishes to alter, demolish or move any part of a protected monument or monument subject to a current procedure must apply for written permission as stipulated in section 11 of the Monuments and Historic Buildings Act 1988, which states that:
1. It is prohibited to damage or destroy a protected monument.
2. It is prohibited, without a written permit or contrary to the stipulations of a written permit:
   a. to demolish, disturb, move or in any way change a protected monument,
   b. to restore, use or allow a protected monument to be used in such a way as to mar its appearance or to endanger it in any way.

Licenses are issued by the Cultural Heritage Agency on behalf of the Minister of Education, Culture and Science. In practice, the Cultural Heritage Agency adheres to a policy whereby, depending on the characteristics of the archaeological monument and its daily use, specified actions may be considered non-disturbing and exempted from the obligation to apply for a written permit.

Fig. 20.18: Spain, Madinat Al-Zahra. General view of the housing of Abd ar-Rahman III the Caliph of Córdoba starting from the 9th century (Juan Carlos Cazalla).

Are owners of listed sites eligible for financial compensation?

Bern (Canton):
Not in canton Bern.

Bavaria:
To a certain degree for additional spending concerning the preservation of sites (i.e. not for excavations).

Czech Republic:
Yes, the owners may ask for the support at the Ministry of Culture of the CR (Monument Restoration Fund).

England:
Owners of listed buildings get no compensation, though it is often the case that a listed property is worth more. There are grants available through a number of routes for the management of some sites such as ecclesiastical buildings at risk or agri-environment schemes on some scheduled sites.

Finland:
No financial compensation.

France:
As the site inventory does not create easements (see point 2 above), land owners cannot claim compensation for their property being listed in the inventory.

Latvia:
In Latvia, owner (manager) of cultural monument shall cover all expenses related to conservation, maintenance, repair and restoration of these monuments.

Following the proposal of the State Inspection for Heritage Protection, state has allocated budget means for research of monuments and conservation and restoration of monuments of low economic value, but municipalities ensure own budget funding for conservation and restoration of local significance cultural monuments. Current financial allocations run short, comprising only one tenth of required minimum. State Inspection for Cultural heritage concludes agreement with respective owners (managers) of cultural monuments. This agreement fixes allocation of state funds for examination of monuments, restoration and conservation of national monuments, and monitoring of expenditures. Surveys for building, drainage, road construction and other economic activities are financed by contractor and invoiced to the owner of works.

Poland:
They may apply to the Ministry of Culture when they can proove loses because of this reason.

Scotland:
-

Slovenia:
Owners of cultural monuments are eligible for financial compensation, if the protection regime worsens the conditions for economic exploitation of the monument and if it is not possible to replace it with another activity within the framework of the protection regime.

Financial compensation can be assessed as a single sum, or in yearly installments.

Fig. 20.19: Belgique, Ramillies (Brabant). Grand Rosière, Tumulus dit d'Hottomont (G. Focant, SPW).

Owners of registered heritage that is not scheduled as a cultural monument are not eligible for financial compensation.

Sweden:
No.

Switzerland (Confederation):
-

The Netherlands:
In the event of a permit application being rejected, owners may claim financial compensation.

| *How are measures for the conservation of sites agreed and financed?*

Bern (Canton):
Measures for the conservation are agreed on a cantonal basis by the cantonal archaeological authorities in accordance with the site's owner. No conservation may be done without the owner's approval.
In Bern, the preservation of a site is the duty of the site's owner. Conservation is therefore done in direct collaboration with the owners. Measures of conservation of sites of national but also of regional importance may be partially financed by federal grants.

Bavaria:
Via the permission-process; principally on a "polluter-pays" basis.

Czech Republic:
Decisions are made either by the County Offices or the Ministry of Culture. The NHI and the IA ASCR may be asked for advice.

England:
This varies depending on the circumstance.

Finland:
No.

France:
Despite the absence as yet of any national policy on the issue, land reserves have been built up to protect known or presumed archaeological sites. Acquired initially by the state, these parcels are now acquired by local authorities, perhaps with financial support from the state.

Latvia:
See above. It depends on the owners.

Poland:
In case of state and communal property – this is administrative decision of the regional Heritage Service. In case of private property – application to the Ministry, see above.

Scotland:
-

Slovenia:
Public tender by owners for funding from the state budget.

Fig. 20.20: Belgique, Durbuy (Luxembourg). Menhirs d'Oppagne (G. Focant, SPW).

Sweden:
Their conservation is financed with state money and administrated by the County Administration Boards.

Switzerland (Confederation):
-

The Netherlands:
There is currently no scheme to encourage conservation measures, though a start is likely to be made on such a scheme in 2009. The Cultural Heritage Agency has made long-term arrangements with other governmental organisations and state-sponsored nature conservation groups that own land where archaeological monuments are situated.

> *Does protection imply preservation in the long term or does the demand for space tend to lead to excavation?*

Bern (Canton):
Long-term preservation is the first aim for the archaeological agencies in all of Switzerland. But economical demands (occupation of the territory by housing, farming, etc.) still are a political priority. Therefore rescue excavations belong to the everyday work of the archaeological services.

Bavaria:
Yes, and mostly yes.

Czech Republic:
The higher status (national cultural monuments, monument reservations) implies preservation of the archaeological terrains, the lower status may tend to rescue excavations.

England:
Preservation in situ is always the preference, but measures aim to strike a balance between protecting what is important and enabling appropriate change. Therefore, there are times when excavation and survey are appropriate, or necessary. Much archaeological investigation is developer-led as part of building projects. Urban archaeology is managed creatively so that the archaeology of a site is fully considered both before and during the works.

Finland:
Outstanding monuments will be protected in the long term while monuments of "less value" can be excavated when needed.

France:
The long-term protection of these property reserves (see above) is in question, and a study is currently under way surveying the practices of regional archaeology services (DRAC) over the last twenty years. Long-term conservation can only be guaranteed with monument historique protection. Without this, the local authority that owns the land reserve can modify its planned use (i.e. allow construction once again), giving rise to a preventive archaeology operation caused by a development project.

Latvia:
Mainly, long term preservation.

Poland:
Both solutions are possible, so each case is analyzed separately by the Heritage Service.

Scotland:
-

Slovenia:
It implies long term preservation in the case of cultural monuments, but excavation in the case of heritage.

Sweden:
It is the responsibility of the County Administration Boards to balance the preservation of the site and the state's interest in the realisation of a development project – the result is often that the Board decides that the site can be excavated and removed.

Fig. 20.21: The Netherlands, Abcoude. Remains of a medieval castle.

Switzerland (Confederation):
The national lists imply preservation on the long term, in particular ISOS and BLN. This is not the case for IVS or KGS.

The Netherlands:
Since, in the past, protection of monuments has been opted for in areas of low dynamism, it has proved possible to provide long-term protection. Nevertheless, some protected monuments have been subject to various types of threat, and have therefore had to be excavated.

III. Questions related to heritage management

Does your country's system involve only administrative protection, or are physical protection measures also taken?

Bern (Canton):
On the cantonal level (managers of the protection), it is not only administrative. Physical protection is accomplished in collaboration with the owner.

Bavaria:
In rare occasions physical protection was able in "archaeological reservations" (on the basis of compensation).

Czech Republic:
Protection is mostly administrative, exceptionally it may also mean e.g. fencing or roofing.

England:
On some marine sites marker buoys are placed to avoid accidental access or collision and on land barriers, signs and other physical markers are placed to avoid animal, human or environmental damage.

Finland:
Physical protection is carried out in the sense of maintenance, by building retaining walls and other support to diminish damages.

France:
The physical measures used to protect archaeological sites are always

negotiated with the land owner, whether public or private, and require close coordination between the archaeologist, the architect and the manager of the archaeological site. Very few archaeological sites in France can be taken as standard references in this respect. The question is under constant examination by those responsible for archaeological heritage.

Latvia:
Legal and private entities have to ensure preservation of cultural monuments in their possession. State owned cultural monuments are protected by their respective tenants. Owners and/or tenants of cultural heritage are obliged to:1) comply with the legislation and regulations, and State Inspection for Heritage Protection instructions on use and protection of cultural monuments;2) inform the Inspection about all damages of cultural monument detected by owner and/or tenant. Monuments of culture are conserved, restored and repaired upon written permission and control of State Inspection for Heritage Protection.

Poland:
-

Scotland:
-

Slovenia:
It only involves administrative protection.

Sweden:
Physical protection is very seldom used because it is vital that the sites are accessible to all.

Switzerland (Confederation):
On the federal level, the protection is only administrative.

Fig. 20.22: The Netherlands, Ubbergen – Duivelsberg. A motte from the early 11th century (P.A.C. Schut).

The Netherlands:
There is no active policy for the physical protection of findspots in the Netherlands. Certain initiatives are however undertaken on an ad hoc basis.

| *Does your country have a programme for monitoring the quality of sites?*

Bern (Canton):
This is a cantonal issue. In canton Bern, a programme exists only for certain type of sites: lake-dwellings and castle ruins.

Bavaria:
No

Czech Republic:
Yes, this is a part of the agenda of the NHI.

England:
Before a designation is decided, field inspectors will assess the quality of the site in question. In some areas post-designation monitoring is also carried out, such as keeping track of the condition of designated wrecks. Archaeological sites are regularly inspected so their condition can be monitored.

Finland:
Not so far.

France:
The expertise of regional archaeology departments and regional offices responsible for Monuments Historiques (which are only concerned with archaeological sites protected as listed monuments), both within the DRACs, remains limited on this subject. Work to coordinate the DRACs with local architecture departments and local authorities with heritage staff is a recent idea to increase efficiency. Certain important monuments – including major archaeological sites – are managed by the Centre des Monuments Nationaux, whose role is currently being redefined, while local authorities were given the option a few years ago of claiming responsibility for monuments

hitherto belonging to the state. The national archaeological database will be able to record details of the condition of sites when the future national application replaces the current application, Patriarche. This should mobilise the DRACs to examine the issue, using common management tools for protected sites currently being developed.

Latvia:
According to Cultural Monuments Protection Law.

Poland:
Yes – regional programmes according to the all-Polish standard, formulated by the Ministry of Culture.

Scotland:
-

Slovenia:
A strategy is absent and monitoring is non-systematic.

Sweden:
No.

Switzerland (Confederation):
-

The Netherlands:
The Archaeological Monuments Inspectorate regularly visits the majority of sites on the list. There is no programme for monitoring the condition of sites.

| *Are monuments and historic buildings inspected?*

Bern (Canton):
Yes (through the cantonal agencies responsible for the preservation of historical monuments).

Bavaria:
Occasionally.

Czech Republic:
Yes, by the NHI.

Fig. 20.23: Germany, Dahlem-Schmidtheim. Mediaeval motte "Zehnbachhaus" (Rheinisches Amt für Bodendenkmalpflege, Bonn).

England:
Yes – as above - prior to designation. Inspection forms an important element of any planning case as well.

Finland:
Yes.

France:
The condition of historic monuments and protected sites should be inspected regularly, although government services will not have the automatic right to make inspection visits.

Latvia:
Yes. State Inspection for Heritage Protection appoints cultural monument protection inspector, subjected directly to the Inspection, in each region and city of Latvia (altogether 33 administrative units). Municipalities are strongly encouraged to create local cultural heritage agencies, and Riga City, Riga Region, Jūrmala, Ventspils and Daugavpils have followed the call.

Poland:
Yes, if the Regional Inspector for Historical Heritage finds it necessary.

Scotland:
-

Slovenia:
Only occasionally.

Sweden:
Only historical buildings are inspected on a regular basis. An inspection is done when a conservation plan is set up and when the County Administration Boards do follow-ups of this plan.

Switzerland (Confederation):
-

The Netherlands:
The Dutch Heritage Inspectorate is responsible for inspecting archaeological monuments, but does not do so in practice.

| How is the law enforced when sites are disturbed?

Bern (Canton):
There are mostly monetary measures fixed in the law: fines to be paid.

When as site has been excavated without a permit: the site has to be put back to the state it was in before and the preservation of finds as well as the evaluation has to be paid for (size of the fine).

Bavaria:
Principally by fines.

Czech Republic:
Through the state or county administration.

England:
There is a range of penalties, from fines to imprisonment, applied for the destruction or damage of sites. Metal-detecting is illegal on scheduled sites.

Finland:
Disturbing archaeological sites is an environment crime, which will be punished according to the penal code.

France:
The voluntary destruction of archaeological remains is against the law (Code du Patrimoine L 114-1 to 5), and recent convictions have strengthened the state and its officers in this protective mission. Offences involving destruction, damage and deterioration to heritage items are punishable under the provisions of articles 322-1 and 322-2 of the French penal code, which explicitly cover the case of land containing archaeological remains and archaeological discoveries made during excavations or by chance.

Latvia:
For failure to fulfill regulations in respect of protection, utilisation, registration, restoration and renovation to cultural monuments, violation of protection zone regime for cultural monuments, and other violations prescribed by legislative enactments, persons shall be held criminally, administratively or otherwise liable in accordance with legislative enactments of the Republic of Latvia.

Poland:
The possessor / user may be accused.

Scotland:
-

Slovenia:
The Inspectorate for Culture and Media of the Ministry of Culture investigates the case and instigates legal proceedings if necessary.

Sweden:
If a site is disturbed the County Administration Boards shall be contacted and they'll determine whether the case should be reported to the police or not.

Switzerland (Confederation):
-

The Netherlands:
To a minimal extent. The criminal justice authorities do not prioritise reports of disturbances at archaeological sites. Prosecutions are extremely rare.

| Does your country have a policy on what developments are permissible on listed sites? Please describe.

Bern (Canton):
This policy depends on the cantons. In Bern, very little sites are totally protected. No development at all is then allowed on their premises. The listed sites are known to the local communities, who determine their own development schemes in accordance with the cantonal authorities. They are obliged to take the listed sites into account when developing their planning. This does not mean that a site has total protection. It only means that the cantonal archaeological agencies have to be informed (see

question II.2) before a site is built on. Developments are allowed as long as the partial preservation or scientific excavation is possible and paid for.

Bavaria:
Principally everything as long as site is preserved ("protective covering"), practically almost everything after "substitute-excavation".

Czech Republic:
There is no formal strategy; it mostly depends on the character of the site. In case of the most important sites attention is paid above all to the authenticity of the place.

England:
We issue considerable amounts of guidance. Because all scheduled Monument applications come to English Heritage, we get involved on a case-by-case basis as well.

Finland:
No.

France:
On the basis of the archaeological inventory (the national archaeological map), zones in which it is presumed that preventive archaeology should be imposed can be defined. Development plans in these zones are automatically examined to measure the impact of the project on any known or potential archaeological remains, and diagnostics are then carried out to identify the heritage and scientific issues at stake and find the most appropriate solution for preserving known remains. If the site cannot be preserved by moving the project or by a technical solution for protecting the site, a preventive dig – "preservation by research" – is imposed by the state. The excavation is the responsibility of the project owner, but the specifications are provided by state, requiring bids from archaeological operators with scientific skills proven at national level. Scientific criteria always take priority in all decisions.
In its responses to local authority development plans, the state may ask the authority to create construction-free zones. For sites discovered through diagnostics whose importance in scientific and heritage terms justifies their preservation in situ and in their entirety, the state can implement protection as a listed monument, creating an easement that extends to the surroundings.

Latvia:
Immovable cultural monuments shall not be displaced or transformed, except cases when State Inspection for Heritage Protection has permitted otherwise. Transformation of culture monuments and substitution of original parts with other parts is approved only in cases, when it is the final resort to maintain a monument or such changes will not affect the heritage value of a monument. Monuments of culture are conserved, restored and repaired upon written permission and control of State Inspection for Heritage Protection. Whereby permit is issued following the review and approval of a project by State Inspection for Heritage Protection. Inspection also provides owners of cultural monuments instructions on use and preservation of cultural monuments.

Poland:
Each renovation must be consulted with the regional Heritage Service and receive its acceptance. The Service

may formulate its conditions (requirements to carry out any protective measures).

Scotland:
-

Slovenia:
There three regimes:
1) Reserve protection (no interventions permitted);
2) Interventions are permitted subject to prior evaluation;
3) Interventions permitted subject to prior excavation or monitoring after an evaluation process.

Sweden:
No we don´t have a policy. The law says in section 6 that "it is prohibited, without a permission from the County Administration Boards, to disturb, remove, excavate, cover over or, by building development, planting or in any other way, to alter or damage ancient monuments and sites."

Switzerland (Confederation):
-

The Netherlands:
A licensing policy is currently being drafted. Generally speaking, physical disturbance of a legally protected monument will not be permitted. Any such permission will be granted only on condition that an archaeological investigation is carried out.

| Is research conducted into factors that impact on the physical quality of sites?

Bern (Canton):
Yes, depending on which kind of sites: Erosion and drying soils in wetlands are two examples which we consider in Bern.

Bavaria:
?

Czech Republic:
It would be needed. Very little has been done so far.

England:
Research is undertaken into all designation cases, depending on the level of understanding and the strength of the case in favour of designation. Care is taken to ensure that the boundaries of a site proposed for scheduling are firmly established.

Finland:
No.

France:
Research work on factors with an impact on the conservation of archaeological sites is relatively rare. Examples that have been carried out include experiments on rising water in Roussillon, work on the consequences of erosion on materials on the Mediterranean coast by the Laboratoire de Recherche des Monuments Historiques and the effect of climate change on cave paintings around the Centre National de Préhistoire.

Latvia:

Poland:
Yes.

Scotland:
-

Slovenia:
No.

Sweden:
Yes in some cases, for example rock-art.

Switzerland (Confederation):
-

The Netherlands:
Yes. The Cultural Heritage Agency studies degradation processes at archaeological sites.

| Are listed sites freely accessible to the public?

Bern (Canton):
The list of the sites is accessible to everybody through the local authorities or the cantonal agency.
In situ, certain sites are accessible with a minimum infrastructure. Sites on local or cantonal property are always accessible.

Bavaria:
Principally yes as long as in fields and forests.

Czech Republic:
Yes.

England:
Some are. Most sites are in private ownership and therefore subject to the owners' decision.

Finland:
All sites are in principle freely accessible to the public.

France:
The Atlas de l'architecture et du patrimoine (architecture and heritage atlas) project, due for publication in September 2008, will have the specific aim of distributing organised information from the national archaeological map on-line. It will offer information about protected zones, zones presumed to contain archaeological sites and zones associated with porter à connaissance planning documents. The Atlas will provide a whole layer of information about known archaeological sites.In parallel, access to the archaeological data in the national database is already and will remain available on request via regional archaeology departments, but this access is limited and controlled to protect site security and the rights of individuals.

Latvia:
Yes, in according to Law "On Protection of Cultural Monuments".

Poland:
Not obligatorily. Some of them are located on the private grounds that are hardly accessible. But they always have to be – for the Heritage Service.

Scotland:
-

Slovenia:
Yes.

Sweden:
Yes.

Switzerland (Confederation):
-

The Netherlands:
There is no general policy on this. It is up to the owner of the site to grant access to the public.

| Do you have a policy on the use of listed sites focused on awareness-raising or public education? Please describe.

Bern (Canton):
In canton Bern, we prepare flyers, web information and on-site information panels for all sites that are accessible to the public. These can be asked for at the archaeological service or downloaded for educative and tourism purposes. General information on inventories is provided by the Archaeological service for the local authorities. The Service has a very extensive public relations policy.

Bavaria:
Limesdevelopmentplan (LiEP), signposting and explanations on the spot, guidebooks etc.

Czech Republic:
Cultural monuments are marked and described in the field. There is no central policy in this field, however.

England:
The Heritage Protection Bill, currently at draft stage, aims to make designation decisions easier to understand by publishing new detailed selection criteria for national and local designation. The public will become increasingly involved, through consultation, in decisions about strategic designation programmes, as well as the current system which allows anyone to put buildings forward for designation. New registers of historic assets will be created that are simple, clear and accessible through a new Heritage Gateway on the internet.

While there is no overarching education policy for designated sites, there are several educational projects which aim to raise public awareness and participation of publicly owned sites. Indeed increasing participation is a major Government policy for culture and the historic environment. Examples include the National Monuments Record (part of English Heritage) on-line databases of images and information about listed and scheduled sites, projects around English Heritage properties, open-house days and events for various groups.

Finland:
Attempts to raise the awareness of the most outstanding archaeological monuments have been made by putting up information boards at the monuments and by publishing information of the sites in a popular way.

France:
Communication about how the inventory of archaeological sites is put together concentrates mainly on on-off events during national days such as the "La science en fête" science festival or "Les Journées Européennes

du Patrimoine" (European heritage days), or open days at sites in operation. It depends on the regional policy of the relevant DRAC, and can in some cases take the form of large educational projects, often in partnership with other organisations (museums, schools etc.) as part of educational activities associated with culture. In this context, and within this strict framework, work on putting together the national archaeological map can be used to illustrate specific activities: introduction to prospecting, map reading, understanding the link between a DBMS and a GIS, analysing reports etc.

The growth in urban topographic atlases relying heavily on the GIS linked to the national archaeological map, the collection of archaeological maps of Gaul, some of which have been produced in close collaboration with the DRACs, and the creation of the Inventaire Général du patrimoine Culturel (general inventory of cultural heritage, which includes archaeological sites on the basis of the data held by the state) entrusted to regional councils, are all opportunities to introduce a wider public to the task of collecting, verifying and organising archaeological data.

Latvia:

Inspection's public relations activities include: regular dissemination of updated information through mass media, press briefings and discussions on various aspects of cultural heritage preservation. Latvian cultural heritage is popularised also through various exhibitions, publications, speeches and lectures.

Inspection organises European Cultural heritage Days in Latvia since 1995. Data on cultural monuments and their preservation is available on web-page www.mantojums. lv. EC campaign Europe, a common heritage has significantly boosted public interest in cultural heritage.Careful treatment of the World culture and nature heritage mainly depends on determined development of social responsibility for locally available heritage values. It may be achieved through early interest in national and provincial history and most vivid part of cultural heritage, its monuments. State Inspection for Heritage Protection prepares publishings for kids, organises creative camps and encourages youngsters get involved in Council of Europe events to help young people understand the essence and role of protection of cultural heritage.

Poland:

This is not within a range of activities of the heritage Service, but several such actions are carried out by the museums, hobby clubs, schools etc.

Scotland:

-

Slovenia:

There is no special policy.

Sweden:

On a national level the National Heritage Boards strive to make the ASIS (see next question) accessible and understandable to the public. On a regional level the county museums have a responsibility to work in many different ways to increase the public's general knowledge about ancient monuments, sites and the historical landscapes.

Switzerland (Confederation):

-

The Netherlands:
No

| *How is knowledge and information on listed sites recorded and made accessible?*

Bern (Canton):
Actually Access-database, GIS-application and homepage service for accessible sites allow accessibility (www.erz. be.ch/site/archaeologie). For 2012 we would like to attain accessibility via inter- and intranet linked to other offices, cantons and local authorities through a GEO-portal. All cantons have homepage access (see www.archaeologie. ch).

Bavaria:
Inventory at the BLfD, public access to reduced/"safe" data on all listed monuments via internet "BayernViewer-denkmal" www.blfd.bayern.de

Czech Republic:
NHI has created web pages where part of this information is freely accessible (MonumNet: http://www.npu.cz/ ; ISAD - Information System on Archaeological Data of The National Heritage Institute in Prag: http://twist.up.npu. cz/

England:
New locally-held registers of historic assets will be created under the new system, which are simple, clear and accessible through a new Heritage Gateway on the internet. Parts of these are already available online, as are other databases such as the photographic archive 'Images of England'. We are keen to make our designations more available, more informative and more effective at raising public interest and appreciation of the assets in their ownership.

Finland:
By this autumn the inventory of the archaeological sites will be accessible on the web.

France:
The purpose of the Atlas is to make it easier to share digital information between departments and everyone involved in heritage on the ground (public establishments, local authorities, research centers etc.). It will make it possible to present this data (as long as it is not confidential) to the general public over the Internet.

The Atlas will be a platform for publishing geolocalised data and maps contributed by decentralised departments and institutional partners, a platform for cataloguing data (metadata) according to the standards of the Géoportail and the European Inspire directive, and a platform for map production. The Atlas de l'architecture et du patrimoine will publish on-line maps of heritage data, and particularly data about archaeological sites, in small and medium scales.The philosophy of the application is to enable users to learn and, where authorised, to download existing archaeological data about French territory. However, certain items of archaeological data will not be accessible directly on-line. Where data is sensitive, the service responsible for the data will indicate its existence and give details of the person to contact to gain real access.

Latvia:
List of state protected cultural heritage monuments is published in Latvijas Vēstnesis (the Official Journal of the Republic of Latvia). List of state protected cultural heritage monuments is also available in the Information Centre of the State Inspection for Heritage Protection at 20 Pils Street, where list can also be found in electronic data base format. Inspection issues object statement defining the status according to filed application
State Monument Register is engaged in exploration of monuments, assessment of their historic, scientific, artistic, architectonic, archaeological, ethnographic or other culture values, recording of monuments and processing of these records, and prepares registration documentation. State Inspection for Heritage Protection supervises registration of cultural monuments, identification and examination of cultural heritage, registration documentation and draft culture monument list and research of culture monuments. All research findings are stored in Centre for Documentation of Monuments.

Poland:
It is officially accessible on the internet – on the web pages of the local authorities and regional offices of the heritage Services.

Scotland:
-

Slovenia:
The data is collected in the Register and is accessible on the WWW.

Sweden:
The Swedish digital sites and monuments record is called ASIS (abbreviation for Ancient Sites Information System). It consists of among other things a geographical database with an application for on-line search. While the application is publicly available for everyone, some of the information is restricted, for instance the position of some sites is not shown. This is due to the risk of looting and vandalism. However, professionals in cultural heritage management, spatial planning, research and education can log in and access all the information in the database. All known sites and monuments are recorded in the ASIS.

Switzerland (Confederation):
Internet for the national inventories: www.isos.ch for ISOS; www.ivs.admin.ch for IVS; www.bafu.admin.ch/landschaft for BLN. The homepage for the KGI is not accessible yet.

The Netherlands:
ARCHIS is a GIS database accessible to anyone working in archaeology. Another system (KICH) available to a wider public (local authorities, planners etc.) contains simplified information on cultural heritage values, including archaeology (www.kich.nl).

Târgoviște, Romania. Târgoviște, fair or place of a fair, is mentioned by the Bavarian Johanes Schiltberger, who took part in the battle of Nicopole (1396), in his travel memories, written after he returned to Germany. The earliest mention of the Royal Court dates to the reign of Michael the 1st (1417-1418), son of Mircea the Old (1386-1418) who in a document speaks: "... from my very royal home, from the very town of my princely court, Târgoviște". Târgoviște played an important political role in the history of Wallachia (today the southern part of Romania) between the XV century and the early XVIII Century and after that remained an important cultural centre. The Royal Palace was first established here in around 1400 and was continuously expanded until the reign of Constantin Brâncoveanu (1688-1714) who was the last prince of Wallachia to maintain Târgoviște as a capital city. The Princely Court of Târgoviște is famous for its "Chindia Tower" (West Tower) built by Vlad the Impaler around 1460 and also for its Grand Princely Church built by Peter Earring (1583-1585) (Ovidiu Cîrstina).

Contributors

Mircea Angelescu	Ministry of Culture and Religious Affairs – National Heritage Department, 30 Kiseleff Street, 1 District, Bucharest, Romania.
Jos Bazelmans	Cultural Heritage Agency (former RACM), Postbus 1600, 3800 BP Amersfoort, The Netherlands.
Roger Bowdler	English Heritage, 1 Waterhouse Square, 138-142 Holborn EC1N 2ST, England.
Eamon Cody	National Monuments Service Environment, Heritage and Local Government Dún Scéine, Harcourt Lane Dublin 2, Ireland.
Bojan Djurić	Department of Archaeology, Faculty of Arts (Oddelek za arheologijo, Filozofska fakulteta, Univerza v Ljubljani), Aškerčeva cesta 2, 1000 Ljubljana, Slovenia.
Sivila Fernández Cacho	Instituto Andaluz del Patrimonio HistóricoCamino de los Descubrimientos s/n 41092-Sevilla, Spain.
Marie-Jeanne Ghenne	Commission royale des Monuments, Sites et Fouilles, Chambre de Hainaut Attachée, Service public de Wallonie, Place du Béguinage 16,7000 Mons – Belgium.
Albert Hafner	Archaeological Service of the Canton of Berne, Department underwater and wetland archaeology, Postfach 5233, CH-3001 Berne/Switzerland.
Kristin Huld Sigurðardóttir	Fornleifavernd ríkisins, The Archaeological Heritage Agency of Iceland, Suðurgata 39, 101 Reykjavík, Iceland.
Ksenija Kovaćec Naglić	Heritage Information and Documentation Centre (Informacijsko dokumentacijski center za kulturno dediščino Ministrstvo za kulturo), Maistrova ulica 10, 1000 Ljubljana, Slovenia.
Jürgen Kunow	Landschaftsverband Rheinland, Rheinisches Amt für Bodendenkmalpflege, Endenicher Straße 133 D - 53115 Bonn, Germany.
Axelle Letor	Université Libre de Bruxelles, Centre de recherches archéologiques (CReA), Avenue F.D. Roosevelt 50, CP 175 B-1050 Bruxelles, Belgique.
Phil Mason	Institute for the Protection of Cultural Heritage of Slovenia (Zavod za varstvo kulturne dediščine Slovenije, Območna enota Novo mesto), Skalickega ulica 1, 8000 Novo mesto, Slovenia.
Christian Mayer	Abteilung für Bodendenkmale Bundesdenkmalamt, Hofburg, A-1010 Wien, Österreich.
Dana Mihai	National Institute of the Historical Monuments, 16 Ienachita Vacarescu Street, 4 District, Bucharest, Romania.
Barbara Mlakar	Directorate for Cultural Heritage (Direktorat za kulturno dediščino, Ministrstvo za kulturo), Maistrova ulica 10, 1000 Ljubljana, Slovenia.
Peter Norman	National Heritage Board, Box 5405, 114 84 Stockholm, Sweden.
Sólburg Una Pálsdóttir	Fornleifavernd ríkisins, The Archaeological Heritage Agency of Iceland, Suðurgata 39, 101 Reykjavík, Iceland.
Brigita Petek	Heritage Information and Documentation Centre (Informacijsko dokumentacijski center za kulturno dediščino Ministrstvo za kulturo),Maistrova ulica 10, 1000 Ljubljana, Slovenia.
Andrzej Prinke	Poznan Archaeological Museum, ul. Wodna 27, 61-781 Poznan, Poland.

Irina Saprykina	Institute of archaeology RAS, 117036, Dm.Ulyanova str., 19, Moskow, Russia.
Marianne Schauman-Lönnqvist	Department of Archaeology, National Board of Antiquities, P.O.box 913, FIN-00101 Helsink, Finlandi.
Peter Schut	National Heritage Agency (former RACM), Postbus 1600, 3800 BP Amersfoort, The Netherlands.
Rikard Sohlenius	National Heritage Board, Box 5405, 114 84 Stockholm, Sweden.
Philippe Vergain	Ministère français de la Culture et de la Communication, Rue Saint-Honoré 182, 75033 Paris Cedex 01, France.
David Villálon Torres	Instituto Andaluz del Patrimonio Histórico Camino de los Descubrimientos, s/n 41092-Sevilla, Spain.
Nathalie Vossen	Cultural Heritage Agency (former RACM), Postbus 1600, 3800 BP Amersfoort, The Netherlands.
Katalin Wollák	Kulturális Örökségvédelmi Hivatal, National Office of Cultural Heritage, 1014 Budapest, Táncsics Mihály utca 1, Hungary.
Leonard de Wit	Cultural Heritage Agency (former RACM), Postbus 1600, 3800 BP Amersfoort, The Netherlands.
Leon Ziengs	Cultural Heritage Agency (former RACM), Postbus 1600, 3800 BP Amersfoort, The Netherlands.
Sandra Zirne	Centre of Archaeology, The State Inspection for Heritage protection, M.Pils Street 19, Riga, LV-1050, Latvia.